drink·ol·o·gy
WINE

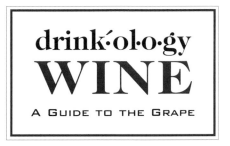

drink·ol·o·gy
WINE
A GUIDE TO THE GRAPE

JAMES WALLER

with a contribution by
ELIZABETH ALDRICH

Illustrations by
GLENN WOLFF

stewart, tabori & chang

NEW YORK

Published in 2005 by
Stewart, Tabori & Chang
115 West 18th Street
New York, NY 10011
www.abramsbooks.com

Wayne Koestenbaum, excerpt from "Twelfth Canto, Part Twelve" from *Model Homes.* Copyright © 2004 by Wayne Koestenbaum. Reprinted with the permission of BOA Editions, Ltd., www.BOAEditions.org.

Library of Congress Cataloging-in-Publication Data

Waller, James.
  Drinkology wine : a guide to the grape / by James Waller ; with a
contribution by Elizabeth Aldrich ; illustrations by Glenn Wolff.
      p. cm.
  Includes index.
  ISBN 1–58479–453–4
  1. Wine and wine making—Amateurs' manuals. 2. Grapes—Varieties.
I. Aldrich, Elizabeth. II. Title.

TP548.2.W35 2005
641.8'72—dc22   2005016944

Designed by Jay Anning, Thumb Print

The text of this book was composed in Adobe Caslon.

Printed in China by Pimlico

10 9 8 7 6 5 4 3 2 1

First Printing

Stewart, Tabori & Chang is a subsidiary of

LA MARTINIÈRE

For Jim O'Connor

He had a weak point—this Fortunato—although in other regards he was a man to be respected and even feared. He prided himself on his connoisseurship in wine.

—Edgar Allan Poe,
"The Cask of Amontillado"

ACKNOWLEDGMENTS

Friends. You can't really enjoy wine without their company—and you certainly can't write a book about wine without their help.

Friends new and old contributed in uncountable ways. A year ago, I walked into a wine shop near my home in Brooklyn, asked to talk to the manager, introduced myself, and bluntly told him, "I'm writing a wine book and need help." That manager, David Kulko (of 7th Avenue Wines & Liquors, in the Park Slope neighborhood), provided incalculable assistance, guiding many of my selections and generously sharing his knowledge of the wine business. The staff at another local shop, the Greene Grape (in the Fort Greene neighborhood), were likewise enormously helpful.

Jay Anning's design and Glenn Wolff's beautiful and informative drawings make the book; one couldn't ask for better collaborators. My old chum Randy Sonderman gave insightful guidance during the book's planning. Betsy Keller, the best person in the world to have at your elbow during a marathon wine-tasting, was unflagging in her support. Joan Smelkinson's welcome stream of emailed wine articles led me places I wouldn't have discovered on my own. Denell Downum was an ace at image research; Michael Ross the perfect winery-visit companion; Bruno Blumenfeld ingenious at chasing down an obscure fact; Christina Zimpel an exemplary model. Arch Brown, Al Sbordone, and Mina Hamilton provided help without which this project could not have been realized. Thanks to all.

The most steadfast help throughout this book's preparation was given by my life-partner, Jim O'Connor. Not only did he prop me up—and keep me going—when I despaired of being able to "explain Burgundy" in two thousand words or less, but he served as the first reader of much of this book, protecting me against my worst writerly excesses and suggesting many an idea that shows up (uncredited) in these pages.

The most pleasurable of the days researching this book were spent in Sicily, where Jim and I and our good friends Jeffrey Edelstein and Mark Finley visited wineries (and a not insignificant number of Greek ruins), got hopelessly lost in medieval hilltowns, and ate Sicilian food and drank Sicilian wine with abandon. Winery owners and staff were, to a person, remarkably gracious; special thanks go to Gianvito Pipitone and Leonardo Nicotra at Firriato, to José Rallo and Wiebke Petersen at Donnafugata, and to Vincenzo Massimo at Florio. Jeff Edelstein deserves special thanks for introducing me to Joel Zack, who generously shared his knowledge of wine-tour planning, and for reintroducing me to Elizabeth Aldrich, whose essay on the wines of Chile makes this book richer than it would otherwise be.

Thanks flow (like wine?) to the members of *Drinkology WINE*'s tasting team: Jim, Jay, Areta Buk, Abyssinian Carto, Eric Mueller, Ramona Ponce, and our tasting-sessions' leader, Rachel Ponce, who shepherded our swirling, sniffing, and sipping with enthusiasm and aplomb.

Researching this book entailed going back to school, and the series of wine courses I took through the New School University's culinary arts program proved essential. All the instructors were excellent, but special gratitude is owed to the wine program's director, Harriet Lembeck. Equally valuable was the gracious assistance given by Bob Pellegrini, owner of the Pellegrini Vineyards winery on Long Island. (And thanks to Roy Ibrahim, of Bistro Les Amis, for putting me in touch with Bob.) Judy Record, of Ariel Vineyards in Napa Valley, gave emergency help for which I'll long be grateful.

My editor at Stewart, Tabori & Chang, Marisa Bulzone, was an ideal reader, and kept my spirits afloat throughout. Thanks go, too, to other members of the STC and Harry N. Abrams staff, including especially Leslie Stoker, Steve Tager, Andrea Glickson, Ron Longe, and Jessica Napp. Finally, this book benefited enormously from the expert manuscript reviews performed by Ray Isle and Nick Fauchald. I take the blame for *Drinkology WINE*'s errors and occasionally outlandish opinions; wherever the book is accurate and sensible, they must share in the credit.

—JAMES WALLER
Brooklyn, New York
May 2005

A NOTE TO THE READER

The wines recommended in this book were, with very few exceptions, purchased at wine shops and liquor stores in New York City. For the most part, I've avoided giving vintages for the wines mentioned, since this book's useful life will extend, I hope, longer than any of the particular wines that I've enjoyed will remain on wine shops' shelves. There is, of course, a real risk in recommending a wine without specifying the vintage, since character and quality differ—sometimes subtly, sometimes greatly—from year to year. A grain of salt therefore accompanies every suggestion. Wine prices differ according to who's doing the selling, and they, too, fluctuate from year to year. The prices given throughout are necessarily approximations, but they closely track typical retail prices during the period of *Drinkology WINE*'s preparation.

—JW

Contents

INTRODUCTION

The Wine Baby

A CLASSIC CASE STUDY

· 1 ·

CHAPTER ONE

Learning to Talk

BASIC WINE VOCABULARY

· 8 ·

CHAPTER TWO

Ambling through the Vintage

A FIELD TRIP TO A VINEYARD AND WINERY

· 38 ·

CHAPTER THREE

Nose, Palate, Body

ANATOMY OF A WINE TASTING

· 73 ·

CHAPTER FOUR

American Roots

AN EXTREMELY TRUNCATED WINE HISTORY

· 121 ·

CHAPTER FIVE
Cabs and Other "Vehicles"
RED WINE VARIETIES
· 132 ·

CHAPTER SIX
Chardonnay and Its Discontents
WHITE WINE VARIETIES
· 158 ·

CHAPTER SEVEN
Fluted Columns
SPARKLING WINES
· 202 ·

CHAPTER EIGHT
A Whirlwind Wine-World Tour
FROM YOUR LOCAL VINO STORE
· 223 ·

CHAPTER NINE
Of Wine Sellers and Wine Cellars
WINE FAQs
· 332 ·

Indexes
· 359 ·

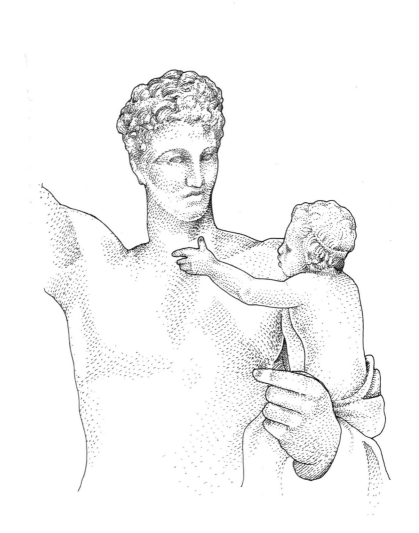

The Wine Baby

IT'S A VERY FAMOUS GREEK STATUE. YOU'VE PROBABLY SEEN PICTURES of it: A naked, lissome young man cradles a tiny baby in the crook of his left arm. The young man's outstretched right arm is broken off at the bicep, but scholars believe that the missing right hand once held a bunch of grapes. The baby's chubby face—with a look that one critic has described as "petulant"—is turned intently toward that missing hand, and it's obvious from the pose that the child once reached toward that now-lost grape cluster, which the young man teasingly dangled beyond the baby's grasp.

The sculpture is called *Hermes with the Infant Dionysus*. Dug up in Olympia, Greece, in 1877 and now in the Archaeological Museum there, it's attributed to the great Classic Period sculptor Praxiteles and was probably carved around 340 BC. Hermes, the beautiful young man in the statue, was the messenger of the gods in Greek mythology; Dionysus, the pouting baby, would grow up to be the Greek god of wine.

Now, don't worry. You haven't mistakenly opened an art history text-book. This is in fact a book about wine. But I begin with a description of this ancient statue because I think it's a perfect metaphor for your—the wine baby's—situation. Like the infant Dionysus, you're filled with desire—in your case, a thirst for some wine *knowledge*. And just like baby D., you feel frustrated—maybe you're even petulant—because gaining that knowledge seems forever outside your reach.

I know just how you feel. I was until recently a classic wine baby myself.

THE WINE BABY EXPOSED

Say you're invited to what promises to be a great dinner party, and you're really looking forward to it, but then the day before, the host calls you and says, "Gee, I'm sorry, but I forgot to ask if you'd mind bringing along a bottle of wine." What a fearsome, humiliating task you've suddenly been saddled with. You walk into your local wine shop and feel like you've entered a library filled with hundreds of volumes written in languages you don't understand—and that it's your job to choose a book that your host will find entertaining and one that, moreover, will expand his or her spiritual horizons. Well, it's probably the case that your host doesn't really much care what you bring, but this is the way you *feel*—and, as the therapists say, let's stay with your feelings for a moment. Feelings are important.

Wine-baby anxiety has a number of dimensions, and you may suffer from any—or several—of them. Maybe you're temperamental and tantrum-prone—an *enfant terrible*—when it comes to wine. "Bring a bottle of wine," that dinner-party host tells you, and you defiantly show up with flowers or dessert instead. Or maybe you're unapologetically "secure" in your ignorance: you don't like wine (you say), and, besides, you think that wine culture is just *stupid*. Or maybe you're just horribly embarrassed. Here you are, all grown up in so many ways, but somehow you've managed to get through this much of your existence without learning a damned thing about wine. Every time you meet a friend in a bar, you cover your ass by ordering a glass of Merlot—not because you really like Merlot but because you (sort of) know what to expect, and, hey, Merlot is easier to pronounce than Côte du Qu'est-ce Que C'est. Every time you try to read the wine column in your newspaper, you feel secretly humiliated: it's so hard to understand that it makes you feel as if you've forgotten your ABC's. And just being invited to a wine tasting is enough to make you break out in a debilitating case of . . . colic? Diaper rash?

The thing is, you've not just being peevish. Wine babies *do* have the ability to reason, and—just like the proverbial paranoiac who has a few actual enemies—they know they face some real hurdles as they try to climb from their highchairs onto the bar stools of wine adulthood. Part of your fear, in other words, is firmly rooted in reality.

SINK OR SWIM?

The world of adults can be very frightening to a little kid, in part because of the things adults say. I wasn't raised by ogres, but, for example, I can remember my older relatives once discussing the best method for teaching children to swim. "Just throw 'em in the water—they'll learn," an uncle of mine averred. And from the child's point of view, adult behavior can be awfully frustrating, too. Your parents, for example, are always taking you to fantastic stores filled with highly interesting things and then, when you see something you want, telling you, "No, you can't have that. We can't afford it." Or, if you dare to pick up some enticing object, you're scolded: "Put that right back. Now!"

The wine baby experiences the same fear and frustration during encounters with the wine-adult world. Reading much wine writing, you feel like a kindergartner being asked to memorize the *Encyclopedia Britannica*. (Sink or swim, kiddo!) But it's not just the amount of unfamiliar information you're being asked to swallow that's so fearsome. The wine world seems terrifically exclusive and forbidding in another sense, as well: the *money* sense. What an incomparable cellar such-and-such a Michelin three-star restaurant has, opines the snooty wine columnist. How lovely the Tuscan vineyards are at harvest time—so gloriously burnished by the late-summer sun. How matchless is the expertise of such-and-such a Manhattan sommelier. This sort of stuff can make you cringe, not just because of the preciousness of the prose but because of the poverty of your own checking account. Without the cash for (lots of) trips abroad, (lots of) fancy dinners, and (lots of) great bottles of wine, how can you—poor, *poor* wine baby—possibly compete? (Hey, just what do you think you're doing with that bottle of Lafite? Put it back. Right now!)

SCOUT'S HONOR

The truth is you *can't* compete. Not at that level—or not yet, at any rate. But you *can* begin your crawl toward that hazily distant land of wine adulthood. And I, in this book, will be your scout. I'm not so far past my own wine-babyhood to qualify as a parental figure—and maybe that's a good thing. Parents too often seem to have forgotten what it's like to be a little kid—they've repressed not just the terrors but also some of the wonder and enthusiasm of childhood. Sometimes they don't really get it when you don't know something *they* think you're supposed to know. And not only that, but adults in general are often so wrapped up in their adult stuff that they neglect to see just how dubious, suspect, and some-times downright comical their "adult" behavior can be—especially when viewed by a reasonably astute child.

So think of me as your scout: you know, the slightly older kid who's explored some of the territory of adulthood and understands a few of its secrets, but who retains enough of the natural, healthy suspiciousness of childhood to zero in on adult pretensions—and occasionally poke fun at them. Think back to your actual childhood: isn't this the way you found out much of what you learned about the adult world and its secrets? (You know exactly what I'm talking about.)

In keeping with my role as scout, let me make you a couple of scout's-honor type pledges:

Number one: This book will not assume that you come to it with any particular knowledge about wine. Having once felt as if I myself were drowning in what the ancient Greek poet Homer called the wine-dark sea, I don't ascribe to the sink-or-swim philosophy.

Number two: I won't assume that you have all the money in the world and all the unstructured playtime needed to spend it—and I promise not to make you feel bad because your resources are less than infinite. I'll therefore assume that you're the sort of person who would rarely spend more than, say, $30 on a bottle of wine bought in a store, and that wines priced from $10 to $20 a bottle fit even more comfort-ably within your budget. I'll assume that you do go out to eat occasion-ally, sometimes to places that have decent wine lists. (Of course, you never *look* at the wine list—too intimidating—but we'll deal with that later.) Here, too, I'll assume that there's a ceiling on what you'll be able and/or willing to spend on the wine—perhaps, at the upper limit and on especially significant occasions, as much as a hundred bucks or so for a very, very special bottle. (If that figure strikes you as awfully steep, keep in mind that restaurants typically charge two or three times the retail price of a bottle of wine, so this is probably what a decent bottle of Champagne will cost in a restaurant.)

Number three: I'm going to guess that you'll be drinking all or most of the wine you buy within a few days or weeks of the time you purchase it. In this respect, you're no different from most wine drinkers; the vast majority of wine sold all over the world is drunk within forty-eight hours after it's bought.

Number four: I promise not to focus too too often on wines that you, in all probability, will be unable to find. This, to my mind, is one of the great annoyances of much wine writing: You'll be reading a magazine article about some magnificent, unusual, not-too-expensive Chardonnay that's being produced by an inventive young winemaker in the Mâconnais region of Burgundy, in France. Your interest is piqued. Then, near the end of piece, the writer reveals that—oh, by the way—this wine is not currently being exported to the United States. And—oh yeah—it's even difficult to find in Paris. Grrr. I don't know where you live, dear reader. I live in New York, which has some of the best wine shops in the country, but—just like you, probably—I buy most of the wine I drink from one of two nearby stores with limited shelf space and a middle-class clientele, and which therefore carry only a moderately diverse selection of (mostly) moderately priced wines. Of course, I can't guarantee that you'll be able to easily find *every* wine or kind of wine I mention, but on this score, too, I promise to keep your possibly limited resources in mind.

Number five: Although I'm convinced that some wine-related travel will considerably broaden your horizons and will deepen your knowledge in a way that mere reading cannot, I'm not going to pretend that you have the time or money to jet off to France, Italy, New Zealand, or the Western Cape Province of South Africa at the pop of a cork. I will talk about the fun of taking a day or weekend to visit wineries in your region. But, for the most part, I'll assume that most of the wine exploring you do will be performed from the vantage of your own dining room or easy chair.

So let's begin. You'll start making progress—you'll see—as soon as you say your first words . . .

CHAPTER ONE

Learning to Talk

(BASIC WINE VOCABULARY)

YOU DIDN'T REALLY START TO GET ON IN THE WORLD UNTIL YOU'D learned a few simple words: some proper nouns (Mommy, Dad), some verbs (give, want), some common nouns (cookie, dolly, truck), an essential possessive pronoun (mine), and one all-important utterance— No!

Well, learning the rudiments of a language is just as critical to your progress as a wine tot. You simply can't go very far until you begin to understand and use the basic vocabulary of a strange language—often deceptively resembling ordinary English—that we may as well call "Winespeak." Without at least a smattering of Winespeak vocabulary, you'll always have difficulty understanding the wine column in your local newspaper and your local wine shop will forever remain an unsettling and confusing environment. You'll be amazed, though, at how much more grown up you'll feel—how much more grown up you will, in fact, *be*—once you memorize and begin to use even a comparatively small set of Winespeak words and phrases.

FIRST WORDS

Let's begin with the simplest and most essential Winespeak word of all. The word **wine** itself.

Yes, yes, I can hear you saying, "What kind of cretin does he think I am? I know what *wine* means!" But—before you fling this book aside in annoyance—ask yourself whether you're really sure you know what *wine* means *in Winespeak*.

Do I sense a little uncertainty creeping in? I won't keep you in suspense. *Wine,* in Winespeak, means the following: *an alcoholic beverage made from fermented grape juice.* Unless preceded by a qualifying adjective—*rice* wine, *elderberry* wine—the word *wine* denotes a beverage made from grapes. Period. You may be interested to know that "an alcoholic beverage made from fermented grape juice" is also the *legal* definition of the word *wine.* Our government, like the governments of other countries, regulates the sale and labeling of alcoholic beverages, and, according to U.S. law, a beverage identified simply as "wine" *must* be made from grapes.

What does _wine_ mean in _Winespeak_?

Easy enough, right? Let's move on to a second word whose Winespeak meaning you're probably also convinced you know: **grape.** I bet you're wrong. First of all, in Winespeak, the word *grape* does not mean an *individual* grape—that is, one little fruit among a bunch. The Winespeak word for that is **berry.** See what I mean about Winespeak being *deceptively* like ordinary English?

Moreover, when they say "grape" or "grapes," Winespeakers do not mean those clustered fruits that you can find in the produce section of your supermarket. Those are *table* grapes, and, with only a few exceptions, the many different kinds of table grapes are never used for making wine. To a Winespeaker, a *grape* is any of the hundreds upon hundreds of *varieties* of grapes from which *wine* is made. Wine grapes—again, with rare exceptions—are never eaten fresh, because they're just too small and seedy to be appealing as fruit. By the way, most wine grapes—there are literally thousands of varieties—are members of a single species: *Vitis vinifera,* or just **vinifera,** for short. The Latin name, appropriately, means "wine grape–bearing vine." (You've noticed that I'm putting important terms in **boldface** type? I'll keep doing that throughout the book to highlight the words and phrases it's especially important to remember.)

So now you know the basic meaning of three—no, four!—Winespeak words. Don't get too carried away with yourself, however, because things immediately get much more complicated. The basic definition of the word *wine* may be simple, but *wines*—in all their overwhelming diversity—are anything *but* simple. To begin to sort things out, you need to know a bit about how wines are *categorized.* The trouble is, there are several divergent yet overlapping ways of categorizing wines. Let me go through these different methods, one by one, and at the end we'll see how they not only diverge but overlap, as well.

RED, WHITE, OR PINK?

You're undoubtedly familiar with the most common way of distinguishing wines from one another: by **color.** Just like the kid who enters kindergarten already knowing how to tell yellow from green from blue, you already know that there are red wines, and white wines, and pink wines. And I bet you even know that pink-colored wines are more commonly referred to as **rosé** wines, don't you? (Believe me, I'm *blushing* with pride!)

But here's something, my little genius, that you may *not* already know: the color of a wine does not necessarily depend on the color of the grapes it was made from. Yes, red wine is made from dark-colored grapes, though most "red" varieties aren't red at all: they're blue, or purple, or blue-black, or nearly ebony. White wine, however, can be made from grapes of any color—pale green, golden yellow, pink, red, even from grapes that are decidedly blackish. How can this be?

Well, peel me a grape. Make it a dark-colored grape. (Or should I say "berry"?) Anyway, if you do, you'll discover that virtually all the color in a grape is in the skin. The stuff inside a red, or blue, or black grape (it's called the **pulp**) is the same pale gray-green as the stuff inside a light green or yellow grape. Red wines are red because the grape juice and skins (and also the seeds, which are called the **pips**) are kept together after the grapes have been crushed. Winespeakers say that red wines are fermented **on the skins**—an upside down–seeming way of putting it,

Peel me a grape

since the skins rise to the top of the tank or vat during fermentation. During fermentation, pigments (as well as other substances) leach from the skins into the liquid—though Winespeakers don't use an impolite word like "leach" to describe this; instead, they say that the pigments are **extracted**. And that extraction of pigments continues after fermentation, during what's called **maceration**—which is a fancy way of saying that the new wine is allowed to sit around for a while, still mixed with the skins, steeping yet more color out of them.

White wines, on the other hand, are made from juice that's been separated from the skins and seeds. As soon as grapes destined to become white wine arrive at the winery, they're destemmed and crushed, and the resulting **free-run juice** goes into the fermentation tank. (After crushing, the grapes are pressed; sometimes the juice from the pressing is added to the free-run juice, but many quality white wines are made from free-run juice only.) At any rate, it doesn't matter what shade the grapes are; the juice is pale in color, and in most cases the resulting wine will be, too. (Granted, some whites are more highly colored than others—but we'll get to the reasons for that in good time.)

Rosé wines, by the way, get their pink color in one of two ways: either the juice is allowed to remain "on" the skins for just a short time—limiting the amount of pigment extracted—or the rosé is created by blending finished red and white wines together.

BUBBLES OR NO BUBBLES?

A second way of grouping wines into categories has to do with whether or not a wine contains any dissolved carbon dioxide (CO_2) gas—and, if so, how much. Wines containing a fair amount of CO_2 *bubble* when they're uncorked; they're known as **sparkling wines**. (No, they're not all called "Champagne." In Winespeak, the word *Champagne* is reserved for the sparkling wines made in the Champagne region of France.)

Wines with no CO_2 don't bubble or fizz. They sit still, and that's what they're called: **still wines**. (The vast majority of wines produced around the world are still wines.) Carbon dioxide is a byproduct of fermentation, but, being a gas, it dissipates during fermentation. When a wine contains dissolved CO_2, the gas has been deliberately introduced into the wine sometime after the initial fermentation, either through a second fermentation in the bottle itself or in an airtight tank or through some other carbonation process. (You'll find more about this in chapter 7, on sparkling wines.)

The distinction between still and sparkling wines isn't quite the whole story, however. There are a number of wines—mostly whites but also a few reds and pinks—that contain a relatively small amount of dissolved carbon dioxide. These wines don't really bubble; they *fizz*—some more, some less energetically. Italy produces some of the best-known of these in-between wines (for example, Lambrusco), and so Italian has a word for them: ***frizzante*** (frih-ZAHNT-tay). So does French: ***pétillant*** (pay-tee-YAW^n). Some Winespeakers adopt one or the other of these words to describe any moderately fizzy wine. (Like standard English, Winespeak is spiced up with numerous foreign words and phrases.)

And then there are a few white wines into which a very small amount of CO_2 is intentionally introduced, just before bottling, to give them a slight but perceptible zing. Though these wines are classified as still wines, they actually squirm around a tiny, tiny little bit. Winespeak doesn't have an official word to designate these wines, though they're often described as "slightly fizzy" (you could have guessed that) or as "spritzy."

ANYTHING ADDED?

The next way of grouping wines into general categories has to do with whether anything has been added to the wine: sometimes more alcohol, sometimes extra alcohol plus other ingredients.

In general, the alcohol level of wine—whether sparkling or still—ranges from about 7 percent to about 14 percent by volume. There's a Winespeak term describing still wines that contain 14 percent alcohol or less: they're called **table wines**. (This traditional term may be a bit misleading, since it seems to imply either that only these wines can be drunk "at the table"—that is, with meals—or that these wines should only be drunk at the table. Neither of these things is true.) By the way, the term *table wine*, like the word *wine* itself, also has a legal meaning:

according to U.S. government regulations, a wine labeled *table wine* cannot contain more than 14 percent alcohol. Now, it's true that there are some wines (including an increasing number from California) whose alcohol level naturally exceeds 14 percent, but they don't fall within the legal definition of table wine and they're taxed at a higher rate.

But there are many kinds of wine—including some of the world's most beloved—that are *deliberately* made stronger than they would otherwise be through the addition of extra alcohol, generally in the form of brandy. These are known as **fortified wines**. Port, Sherry, Madeira, and Marsala are the most famous fortified wines.

But, once again, this simple, two-part distinction doesn't tell the whole tale. First, fortified wines like Port and Sherry also differ from table wines in the manner in which they are *aged*. Second, there is a large subcategory of fortified wines that are better known by another name: they're called **aromatized wines**. As that name implies, the smell and taste of these fortified wines have been altered and intensified through the addition of *aromatic* ingredients, including flowers, herbs, and fruits of various sorts. The best-known aromatized wines—because they're essential ingredients in so many mixed drinks—are dry vermouth and sweet vermouth, but there are many others, including French aperitif wines such as Lillet and Dubonnet.

DRY OR SWEET?

A fourth way of distinguishing among wines focuses on how sweet (or not) a wine is. A wine's sweetness—no surprise—has to do with the amount of sugar in it. If a wine contains no sugar, or an amount so small as to be imperceptible, it is called **dry**. (In Winespeak, dry is the opposite of sweet, not of wet.) If a wine contains a little bit of sugar—maybe

10 to 20 grams per liter—Winespeakers call it **off-dry** or perhaps *medium dry*. It takes yet more sugar (about 20 to 30 grams per liter) for Winespeakers to describe a wine as *sweet*, or perhaps *semisweet* if the sweetness isn't terribly pronounced. Extremely sweet wines, which can contain as much as 600 grams of sugar per liter and which are also often viscous, or honey-like, in texture, are often referred to as **dessert wines**, because they're most often drunk with—or even *as*—the last course of a meal.

How a wine becomes dry or sweet is a topic we'll deal with later. But just to tickle your interest, let me say here that a wine's sweetness doesn't necessarily have to do with how ripe (and therefore how sweet) the grapes it was made from were when they were harvested.

WHAT'S ITS NAME?

Has your attention deficit disorder kicked in yet? I rather hope not, because we have yet to tackle the most complicated way of categorizing wines: by how they are *named*.

There is no easy way to explain this system of categorizing wines, because it isn't a *system* at all—or not in the sense of something logical, sensible, and well-ordered. Rather, it's the result of differing national traditions and divergent wine-industry practices, some ancient and some relatively new. It's kind of a mess, in other words, but you're forced to negotiate this jumble every time you walk into a wine shop, so it's a good idea to be at least minimally prepared.

So let's wade right in. Wines are named in five basic ways:

- Some wines are named for the *kind of grape* they're made (or mostly made) from.

- Some wines are named for their *place of origin*—for the place the grapes are grown and the wine is made.
- Some wines have what are called *generic* names.
- Some wines are known by *proprietary* names.
- And some wines are named for the *style* of wine they represent.

I'll start explaining what each of these means in just a sec, but let me first warn you that this five-bullet scheme is a gross oversimplification. (One of the vicissitudes of learning about wine is that you quickly realize that just about anything you say about wine *in general* will be a gross oversimplification.) The truth is that most wines have several names—including, of course, the name of the wine's maker. But the maker's name isn't what I mean here; rather, I'm talking about the name that identifies what *kind* of wine a given bottle is.

Kind of Grape. Let's start with the simplest (or what seems the simplest) method for naming a wine: calling it after the kind of grape it's made (or mostly made) from. This sensible, consumer-friendly way of naming wines—the one with which we Americans are most familiar—is actually fairly new in the history of wine. It had never existed before the 1930s, when this method of naming was first adopted by some California wine producers, and the practice didn't really gain wide acceptance until the 1970s, when other U.S. winemakers as well as producers from other New World regions—that is, wine-producing regions outside the "Old World" of Europe—began following suit. (As Winespeak differs from ordinary English, so wine geography differs from the geography you learned in school. **Old World** encompasses those countries—France, Germany, Greece, Italy, Spain, and so on—

whose winemaking traditions stretch uninterruptedly back to antiquity or at least the Middle Ages. **New World** covers all the "upstarts": the countries where making wine from grapes is a more recent, or recent-*ish,* phenomenon. North and South America belong, of course, to wine's New World, as do Australia, New Zealand, and even South Africa, where wine has been made for nearly 350 years.)

A wine named after a grape is called a **varietal** wine, and today the great majority of fine table wines made in the New World are varietals.

Varietal—repeat the word (vuh-RYE-uh-tull) and make a careful mental note here, so that you'll remember to avoid an all-too-common mistake. The term *varietal* refers to a *wine* named for a grape, *not* to the grape itself. Chardonnay is a *variety* of grape, but a wine called Chardonnay is a *varietal* wine, as are any number of other wines named according to the same principle: the uncountable Sauvignon Blancs, Pinot Noirs, Cabernet Sauvignons, and so on and so on. (For a quick overview of the world's eight most important grape varieties—all of which are used to make varietals as well as other wines—see the side-bar on pages 32–33.) And while you're at it, make another mental note here: a varietal wine isn't necessarily or even usually made *entirely* from the grape it's named for. In the United States, for instance, winemakers are legally allowed to call a blended wine by a varietal name if at least 75 percent of the blend consists of wine made from a single grape variety.

Wine geography differs from what you learned in school

You might also want to note that some winemakers in America and elsewhere put varietal-type I.D.'s on blended wines even in cases where no single grape is responsible for 75 percent or more of the blend: these days, you'll find some wines labeled "Chenin Blanc–Viognier," for

HELLO, DOLLY?

Clone. The word conjures images of genetic engineering: of the creation, by test-tube means, of individuals (whether sheep, or—yipes!—human beings) that are identical in every way to their (single) parent. In common parlance, the term *clone* connotes advanced reproductive technology, a field that's both highly controversial and more than slightly frightening. So if you overhear a couple of Winespeakers talking about "clones," you should probably be forgiven for leaping to the conclusion that they're discussing some sort of high-tech genetic modification of grapevines. "Oh my god," you might think, "I only eat *organic* food. I'm certainly not going to drink wine made from a *clone!*"

Well, drink up: Although in Winespeak the word *clone* does have to do with genetic engineering, it's "engineering" of a decidedly old-fashioned sort. Grapevines, you see, aren't generally raised from seeds; for centuries, they've mostly been propagated *vegetatively*, which means that new vines are created from cuttings from existing vines. (In the old days, new vines were often created simply by sticking one of a vine's **canes**, or branches, into the soil; it would grow roots, and that would be that.) Since a vegetatively propagated vine has only one parent (so to speak), it's genetically identical to that parent—it is, in effect, a clone.

By "clone," however, Winespeakers usually mean something that's a tad more technical (if not exactly technological). Though grape growers have long engaged in what's now called **clonal selection**—preferring to take cuttings from their most vigorous vines or from those that, year after year, produce the best grapes—the practice has in recent decades become much more methodical (and commercialized). In older vineyards all over the world, the hunt is on to find especially promising vines of each major grape variety—vines that produce wine grapes of high quality and distinctive character. Cuttings (clones) from these **mother vines**, generally identified by a number, are propagated and sold to nurseries—and thence to growers—internationally. As little as twenty years ago, a grower wanting to plant, say, Merlot vines would contact the nursery and say, "Hey, I need some Merlot." Today, however, a grower can pick and choose among the diversity of Merlot clones on the market—ordering Merlot clone number 8, say, or 181, or 314, or (more likely) some combination of different clones, each of which is known to flourish under a certain set of climate and soil conditions; to provide a yield that's high, or medium, or low; and to produce wine with recognizable, more or less well-defined flavor characteristics.

Growers plant the different clones in separate parcels, and winemakers often ferment the juice in separate batches, bringing the different clonal wines together only when blending their varietals. Some producers are now listing the clones used in these "blended" varietals on wine bottle labels, thus adding another layer of complexity to the job of label-deciphering. And some single-clone varietals are now being brought to market: you might, for example, find a California "clone 6 Cabernet Sauvignon" on a wine shop shelf or restaurant wine list. (Wines made from different clones of the same variety really do taste different—even wines from the same year, made from grapes grown in the same area and produced by the same winemaker.)

If nothing else, clones give wine snobs something new to be snobbish about. Right now, somewhere in the world, there's probably a conversation going on that sounds something like this:

> **Wine Snob #1:** You won't *believe* it, but I had an absolutely superlative Cabernet clone 4 yesterday evening.

> **Wine Snob #2:** Oh, *really?* That *is* astonishing. I always find a clone 337 to be so much more formidably structured. I mean, you pay through the *nose* for a 337, but . . . .

example (indicating that the wine is a blend of wines from these two grapes), or "Cabernet Sauvignon–Merlot"—and sometimes the labels give the exact percentages of each. And to add yet another twist to varietal naming, some winemakers—relatively few so far, but their numbers are increasing—don't just put the name of the grape variety on the label, but tell you which **clone** of that variety was used to make the wine. The sidebar on pages 18–19 explains the meaning of this scary-sounding term.

Varietal versus Place Names. Sorry, but here we've got to pause before going on to the next method of naming wines—that is, by place of origin—because to grasp the difference between varietal naming and place-of-origin naming you've got to understand a philosophical divide that, historically, has separated the new from the old wine worlds.

If you walk into a wine shop and tell the salesperson you want a Sauvignon Blanc, or a Pinot Noir, or a Cabernet Sauvignon (for example), he or she will most likely steer you toward the New World wines: a shelf containing a range of different New Zealand Sauvignon Blanc varietals, say, or the one holding the Oregon Pinot Noirs, or the Chilean Cabernets, or whatever. In all probability, the salesperson will *not* lead you to the French wines section, despite the fact that many very well-known French wines are made from these same kinds of grapes: Loire Valley wines such as (white) Sancerre and Pouilly-Fumé are made from Sauvignon Blanc; red Burgundies from Pinot Noir; and Cabernet Sauvignon is a major component of many red wines from Bordeaux.

So why is it that you'll be shepherded in one direction rather than the other? Well, simply because you, the customer—no matter how unwittingly—have used New World rather than Old World nomenclature. In general, the Old World winemaking bastions of France, Italy, Spain, and some other European countries name their wines for *places,* not grapes.

This New World–versus–Old World divide is a matter of conventional practice, but these conventions are rooted in a profound philosophical difference. The New World winemakers who adopted and promoted varietal naming believed that the kind of grape used to make a wine is the predominant factor determining that wine's character. By contrast, the Old World—epitomized by France—continues to resist varietal naming because its wine industries largely adhere to the philosophy that a wine's character is fundamentally determined by local winemaking traditions and, especially, by the whereabouts of a vineyard and by the land's physical characteristics. In Winespeak, this combination of geographical location, soil composition, climate and prevailing weather, exposure to the sun, and so on goes by a fancy name: it's called ***terroir***— a French word that, among other things, is very difficult for a non-francophone to pronounce. For my stab at a definition of *terroir*, see the sidebar on pages 22–23.

Now, let me retract, or strongly modify, what I've just told you. In reality, this distinction between grape variety and *terroir* is *never* so starkly drawn. New World winemakers certainly recognize the importance of where the grapes are grown in determining what a wine is like. (How could they not? For one thing, certain kinds of vines simply don't do well in certain places, while others flourish in those same locales.) And, as I've already indicated, Old World wines are typically made from specific grapes or combinations of grapes. In fact, France, Italy, Spain, and other Old World countries strictly regulate the kinds of grapes that can be used in particular kinds of wine. The difference, historically, has been one of *emphasis* rather than out-and-out opposition.

Not only that, but this philosophical divide is, it seems, gradually collapsing. To an ever-increasing extent, New World winemakers are paying homage to *terroir* and emphasizing their vineyards' specific virtues in marketing their products. By the same token, some Old World winemakers are clamoring for their countries' regulatory institutions to allow them to apply varietal labels to their wines, largely because varietal names are so easily recognized and understood by consumers, especially American consumers. And some Old World producers, in defiance of tradition and regulations, go ahead and give their wines vari-

TERROIR-ISM

The mere whisper of the word *terroir* can set a wine novice atremble. First off, for the non–French speaker, the word is *really* hard to say. It's pronounced "teh-RWAH," more or less, though this lame phoneticization can't really convey the throat-scraping power of the word's several guttural French "r's." For the impressionable wine newbie, anybody who *can* say the word immediately assumes an air of mysterious and intimidating authority.

But don't let yourself be so easily *terroir*-ized. Even if you won't ever learn to pronounce *terroir* flawlessly, you can at least understand what it means.

My French-English dictionary defines *terroir* as "soil," but that's only part of its meaning in Winespeak. For a Winespeaker, *terroir* embraces all the natural physical attributes of a particular vineyard: not just the geological composition of its soils and subsoils but also the vineyard's climate (or, better, its *micro*climate), its placement on flat or sloping land (and, if the latter, the angle of the slope and the vineyard's orientation to the sun), even the depth of its water table. Obviously, each and every place on earth possesses a unique combination of such attributes, and *terroir* is thus the natural, physical *individuality* of a vineyard.

etal names anyway, so that it's more and more common to find French or Italian wines labeled "Merlot" for instance, or "Chardonnay."

Confusing? Just wait.

Place of Origin. In a sense, of course, *all* wines are categorized—on the most superficial level—by where they come from, and you'll find that in virtually every wine shop, wines are broadly grouped together by their countries of origin. Even very small shops (such as the one around the corner from my house, which carries only a few dozen different wines)

But *terroir* isn't just a descriptive term; it's also a subtly prescriptive one. People who are fond of the word *terroir* tend to use it (or *over*use it) as shorthand for a whole philosophy of winemaking, one that emphasizes the primacy of the vineyard in producing a wine's distinctive personality—as opposed to emphasizing the role of the particular grape variety, for example, or the winemaker's skill in crafting the wine. From the *terroirista*'s point of view, a wine should reveal and **express** its *terroir*, and wines that do not (because they are blends of wines from different *terroirs*, for example, or because the winemaker has intervened too forcefully in the winemaking process) are decidedly inferior . . . if not downright meretricious.

And there's another subtlety you might want to be aware of. The partisans of *terroir* tend to reserve the term's application only to vineyards that they, for whatever set of reasons, consider worthy. *Terroir*—though this usually goes unstated—is also term of approbation, of approval, and one just doesn't speak of the *terroir* of a second-rate vineyard. Land that's good for growing grapes that make high-quality wine has *terroir*; land that isn't somehow doesn't.

arrange foreign wines by country and American wines by state. But—here's the clincher—these broad geographic designations are *not* what I mean when I say that *some wines are named for their place of origin.*

I mean that the *primary* name by which a wine is called—the name you'd be most likely to ask for it by in a wine shop or restaurant—is the name of the region, or district, or village, or even the specific piece of property where the grapes were grown and the wine was made and bottled. In general, this is the way that wines have traditionally been named in France, Italy, Spain, and some other European countries.

To illustrate, I've just pulled three bottles off my wine rack and set them on my desk to look at: one bottle from France, one from Italy, and one from Spain. The French wine is a Sauternes. The Spanish wine is a Rioja. The Italian is a Soave Classico. Each of these names communicates that the wine was made in a certain place: the Sauternes in a section of Bordeaux, in southwestern France; the Rioja from an area of north-central Spain; and the Soave Classico from a particular zone of the larger Soave district in the Veneto region of northeastern Italy. Now, experts in such matters will know that each of these wines is made from certain varieties of grapes. The Sauternes was made from a combination of Sémillon and Sauvignon Blanc grapes; the Rioja is a blend whose major component is wine from a grape called Tempranillo; and the Soave Classico, another blend, is based mostly on the Garganega grape. The thing is, you would never be able to find this out from reading the front labels of these bottles.

You may not find the grape on the label

Don't get too fretful. You don't have to commit to memory any of the factual information in the previous paragraph. For the moment, all you have to remember is that when a wine is primarily known and identified by its place of origin, the label will not *necessarily* let you know what kind of grape or grapes the wine is made from. In fact, it's more than likely that it won't.

In France—which has the richest and most complex wine culture in the world—the system for assigning geographical names to wine is especially daunting to the novice. It's called the **Appellation d'Origine Contrôlée** system, which roughly translates into English as "controlled [place] name of origin." If your French is in need of some brushing up, don't worry about how to pronounce the term: you're allowed to say "AOC," or, even better, just "AC," for short. For the moment, all you need to know about this mind-bogglingly complex regulatory system—it's run and enforced by a sizable French-government agency—is that it permits a wine producer to give its wine a certain geographical **appellation** based on the location of the vineyard *and* the quality of the wine. In other words, the AC system both names and *ranks* wines. The same is true, for example, of the Italian regulatory system, which was instituted later than the French system and used it as a model.

Now, these appellation systems weren't invented from whole cloth. The practice of naming wines for places grows out of centuries-old traditions: Burgundies have always been called "Burgundy" because that's the region of east-central France that they come from; Chiantis have always been called "Chianti" because that's where, in the Tuscany region of Italy, they're made. But what can make appellations so opaque to the newcomer is that they don't just specify large-ish regions. The geographical nomenclature can be quite specific—in many cases denoting subregions within the larger territories and even subsubregions within those smaller areas. In other words, the designations are often (more or less) *concentric*—like the layers of an onion.

To illustrate, let's stick with France: the Bordeaux appellation, for example, covers a comparatively huge swathe of territory in the southwestern part of the country. Much of this territory is just "Bordeaux," but within the region's boundaries there are more than fifty subregions—each a distinct appellation—many of which are, in fact, smaller subdivisions of *other* appellations. Thus, Bordeaux contains (among other subdivisions) the appellation known as Haut-Médoc, and Haut-

Médoc, in turn, is itself subdivided into a number of smaller, **communal appellations** (village, or community, appellations), one of which is called Margaux. When an appellation contains other, smaller appellations that themselves contain other, yet smaller appellations, it's true as a *general* rule that the best wine comes from the *smallest* of these appellations—or, to continue with the onion metaphor, from the *inmost layer.* Thus a Margaux AC wine is likely to be better than an Haut-Médoc AC wine, and the Haut-Médoc, in turn, is likely to be better than a Bordeaux AC wine. This is the *ranking* dimension of the AC system that I mentioned, above. Or that's the way the system is set up, at any rate—with regulations concerning the quality of the grapes, the specific winemaking methods used, and the quality of the finished wine often growing stricter as the territory contracts. Unfortunately for the unschooled consumer, there are lots—*scads*—of exceptions to this general rule.

As if this weren't complicated enough, the AC system is overlaid with other, regional classificatory systems—including four in Bordeaux itself—that further discriminate among wines of higher and lower quality. We'll wait till later to wrangle with these intricacies, but, just to ice this half-baked cake, let me mention that there is one French wine-producing region—Alsace—whose wines are also given *varietal* names under the AC system.

> # The AC system wasn't devised to confuse you—it just seems that way

Now, I'm willing grant that the AC system and similar systems in other European countries were not devised to befuddle and defeat the likes of you and me. It just *seems* that way. So let's say *ça suffit pour le moment* and turn—quickly, please!—to a few other, mercifully simpler, methods for naming wines.

Generic Names. Few if any people who really care about wine pay any attention at all to wines with **generic names**. Generically named wines—the various California "chablis" and "burgundy" jug wines, for example—are cheap, mass-produced, and uninteresting even if reliably consistent. (Today, "jug" wines are as likely to come in a cardboard box, with an airtight plastic bladder inside, as in a glass jug.) You might think of generics as wine's equivalent to Kraft cheddar if not actually to pasteurized process cheese food. Still, it's worth mentioning them here, since their names are sometimes deceptive and might produce a moment of confusion in a wine novice's mind.

How, you might ask yourself, can a California wine be a *Chablis* or a *Burgundy*? Aren't those the names of French wines? Well, yes they are. Because Chablis and Burgundy (Fr., Bourgogne) are French appellations, a California wine cannot, by definition, be a Chablis or a Burgundy—nor can it be a Chianti, for that matter (Chianti being an Italian geographical denomination). But that hasn't stopped some New World makers of mass-market wines (including some Australian companies, as well) from slapping deluxe Old World names on their mediocre products. For the most part, such makers don't even bother to imitate the Old World wines

But isn't Burgundy in France?

whose names they steal. A real (red) Burgundy, for example, is made only from Pinot Noir grapes, but a California "burgundy" might be made from any number of red-wine grapes, probably *not* including Pinot Noir. A real (i.e., French) Chablis is made only from Chardonnay grapes and is ineffably dry, but a California "chablis" might be stewed up from numerous white wine grapes, and might be ineffably icky.

It's true that the generic use of such names has fallen off in recent years, as consumers have become more sophisticated and as European countries—which forbid the importation of such mislabeled wines—have become adamant in their objections to the practice. But it hasn't disappeared. The E&J Gallo company still markets a "hearty burgundy," and Almaden still has a "chianti" and a "chablis" (and even a "light chablis") in its lineup. Still, it's likelier these days that a generic wine will simply be called red (or white, or rosé) table wine. And that's about as generic as you can get.

Proprietary Names. Some wines (more and more all the time, in fact) are known by **proprietary names**—that is, by names that winemakers simply *make up*. For example, there's a very creative California maker called Bonny Doon Vineyard, all of whose wines have proprietary names. Some of Bonny Doon's wines' names are witty (or possibly just silly): there's the Critique of Pure Riesling, for instance, and Le Cigare

Volant—the latter, whose name means "Flying Cigar," is a blended red wine that's Bonny Doon's knockoff of the Châteauneuf-du-Pape wines of France's southern Rhône Valley. Wines with proprietary names can be ordinary or extraordinary. One of the most famous such names is Mouton-Cadet, made by the French winemaking company Baron Philippe de Rothschild, which also makes the world-famous, exorbitantly expensive Château Mouton-Rothschild. Unlike their celebrated relative, Mouton-Cadet red and Mouton-Cadet white are reliable but unremarkable Bordeaux wines. But some Italian proprietary-name wines—Tignanello, for instance—are widely regarded as among the best wines that Italy produces (and are also among the priciest).

Style. Finally, there are some wines that are named for the particular *style* they embody. For example, a number of American makers produce what are called **Meritage** wines. These blended wines imitate the blended wines of the Bordeaux region of France—or, rather, they use various combinations of the same varieties of grapes traditionally used in Bordeaux wines. Now, *Meritage* (rhymes with "heritage") isn't a geographical designation, and it's certainly not a varietal (these wines are blends, some of them complex blends), and it's not a proprietary name in the sense of belonging to only one wine. And even though Meritage wines constitute a genre, you'd hardly call them "generic," which has a disreputable connotation. So for lack of a better term, let's call this kind of name a *style* designation.

Phew. I think we're done with the name game, at least for now. To help you sift through all the information that's just been dumped on you, the table on the next page summarizes the various ways of classifying wines and the major groupings within each of those broad categories.

CLASSIFYING WINES

Mode of Classification	Major Groupings
By color	Red White Rosé (a.k.a. pink, or blush)
By absence or presence of dissolved CO_2	Still Sparkling *Frizzante*, or *pétillant*
By absence or presence of additives (alcohol and other ingredients)	Table wines Fortified wines Aromatized wines
By level of sweetness	Dry Off-dry, or medium dry Semisweet Sweet Dessert (i.e., extremely sweet)
By name	Varietal names Geographical names Generic names Proprietary names Style-based names

You may recall that near the beginning of this section, I said that all these ways of categorizing wine are *divergent yet overlapping*. Well, we've covered the divergent part; now, let's talk about the overlap.

It's simple, really: Any wine you can think of can be classified in several different ways, and to begin to describe it, you have to use multiple categories. To take a few examples from wines already mentioned:

- A brut Champagne is a dry white (or possibly rosé) sparkling wine made in the Champagne region of France.

- A California Cabernet Sauvignon is a dry red varietal table wine.

- A Sauternes is a white dessert (i.e., very sweet) wine made in the Sauternes appellation of Bordeaux, France.

- Bonny Doon's Le Cigare Volant is a proprietary-name dry red table wine.

- Almaden Light Chablis is a sham.

Oh, wait. I flubbed that last one, didn't I? I guess I need to do some growing up, too.

IT WAS A VERY GOOD (OR BAD) YEAR

You need, I think, just one more vocabulary lesson before moving out of this stifling nursery-school classroom. The vocabulary word is **vintage**, and, as you might guess, the meanings of *vintage* in Winespeak don't quite correspond to its meanings in ordinary English. It doesn't mean "old," for example, and usually—there are some exceptions, which we'll get to—it does not, in and of itself, connote anything about quality or value.

The original meaning of *vintage* is the actual *harvest* of the grapes, as in, "The vintage began on October 3 and went on through the first

THE BIG SIX (PLUS TWO)

Introductory wine classes sometimes concentrate on the so-called Big Six: the six most important "international" grape varieties, used to make many of the world's best-known wines. The theory is that by learning a little something about just these six varieties, you'll acquire a basic handle on the wine world—its connectedness *and* its diversity. Not a bad pedagogical tack at all, but I think that this exclusive Group of Six needs to be expanded to admit at least two more members. Here are grapes most wine educators define as the Big Six, the three reds and the three whites:

Red Wine Varieties	White Wine Varieties
Cabernet Sauvignon	Chardonnay
Merlot	Riesling
Pinot Noir*	Sauvignon Blanc

And here are my candidates for club membership: Syrah (a.k.a. Shiraz) in the red group, and Pinot Gris (a.k.a. Pinot Grigio) in the white. And, yes, it is inconvenient that each of these grapes has two different names. (The names vary according to where the grapes are grown.)

What do all these varieties have in common? Well, first off, they're all strains, or breeds, of *Vitis vinifera*. But that's not so remarkable, since the vast majority of grapes used to make wine belong to this species. More telling is the fact that seven of the eight varieties originally appeared, centuries ago, in France. Even Riesling, the lone, German-born exception, is an important grape in the French region of Alsace. Of the French varieties, all are used, either by themselves or in combination with other grapes, to make one or more of the great wines for which France is so renowned: most red Bordeaux are made primarily from Cabernet Sauvignon and/or Merlot. Dry white Bordeaux are partly made from Sauvignon Blanc, and many Loire Valley whites are composed of Sauvignon Blanc alone. Many red Rhône wines employ Syrah, either solely or in blends; Chardonnay is the basis of the white wines of Burgundy, including Chablis. Pinot Gris is a notable, varietally named wine of Alsace. And all red Burgundies except Beaujolais are made from Pinot Noir. (Pinot Noir is also used in many Champagnes—sparkling *white* wines—which is why there's an asterisk next to it on the "red wine varieties" list.)

Just as important, all these varieties have "traveled" very well—and very extensively. Each is now widely grown elsewhere in the world, and together they're the basis for the world's most popular varietal wines, including (among many, many others) California Cabernets and Chardonnays, Oregon Pinot Noirs, Washington State Merlots, and Sauvignon Blancs from New Zealand and South Africa. To my mind, the burgeoning world-wide popularity of Australian Shirazes and Italian Pinot Grigios (not to mention Pinot Gris varietals from Oregon) makes club membership for Syrah/Shiraz and Pinot Gris/Pinot Grigio imperative.

As with NATO and the European Union, there will always be new contenders for membership in the elite group. Among the up-and-coming is a red wine grape called Malbec. It, too, is natively French—it's one of the traditional grapes of Bordeaux—but its importance there has declined markedly over the past century. What makes it a contender on the world scene is its vitality in Argentina, where it is extensively cultivated and produces some knockout wines. And, personally, I'm also keeping my fingers crossed for Chenin Blanc, another French grape (the white wines of Vouvray are based on it) that does beautifully in the hands of some California and South African winemakers.

So drink up—every time you quaff a wine, you're casting a vote in an ongoing international popularity contest, and every vote counts.

week in November." By extension, the word came to mean the *year* during which the grapes in a given wine were harvested: a wine labeled "Cabernet Sauvignon 2001" is a *vintage 2001* Cabernet. Some wines are **vintage wines** and some aren't; **nonvintage wines** (sometimes identified with the initials "NV") are *blends* of wines made from grapes harvested in two or more different years. Easy enough, huh?

Well, not so fast. Remember, we're talkin' Winespeak here. If a wine label shows a vintage year, it doesn't necessarily mean that *all* the grapes used to make that wine were harvested during that year—just that *almost* all of them were. U.S. law permits a winemaker to put a vintage year on a wine's label so long as at least 95 percent of the grapes from which it was made were harvested that year.

The mere fact that a wine is identified as belonging to a particular vintage says *nothing whatsoever* about how good it is. Vintages vary in quality. In any wine grape–growing locale, some years are excellent, some years are decently good, some are just O.K., and some are awful. The quality of a vintage is mostly the result of the weather during the growing season. Were there any late frosts that killed some of the vines' buds? Was there a good balance between rain and sun over the summer? Were the weeks leading up to the harvest dry and warm (good) or wet and cold (bad)? So to know what, exactly, a particular vintage signals, you've got to know what the weather that year was like in the place the grapes were grown.

Now, don't panic. Nobody's asking you to pore over the meteorological records of Bordeaux in 1998 or the Napa Valley in 2001. The work of gathering weather data from all the world's wine-producing regions, year by year—and of evaluating, in overall terms, the wine produced in each region each year—has already been done for you. It appears in the **vintage charts** compiled by various wine industry–related organizations and publications. (*Wine Spectator* magazine, to take just one example, publishes vintage charts for most important winemaking areas. The charts are available on *Wine Spectator*'s website, www.winespectator.com, but you've got to be a member of Wine Spectator Online, at a cost of about $50 per year, to access them. Like other vintage charts, those published by *Wine Spectator* also tell you whether the experts consider wines of this or that vintage to be ready to drink yet—that is, whether they've been in the bottle long enough to be at their peak. The *Spectator*'s charts also give point-scores to vintages. We'll be talking about both of these matters—bottle ageing and wine scoring—in chapter 3.)

So how much do you, a wine newbie with no head for facts and figures, need to know about the relative quality of various vintages in any given winemaking region? *Nothing.* Or not in the sense that you have to *memorize* anything. If you need to know whether a particular vintage is considered good or not, you can simply consult a vintage chart for that region—and many wine shops keep vintage charts on hand to help their customers in making decisions. But you may find the following two principles helpful:

- In general, vintage matters less for New World wines than for Old World wines—particularly Old World wines from more northerly areas where there's greater variation in the weather from year to year. So if you're buying a moderately priced wine from California, or Australia, or Chile, don't worry too much about vintage. Such wines tend to be more consistent from year to year than, say, wines from Burgundy, whose weather is much less predictable.

- Note that in the previous item I say, "if you're buying a *moderately priced* wine." If you're shelling out a lot of dough for a premium bottle of wine *from anywhere*, you might want to try to make sure that it's the best available vintage. Say you're feeling flush and decide to treat yourself to a fifty-buck wine, a California Cabernet, maybe. You walk into a wine shop and on its shelves find two different Napa Valley "Cabs," by two different makers, at about that price point. You've never heard of either label, so that can't help you decide. You ask a salesperson for advice, but he turns out to be an obnoxious **cork dork** who rattles off a bunch of "information" that you're too embarrassed to admit you don't under-stand. Then you notice that one of the Cabernets is a 2000 and the other a 2001. Well, ask the guy if he's got a vintage chart you can look at. It *may* help you choose one over the other.

Unfortunately, however, the second of these principles is hardly fool-proof. The ugly truth is that a vintage chart can provide only a moder-ately trustworthy clue as to how good or not a wine of a particular vin-tage might be. Why? For the simple reason that even in a "bad" year, some winemakers within an afflicted region may manage to turn out exceptional wines, and even in a "good" year some makers will produce mediocre wines. Vintage charts are like actuarial tables: they give prob-abilities, not certainties. (It also merits mention that vintage charts themselves are to some extent *opinions*—that is, that the vintage charts published by one person or organization may differ from those pub-lished by another.)

Though you're wishing it were so, we're not yet quite through with vintage's Winespeak meanings. As I hinted above, the appearance of a vintage year on a wine bottle's label does, in a *few* cases, indicate that the wine is of better-than-average quality. This is true of Champagne and Port. Now, Champagne and Port are about as unlike one another as wines can get, but they do have something in common. Most Champagnes and most Ports are nonvintage wines—blends of wines from different harvests. There's a reason for this: if you blend wines of various vintages together, you can achieve a more or less consistent taste, or "style," over time. But every so often a year is *so* good—producing grapes of such high quality—that a Champagne maker or Port maker may decide to **declare a vintage year** and bottle a wine made from that year's grapes alone. Vintage Champagnes and vintage Ports are therefore often extraordinary wines—*but* (and this is an important "but") they are sometimes very different in character from the nonvintage wines made by the same maker.

So *vintage* (in Winespeak) doesn't mean "old," and it only sometimes means "good," and knowing a wine's vintage may or may not be helpful in determining its quality. Now that that's settled . . .

CHAPTER TWO

Ambling through the Vintage

(A FIELD TRIP TO A VINEYARD AND WINERY)

I KNOW, I KNOW. YOU DON'T *CARE* HOW WINE IS MADE. AFTER ALL, you're not about to plant a bunch of vines on your quarter-acre lot or set up a DIY winemaking operation in your underutilized powder room. You care about how wine *tastes*—and besides, you probably have an uncomfortable premonition that *really* understanding grape growing and winemaking would require a fair amount of technical knowledge about botany, chemistry, and the rest. (You'd be right on that score.)

The problem with your blissfully ignorant, entirely reasonable attitude, however, is that you can't really understand wine unless you know at least a little bit about how it's created. And so this chapter proposes to equip you with *just enough* knowledge to enhance your experience of wine, but not so much as to give you a headache. (We'll let the wine itself do that.) En route, you'll be expanding your Winespeak vocabulary—since so much of that distinctive language's terminology is drawn from the lingo of the grape grower and winemaker.

Words, Words, Words

We're going to learn about grape growing and winemaking in a highly sensible way: by visiting a vineyard and winery. But before we start that journey, I'm afraid there are just a few more essential Winespeak terms I think you ought to know.

The creation of wine is a three-phase process—we'll witness part of each phase on our winery visit—and there's a word for each: *viticulture, vinification,* and *élevage*. Though the terms sound forbidding, their meanings are fairly straightforward:

Viticulture, whose prefix comes from the Latin *vitis,* for "vine," is the specialized form of agriculture that concerns the cultivation of grapevines and the nurture and harvest of their fruit. Everything that happens in the vineyard—up to and including the picking of the grapes—is viticulture.

Vinification, whose prefix *vin-* comes from the French word for "wine," begins when the harvested grapes arrive at the winery. Basic vinification techniques differ according to whether red, white, or rosé wine is being made, but in any case the central event in vinification is **fermentation**—a natural process that winemakers attempt to direct or control. (For a look at why fermentation *needs* to be controlled, see the sidebar on pages 40–42.)

The third term, **élevage,** is the toughest of the three for not-yet-fluent Winespeakers. It comes from French, obviously. Pronounced eh-luh-VAHZH, it means "raising" (in the sense of the raising of children), and it covers everything that's done to wine from the time fermentation is completed until the wine is bottled and sometimes even beyond. You might think of élevage as "wine rearing": a process that turns untamed, juvenile wine into something more mature and well-behaved.

CONTROLLED VIOLENCE

Fermentation is something that happens naturally, all by itself. Frankly, *fermentation* is nothing more than a polite word for a kind of *rotting*. As soon as a ripe fruit is picked—or as soon as its skin is pricked or bruised—that fruit begins to ferment.

The world, you see—or rather you *don't* see—is thrumming with uncountable microbes, including endless platoons of single-celled buggers called **yeasts**. Yeasts live blessedly simple lives, existing for two purposes only: to eat carbohydrates and to reproduce, which they do by budding little yeast cells right off themselves (no sex partner required). So as soon as a yeast cell (a spore, really, but we won't get into that) sidles up to something wet and sugary or starchy, it starts chowing down—and making lots of babies, which quickly follow in the same career path as their parent.

Now, as I'm sure you're aware, digestion produces byproducts, and luckily for human beings, the two main byproducts resulting from yeast's carb consumption—carbon dioxide and alcohol—are very useful and desirable. Where yeast have access to lots of oxygen, they mostly produce CO_2. That's what happens in bread dough leavened with yeast: the CO_2 creates little bubbles in the dough, causing it to rise. But where yeast are deprived of oxygen, as they are in a liquid-filled tank or vat, the little sots also produce a lot of alcohol—specifically, the potable, intoxicating kind of alcohol called **ethyl alcohol** (a.k.a. **ethanol**). As we'll see, their gluttony is their undoing, since the alcohol they create eventually poisons them, but we'll return to that moral lesson in a moment.

Given the right environment (plenty of food, a comfy temperature), yeast reproduce *very* rapidly—they put rabbits to shame. And as a yeast population increases, what began as a nice family meal quickly turns into an outright feeding frenzy. Once it gets going, fermentation is a *violent* process.

(There's a good reason that our word "ferment" can connote a situation that's heating up, restless, ready to explode.)

So, really, a winemaker doesn't *have* to do anything to encourage or direct fermentation: fruit juice and ambient yeast do the trick all by themselves. But the rapidity with which fermentation can progress points to one important reason that winemakers try to control it. If fermentation proceeds too quickly—gets too "hot"—the quality of the wine (especially white wine) may be negatively affected. By the same token, a winemaker might want to hasten fermentation for some wines, or to make sure that the process doesn't get interrupted, as it might, for example, if it becomes too chilly for the yeast to remain active. The speed at which fermentation occurs is controlled by regulating the temperature either of the fermentation vessel itself or of the space housing that tank or vat. Red wines are usually fermented quickly, the process lasting only a few days; for whites, however, fermentation is often deliberately protracted in refrigerated tanks and might go on for weeks or even months.

Winemakers also control fermentation by choosing the *kind* of yeast used. Though winemaking yeasts all belong to the same species, there are lots of different strains, with different traits. Some occur naturally—they're just hanging around, waiting for their next meal-ticket—but yeasts are also specially bred, or **cultured,** to enhance certain traits. For winemaking purposes, the most important of these is a yeast's tolerance for alcohol. Some wild yeasts have a very low tolerance: they'll die off if the alcohol in solution reaches a level as low as 5 percent; some cultured yeasts, by contrast, can really hold their liquor, surviving at alcohol levels of up to 20 percent.

Why is this important? Well, in the majority of cases, it's desirable that the fermentation be *completed*—that is, that the yeast consume *all* the sugar in the grape juice and that the wine be **fermented to dryness**. If a yeast's alcohol tolerance is too low, it may die before fermentation is finished. But even when it's a sweet, rather than a dry, wine that's being made, the yeast needs to be hardy enough to survive until the desired alcohol level is achieved. Although it's true that some winemakers continue to rely on naturally occurring yeasts to ferment their wines, most contemporary winemakers inoculate the tank with one or another strain of cultured yeast to prevent what's called a **stuck**—that is, incomplete—fermentation. (By the way, some winemakers choose specific cultured-yeast strains rather than others because they also believe that different yeasts impart subtly different flavors to the wine.)

For now, there's just one more thing that you should know about fermentation. Unfortunately, it can be a little bewildering to the non-microbiologist, but here goes: the yeast fermentation of a wine is often accompanied or followed by a secondary fermentation, known as **malolactic** (mal-oh-LACK-tick) fermentation. This fermentation is performed by bacteria that convert the sharp, stinging *malic* acid naturally present in grape juice into another, much milder kind of acid, called *lactic* acid. Malolactic fermentation softens a wine's apparent acidity and can give wine a flavor often described as "buttery" (which makes sense, given that lactic acid is the main acid present in cultured dairy products, such as buttermilk). It's desirable for some wines (most reds and a few whites, like Chardonnay) to undergo this secondary fermentation, but it's not so good for others—especially those white wines that are prized for their crisp acidity. Winemakers therefore use various techniques either to encourage malolactic fermentation or to prevent it from happening. (Don't confuse the [secondary] malolactic fermentation with the "second fermentation" to which many sparkling wines are subjected. That is also a yeast fermentation. But don't worry: all will become clear in chapter 7, on sparkling wines.)

You're maybe noticing that Winespeak terms are often rooted in or come directly from foreign languages? Well, think about it: Although the Romans introduced grapevines to England after they'd conquered it and although some wine is made—and a great deal is drunk—there today, the British Isles' rainy, cool climate doesn't generally lend itself to viticulture, and Anglo-Saxon therefore wasn't rich in wine-related words. Besides borrowing from Latin and French, Winespeak also cadges from ancient Greek, as in the word **oenophile** ("wine lover"; pronounced ee-no-FILE, it's a compound formed from the Greek words *oinos*, "wine," and *philos*, "loving"). Greek also gives us **enologist** (an expert in the scientific aspects of winemaking), whose prefix, despite the different spelling, also comes from *oinos*.

Enologists, while we're on the subject, are often freelance consultants—big winemaking operations have their own enologists; smaller wineries hire freelance enologists when they need advice. An enologist isn't necessarily a **winemaker** (or vice versa), and, actually, *winemaker* is a somewhat ambiguous word. It can be loosely used to mean any wine producer (person or company), but it also means that staffperson at any winery who's responsible for making all the decisions about how the wines are vinified and the kind of élevage each wine undergoes.

O.K., I'll stop! I promised you some R&R from the vocabulary exercises, so off to the country we go.

A Gentleman and His Vines

Bob Pellegrini is a small man with longish gray hair, a pleasantly rumpled look, large, expressive hands, and a genial, self-effacing manner that you wouldn't necessarily expect from someone who's the owner of one of Long Island's most long-established winemaking operations.

Bob and his wife, Joyce, established their winery, Pellegrini Vineyards, back in 1984, when there were only half a dozen other wineries on Long Island's North Fork. Today there are more than twenty-five, and this little finger of land poking between Long Island Sound and the Great Peconic Bay is an up-and-coming wine-producing area.

A mutual friend put me in touch with Bob. When I called him, he was quick to invite me and a companion to join him at the winery for a personal guided tour—a visit that turned out to be the best, most thorough and informative, winery tour I've ever had. And so I thought I'd let you experience it vicariously. Not because Pellegrini Vineyards is a typical, or representative, winemaking operation. But rather because all the issues Bob talked to us about—forthrightly and at length—are the kinds of issues *any* wine producer, anywhere in the winemaking world, would encounter. The kinds of grapes Bob's decided to grow, the wines he makes from them, and the methods he uses to create those wines—these are all *particular* decisions arising from the North Fork's distinct *terroir* and climate and from Bob's (and his winemaking staff's) own take on common winemaking practices. But I think our visit to Pellegrini Vineyards told me more about winemaking *in general* than any abstract summary could—and I'm hoping it does something similar for you.

Wine, needless to say, begins in the vineyard. (There's an old saw that declares, "Wine is *made* in the vineyard," pointing to the central, undeniable importance of the quality of the grapes to the quality of the wine that's ultimately made from them.) Appropriately, the vineyard is where our tour of Pellegrini commences.

We arrive on a blustery, overcast, chilly Saturday afternoon in late October. Bob greets us and immediately leads us out to Pellegrini's main vineyard, which occupies several acres of (very) gently rolling land just behind the winery compound. Though by the calendar we're more than a month into fall, the vines are still mostly green. The harvest, we soon learn, has been going on for almost a month: it's almost finished, though there are still some grapes waiting to be picked.

Bob Pellegrini is now both a grape grower and a wine producer. His wines are **estate bottled,** which just means that the wine is made from grapes grown on site—vineyard and winery are parts of the same operation. But this wasn't always the case. When, more than twenty years ago, he first set up his winemaking business, he bought his grapes from other, local producers while he waited for his own, newly planted vines to mature. It generally takes about three years, he explains, for a young vine to begin reliably bearing fruit. (Most vines, by the way, have productive life spans of twenty-five to forty years, though there are plenty of instances of vines producing good—even superlative—fruit for one hundred years or more.)

As we look out over the vineyard—and the handsome white gazebo plunked down in the middle of it—Bob tells us that his intentions as a winemaker were (and remain) pretty straightforward: "I wanted to create well-made, reasonably priced wines that—though I'd use international varieties— would express the North Fork in all its distinctness." Embedded in that remark is an acknowledgment of the first decision a wannabe wineproducer has to make: which kind or kinds of vines to plant. It's a decision that's based partly on local experience—and by the time Bob arrived on the North Fork, the handful of growers who'd preceded him had had good luck with a few of the well-known varieties you began to learn about in chapter 1. But it's based, too, on an educated guess about which grape varieties are likely to flourish in a given place, with a given climate.

> **It takes three years for a vine to begin reliably bearing fruit**

TRAINING MANEUVERS

Viticultural success is largely a result of three factors: location, location, and location. The reason that the winemaking industry has expanded so dramatically on Long Island's North Fork over the past two decades is that this sliver of land turns out to be a fairly good place to grow a fairly wide range of grapes—not just the white-wine varieties that tend to do well in cooler climates but also a number of slower-ripening red-wine grapes, which demand longer growing seasons than can generally be found this far north. The key, Bob tells us, is the North Fork's position between two large bodies of water, combined with how very *narrow* this eyelash of land is. Not only do the sound (to the north) and the bay (to the south) considerably moderate temperatures during summer and winter alike, but because the landspit is so skinny—there's no place on the North Fork that's more than a mile from the water—the whole peninsula enjoys the water's moderating influence. The growing season here averages 220 days annually: equivalent to that of Virginia or North Carolina. Even during the coldest winters, temperatures seldom fall low enough or remain below freezing long enough to kill the buds—from which the next year's new growth will sprout—on *Vitis vinifera* vines.

The North Fork has another advantage besides its mild climate. "Remember," says Bob, "it's really a sandbar." The North Fork's relatively thin topsoil is, he explains, about 30 percent sand, and the subsoils underlying it are a mix of sand and gravel. Why is that a good thing? For the reason that grapevines *like* relatively poor soils and are especially fond of soils with good drainage. As a general rule, the best grapes result when vines are forced to do a little work to find water and nutrients. Put a grapevine in a place with rich, well-watered soil and it may *seem* to do well, putting out scads of leaves and piles of fruit, but this apparent abundance is deceptive—so much growth diminishes the fruit's quality. That's why producers of fine wines are so concerned about controlling **yield**. If a vine's producing too many grapes, the grapes won't have as high a concentration of sugar and flavor as those from a vine with a lower yield. And one way to control yield is to plant vines in places where they'll suffer a little bit of environmental stress—in places with sandy soils and subsoils, or where the land is calciferous (chalky), or slatey, or

Poor soils can make for great grapes

gravelly. (There are other ways of controlling yield: for example, some growers perform a so-called **green harvest** during the summer, getting rid of "excess" clusters in hopes of intensifying the concentration of the remaining grapes.)

Based on his neighbors' experience and his own educated guesswork, Bob ultimately decided to plant his vineyards —the one behind the winery and another, smaller property a few miles east on Route 25—with six different varieties. Four of these belong to the "Big Eight" discussed in chapter 1: the white-wine varieties Chardonnay and Sauvignon Blanc and the red-wine varieties Cabernet Sauvignon and Merlot. But two of the varieties Bob raises may be unfamiliar to you: a red-wine grape called Cabernet Franc, which is a component of many of the blended wines of Bordeaux (and wines modeled on them), and a white-wine variety called Gewürztraminer, which originated in Italy but is most often associated with Alsace and Germany. (Hence the German name, which is pronounced geh-VERTZ-trah-mee-ner, in case you're wondering.)

As time's gone on and Bob's expanded Pellegrini Vineyards' holdings, he's become more selective with the new vines he buys. "Twenty years ago," he recalled, "we didn't know anything about clones. Merlot was Merlot was Merlot." Nowadays, though, various clones of numerous varieties are available from American nurseries, and some of the more recently planted areas of Pellegrini's vineyards are dedicated to specific Merlot clones, which are harvested separately, vinified separately, aged separately (at least for a while), and then blended to make Pellegrini's Merlot varietals.

Deciding which vines to plant is just a preliminary step in the viticultural process, however. Next, you've got to decide how many vines to plant per acre—and how wide apart to space the rows. Doing so involves a delicate balance: you want to ensure an adequate (but not too great!) per-acre yield, but you also have to allow enough room between rows so that a tractor can efficiently navigate the vineyard. At the majority of modern vineyards, Pellegrini included, most of the harvesting, and most of the work of caring for the vines, is performed mechanically. (At Pellegrini, only the Gewürztraminer grapes are harvested by hand.) Caring for the vineyard is, by the way, a year-round effort. In winter, the vines are **pruned** to control the next season's growth; in summer, they're subjected to what's called **canopy management**—a technical term for the cutting away of superfluous foliage to ensure that the vine doesn't waste too much energy on its leaves and that just the right amount of sunshine reaches the ripening grapes. On the question of how far apart to plant his vines, Bob admitted that he's still experimenting. In different sectors of the vineyards, he's planted the rows at different intervals, not yet certain which (if any) of these patterns will achieve the elusive balance between yield and efficiency.

Bob talks with us, too, about the method he uses for **training** his vines—though I've got to admit that here he begins to lose me! (I consider it a mercy, as should you, that neo-oenophiles don't have to know nuthin' 'bout trainin' no vines.) What I *do* manage to grasp is that grapevines *need* to be trained, that is, they have to be supported by some structure (often a **trellis**) or else—being vines that evolved, originally, to hang on trees—they'll fall over. The particular method Bob uses is called the *cordon* method, in which the part of the vine called the cordon (extending upward from the trunk) is forced to grow horizontally along a wire strung between posts. The branches emerging from the cordon grow upward, supported by the other wires of the fencelike trellis.

I'd noticed that all the vineyards we'd passed en route to Pellegrini seemed to employ the same training system, and Bob confirms it's the preferred method on Long Island. The visual result is strikingly architectural: the long rows of meticulously trained vines, their strictly "managed" foliage nearly flat against the supporting trellis wires. It's true that every agricultural landscape displays human beings' reshaping and ordering of nature—that's part of farmland's beauty, I think—but nowhere is this truer than in a vineyard.

Concluding this first part of our lesson, Bob points out that strung along each of his trellises is a length of rubber tubing: the whole vineyard is equipped with a drip **irrigation** system. Whether or not to irrigate is, it turns out, a contested issue in wine grape–growing circles. Though it's common in the New World, especially in areas subject to periodic drought, Old World winemakers tend to look down their aquiline noses at the practice, believing that it impairs the quality of the grapes. (In fairness, some Old World regions receive regular-enough rainfall that irrigation is unnecessary.) Bob *does* seem the eensiest bit defensive about his decision to install the drip system: Pellegrini uses it, he insists, only during protracted dry spells, when the earth is desiccated and hardened and the vines' leaves are beginning to shrivel and brown—a sure sign that photosynthesis has stopped, shutting down the grapes' growth and ripening.

SNIP SNIP HERE

But enough talk. It's time we had a close-up look at the harvest, which, as I mentioned above, is still going on nearly a month after it began. Bob tells us that they're finishing up with the Gewürztraminer vines today. To see the work in progress, though, we have to travel to Pellegrini's other vineyard. (All the grapes in the main vineyard have been harvested.)

We hop in Bob's car, and as he drives Bob voices annoyance about the weather. (Grape growers, like all farmers, do a lot of fretting about the weather.) Eastern Long Island, he explains, usually enjoys a glorious Indian summer during late October—a period of warm, sunshiny days that help bring the late-harvested red grapes to perfect ripeness. This year, it just ain't happening: the North Fork has had a week of overcast skies and chilly temperatures, and today—with thick cloud cover and the thermometer hovering in the mid-50s—is no exception. Bob's not over-anxious. This growing season, he says, has been an exceptionally good one, and, in any case, most of the crop has already been brought in. Still, he's been hoping to give some of his Merlot vines just a little more time to finish their work. The forecast, he says, is now calling for warmer weather and clearer skies, so he'll hold off for a few more days before bringing in the last of the Merlot crop.

In response to a question, Bob explains that Pellegrini Vineyards uses all the usual technical methods for determining the right moment to pick the grapes, including tests of the ripening grapes' **pH** and **Brix**—commonly employed scientific measures of grapes' acidity and sugar content, respectively. "But we don't just depend on what the numbers tell us," Bob says. "We're also always *tasting* the grapes." It's the good old-fashioned human tongue that provides the final litmus on when the grapes are ready to be picked.

Within just a few minutes we're turning into the drive leading to Pellegrini's second vineyard. As soon as we're on the property, we see the Gewürztraminer vines—and the workers harvesting their grapes. It's fastidious work and looks both boring and difficult. The little clusters, only a few per vine, hang near the bottom of the trellises, below the vines' foliage. The workers are spread out along the row, and each is moving from cluster to cluster, crouching down, snipping the stem with scissors, and carefully laying the bunch alongside others in a plastic tray.

I'm surprised by the color of the grapes (Bob calls it "mahogany," but it's more like a rosy butterscotch) and by their small size—the berries aren't much larger than peas. But what's more surprising is the raggedy appearance of the clusters. On most of the bunches, only about half the berries appear to be fully developed; the rest are stunted or missing. Bob explains that this is typical of Gewürztraminer's performance on the North Fork. In some rare vintages, the **fruit set** is good and all the berries mature. Sometimes (equally rarely), the clusters are nearly bare of fruit. But usually North Fork Gewürztraminer growers end up with these tattered, half-eaten-looking bunches.

Leaving the workers behind (and, for my part, feeling guilty relief after viewing their hard labor through the window of an automobile), we tool around the rest of the vineyard. Most of the rows here are planted with Merlot—the very vines that Bob wants to give a little more **hang time** to, before harvesting. The Merlot clusters—each a compact, triangular pendant of nearly black fruit suspended below the vine's foliage—are certainly a lot more attractive than the Gewürztraminer, and they certainly look ripe to me, but then what do I know?

Cold Soaks and Monster Mashers

Within a few minutes we're back at the winery and ready to move from the viticultural phase to phase 2—vinification. The **destemming** and **crushing** operations are quiet today, so we're skipping ahead to fermentation, though we do pause to have a look at Pellegrini's state-of-the-art **bladder press**, a large, sleek metal cylinder that, Bob explains, contains a huge "balloon." When crushed grapes are added to the press, the balloon is gradually inflated, squeezing them against a perforated interior wall; the press juice flows through the perforations and then travels through airtight channels into the fermentation process.

It's been obvious since our earlier arrival at the winery that fermentation is going on: the smell of fermenting grape juice—it's called **must** at this stage—pervades the whole place. The odor is deeply organic: it smells like wine, yes, but there's also something bready about it (the yeast), and something slightly putrid, too—not an unpleasant smell, but not exactly appetizing, either. It's one of those profound odors that doesn't disappear; you're always aware of it. And it grows much more intense when we, following Bob, go through an exterior door into the fermenting room.

This is a cavernous, high-ceilinged space, with several ranks of enormous stainless steel tanks resting on its floor. We're far above, on a railed balcony that partly encircles the room, more or less level with the tops of the tanks nearby. The tank closest to us is open, its lid suspended from a chain, and we can see that it's filled with red-wine must—a pulpy, chunky-looking mixture of crushed grapes, skins and all. I know that red wines are fermented "on the skins," but here I am, actually *seeing* red-wine fermentation for the first time . . . or so I think.

As it happens, that's *not* what I'm seeing. A winery worker is perched at the top of the tank, fiddling with something. He looks up when we enter, smiles winningly, and greets Bob, who introduces the young man—John—to my friend and me. "Tell them about what you're doing," says Bob, and John explains that the must in this tank is being readied for a **cold soak** prior to fermentation. This tank, like the others in the room, is sheathed in diamond-patterned stainless steel; we learn

Cold soaking = macerating *before* fermentation

that beneath that jacket is a network of tubes through which liquids—either hot water or a refrigerant—can pass, heating up or cooling down the tank, as desired. For the cold soak, which will last for a few days, the temperature inside the tank is being brought down to a point low enough to prevent fermentation from commencing. John tells us that cold soaking can sometimes improve the extraction of pigments and other substances, especially **tannins**, from the skins. (Do you remember the Winespeak word *maceration*, introduced in chapter 1? Well, cold soaking is a *pre*-fermentation maceration. And tannins, which we'll look at more closely in the next chapter, are the compounds that give some red wines their astringent mouthfeel, and that help a red wine last—even to grow better—once it's been bottled.)

Since John seems eager to talk to us, I decide to ask him a question that's occurred to me. I've read that as a red wine ferments, the skins and seeds rise to the top, forming what's called a **cap**, which has to be broken apart periodically and punched down into the fermenting juice to ensure that the liquid remains in contact with the skins. I'm wondering,

I say, just how *tough* this cap is. How hard is it to bust it up and force it back down into the wine? (Don't ask me where this question is coming from: probably from some mud-pie-remembering little-boy place deep inside me.) Well, John has the answer ready to hand; he points to a scary-looking device suspended near the red-wine fermentation tanks. It has a long steel arm ending in a big metal disk. This is the monster masher that's used to break up the caps, which can become very tightly compressed indeed.

We chat for a moment longer, with Bob explaining that Pellegrini also uses another common method of maintaining contact between the fermenting liquid and the skins, which involves pumping the liquid up and over the cap, again and again. Then we say our goodbyes to John and head out of the fermentation room. As we're leaving, Bob points to a set of larger steel cylinders on the other side of the room; these are the white wine fermenting tanks, which unlike the tanks for red wine don't have removable lids. (Many white wines are particularly susceptible to the ill effects of **oxidation**, so contact between the wine and the air must be kept to an absolute minimum between the time the fresh juice is pressed and the moment, at long last, that the bottle of wine is opened by the consumer.) The white wine tanks are also in use at the moment, but unless you're an expert who can interpret their dials and meters, there's nothing much to see. For the casual wine tourist, white wine fermentation seems pretty boring as compared with red. No cold soaks, no caps in need of a good, hard punch—just these silent silos . . .

But maybe not always quite so boring. We head down a set of stairs and through a couple of doors. We're on our way to the **cellar**, but en route we pass through a long corridor lined, on either side, with oak barrels. At first I think we're already in the cellar, but Bob explains that this, too, is a fermenting room. And, yes, now I see (and hear) that there is some perceptible activity here. Set in the aperture at the crest of each barrel—it's called the *bunghole*—is a little glass valve, and there's some visible, faintly audible bubbling action going on inside the valves.

Most of Pellegrini's wine, red and white, is fermented in the steel tanks we've just left behind, but a portion of the Chardonnay crop is, as we're witnessing, **barrel fermented**. This isn't uncommon: many winemakers prefer to ferment some white wines, especially Chardonnay, "in oak," believing that the wood's presence at this early stage softens the wine and lengthens its "finish"—that is, the persistence of its flavor in the mouth when drunk. (At Pellegrini, the oak-fermented Chardonnay is blended with steel-fermented wine to create the company's premium Chardonnay varietals.) The valves atop the barrels are *fermentation traps*, which enable the release of CO_2 produced during fermentation without allowing any oxygen back inside the barrel.

Fermentation isn't oak barrels' primary winemaking purpose, though. As you probably already know, many, many fine wines—reds, especially, but also some whites—are **aged**, or **matured**, in oak. Ageing is the central step (it can actually comprise several steps) in the third phase of winemaking: élevage. Actually—as Bob informs us—the barrel-

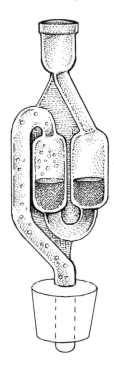

FERMENTATION TRAP

fermented Chardonnay will begin its ageing in these same barrels, where it will rest for a time on its **lees** before being **racked**. And, yes, those are two more Winespeak terms whose meanings you should know: The lees are the gunk—mostly composed of dead yeast cells—that settles to the bottom of the vessel as fermentation draws to a close. Most newly fermented wines are immediately separated from the lees by being carefully racked—which simply means transferred—to another container. But some whites, especially Chardonnay, are often left on the lees for a period following fermentation, because it's believed that **lees contact** enhances their complexity and imparts a desirable creamy taste to the finished wine. Bob tells us that the lees are occasionally stirred up to maximize their contact with the maturing wine.

SPICE RACK

Until now, Bob Pellegrini has been voluble and informative, but after we've passed through the corridor where the Chardonnay's being fermented and into the cellar, he waxes positively poetic. Like all well-kept wine cellars, Pellegrini's is pleasing to look at: the ranks of neatly stacked wooden barrels; the dim, even lighting; the overall orderliness of the place all convey the impression that winemaking is a particularly painstaking and patient endeavor.

But Pellegrini's cellars are somewhat unusual, too—and Bob's very proud of the difference. Unlike many cellars, whose floors are made of impermeable concrete, the floors here are composed of gravel, which allows moisture from the soil below to permeate the cellar, aiding in maintaining high humidity throughout the space. That's one of the essentials of a well-functioning cellar. The other is a constant, cool temperature, which has traditionally been achieved by locating the wine-ageing rooms below ground level (that's right: in the cellar). Nowadays, of course, cellar temperatures are also controlled through carefully monitored air conditioning. These two factors—high humidity and a cool, even temperature—are crucial because, together, they limit the amount of evaporation from the barrels.

Even barrels made of tight-grained oak, Bob explains, are slightly porous. That's a good thing, because it allows for a very gradual oxidation of the wine maturing inside them. (Long-term barrel ageing is reserved for red wines and just a few kinds of whites; as noted above, many whites are seriously

> **Barrels permit the gradual oxidation of the wine inside**

damaged by even minimal contact with oxygen and so are stabilized and aged—much more briefly—in inert steel tanks.)

But this slow, osmotic interaction between the contents of the barrel and the surrounding atmosphere also presents the winemaker with a problem. Over time, the volume of maturing wine in the barrel diminishes, evaporating through the fine pores in the wood and creating an air pocket inside the barrel. That air pocket contains *too much* oxygen, an overabundance that might encourage bacterial growth and (oops!) turn the wine to vinegar. Even under "ideal" cellar conditions, some evaporation is inevitable. Bob says that, if left alone, a barrel can lose as much as 10 percent of its volume per year. Because of the danger to the developing wine, that can't be allowed to happen, so winemakers regularly **top up** the barrels, uncorking the bunghole and pouring in additional wine to fill the space. (Winespeak vocabulary alert: the air pocket inside a barrel is called the **ullage**, pronounced UH-lij; the word is also used to denote the airspace between the surface of the wine and the cork in a bottle of wine.)

But I can hear you murmuring: where's the *poetry* in this? Well, we're about to get to it, because at this point Bob begins to rhapsodize about **oak**. For the winemaker, he says, oak barrels are like herbs and spices. As a chef employs the ingredients in a spice rack to enhance and complete a dish, a winemaker uses different oaks to confer subtle but unmistakable flavors to a finished wine. I've never heard it put this way before, and the analogy strikes me as apt and, well, beautiful.

Pellegrini Vineyards uses three kinds of oak barrels: French, American, and Hungarian. Though many a wine snob believes that French oak is vastly superior to any other kind, Bob insists that this isn't the case—different, yes; necessarily better, no. As he tells it, there was once a time when even French winemakers preferred oak barrels from eastern Europe, especially Hungary, to those made from their own homegrown wood. But that came to an end with World War II. Not only did the conflict interrupt trade, but afterward, with the communist takeover of eastern Europe, Hungarian barrels were no longer available in the west, and French oak became the gold standard. It's only been since the lifting of the Iron Curtain that Hungarian barrels have again been sold internationally, and, according to Bob, they're well on the way toward reclaiming their former reputation.

Bob doesn't sneer at American wood, either. American oak barrels' poor reputation, he tells us, is an artifact of the past, when most of the barrels produced by U.S. coopers (barrel makers) were destined for the

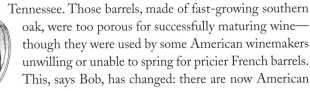

bourbon and sour mash whiskey distilleries of Kentucky and Tennessee. Those barrels, made of fast-growing southern oak, were too porous for successfully maturing wine— though they were used by some American winemakers unwilling or unable to spring for pricier French barrels. This, says Bob, has changed: there are now American coopers manufacturing barrels specifically for the wine industry—and using slower-growing, and therefore tighter-grained, northern oak in their products.

And speaking of price: Besides the weather, there's one other thing that wine producers love to complain about, and that's the cost of doing business. Bob's no exception, and he launches into a riff about the high price of European, especially French, barrels—a cost that's been steadily escalating because of the decline of the dollar against the euro. He's paying, he says, about $700 for each new French barrel he buys. (The price may have gone up even further since the time of our visit.) And he delivers a fact that I find interesting: barrel ageing adds, on average, about a dollar to the cost of a bottle of wine.

What makes the high cost of barrels difficult to bear is that an oak barrel has a limited life span. Bob explains that about half of the "stuff"— not just flavors but also **wood tannins**—that an oak barrel imparts to wine is exhausted during the first use. Oak barrels, you might say, have a kind of half-life: after a barrel's been used twice, three-quarters of the flavors and tannins have been used up; after three uses, seven-eighths, and so on. Older barrels do have their purposes: for example, the barrels that Pellegrini uses for fermenting Chardonnay aren't new, and red wines are often racked from newer to older barrels as maturation progresses. But even so, after seven or eight years, a barrel has concluded its useful wine-making life—and there's nothing for Bob to do with it except to saw it in two and sell the half-barrels as planters, at thirty-five bucks apiece.

The poetic rhapsody of a few minutes before has, it seems, turned into a rather glum cost-benefit analysis. It's high time we cheered ourselves up—by proceeding to the tasting room. (But for just a little more on the uses—and abuses—of oak, see the sidebar on the next page.)

"Oaky" Isn't Okey-Dokey

Wood is Wineslang for oak barrels, as well as for the flavors and tannins that oak bestows on wines that are barrel fermented and/or barrel aged. If you don't have a clue what oak tastes like, pour yourself a glass of an "oaked" California Chardonnay. (To be sure the wine's spent some time in barrel, ask your wine-shop salesperson, since some California Chardonnays are not oaked.) I suggest Chardonnay rather than one of the multitudes of oaked red wines because there's often too much else going on in a red, and it's easier to discern the effects of oaking in a (comparatively) simpler white wine. Tasting the Chardonnay, you'll probably notice the following things:

First, it's ever so slightly prickly in the mouth (it won't have the mouth-puckering power of many reds, but a vague astringent quality may still be noticeable). This effect is produced by the **wood tannins** that migrated into the wine during barrel fermentation or ageing. (Remember that *grape* tannins are more or less absent from white wines. Non-oaked whites therefore have so little tannin that it's imperceptible.)

Second, you may taste a creamy or buttery flavor. This may partly be the result of malolactic fermentation (see page 42), but it may also come from the oak. You're also likely to perceive a definite vanilla flavor—sometimes it's quite pronounced—and this is certainly due to the oak. Barrel fermentation/ageing may also produce a range of other flavors, including cloves, almonds, and caramel, but whether you'll perceive these in the wine you sample is anybody's guess. Finally, you may actually taste *wood.* At its best, this effect will be a gentle undertone, complementing the wine's other flavors; at its worst, your mouth may taste as if you've been gnawing on a two-by-four. Wines with a profoundly woody flavor are often described as **oaky**—usually a term of disparagement.

The particular influences that an oak barrel has on a wine have to do not just with country of origin—and therefore the type of oak it's made from—but also with other factors, including how the wood was *seasoned* (that is, dried and aged after being cut) and the degree to which it was heated, or "toasted" (to make it pliable enough to bend into the barrel's staves). The size and age of the barrel also make a difference. The influence is greater in smaller than in larger barrels (because of the higher surface-to-volume ratio), and, as Bob Pellegrini told us, younger barrels produce stronger effects than older barrels. Don't be misled into thinking, however, that smaller means better: if a barrel is too small, the oak effects will be too pronounced. And although brand-new barrels are prized—you'll often read wine writers raving about a winery's (costly) decision to employ only "new French oak *barriques*" for ageing its wines—new barrels aren't appropriate for every barrel-aged wine. (A *barrique*, by the way, is particular size of barrel—it holds about fifty-nine gallons—traditionally used in the Bordeaux region of France.)

Wood has played an extremely important role in the history of wine. Before glass wine bottles came into widespread commercial use in the eighteenth century, wine was usually transported in, and sold from, wooden barrels. And vats and barrels made from a variety of woods other than oak were used, historically, for fermenting, ageing, and storing wine. Chestnut barrels were, for instance, in widespread use in Italy up until a few decades ago. In recent times, though, a consensus has developed among winemakers worldwide that for ageing wine, oak is superior to any other wood, and the use of other kinds of wood has largely (though not totally) disappeared.

Oak barrels, as Bob Pellegrini bemoaned, are expensive, and some producers of less expensive wines resort to a vastly cheaper alternative, flavoring their wines with *oak chips* or even oak shavings. The chips, usually added to the must at the time of fermentation, *do* do the job—sort of. They certainly give the resulting wine an oak flavor—often much too strong an oak flavor. Remember: oak's O.K., but oaky isn't okey-dokey, and the substitution of oak chips for genuine barrel maturation is derided by serious wine drinkers.

Room with a View

A winery tour has to end in a tasting. (Otherwise, what's the point?) Leaving the cellar, Bob guides us to Pellegrini Vineyards' handsome tasting bar, but it's immediately obvious we won't be able to conduct our tasting here. The large room is overflowing with wine tourists, all of whom appear to be having an *extremely* good time: their alcohol-loosened voices reverberate in the cathedral-ceilinged space, creating an almost painful din. Business is obviously good—a little *too* good. One of the pourers behind the bar shouts at Bob that the staff's at wit's end; they've run out of glasses, and the carloads of autumn-weekend revelers keep on arriving.

For a moment, I think we're going to have to bag it. But I'm forgetting that Bob's the boss: glasses for our tasting *will be found.* Bob grabs a few bottles from the bar and signals us to follow him. We retreat across the compound's courtyard into another building, where he leads the way upstairs to a loft-like conference space that a wall plaque identifies as the Vintner's Room. It's a beautiful room, with large windows that offer views (at the back) of the vineyards and (at front) of the highway and the fields and woods behind, with the Great Peconic Bay dimly visible in the distance. Within moments, glasses, more bottles of wine, and a pitcher of water arrive, delivered by Joyce Pellegrini, who, because she has to lend a hand in the tasting bar, can't stay with us.

Our tasting commences. Mercifully, from here we can neither see nor hear the madding crowd across the courtyard. Over the next hour or so, we sample eight of Pellegrini's wines: three white table wines, four reds, and, as a finale, the ice wine that Pellegrini makes from a combination of Gewürztraminer and Sauvignon Blanc grapes. (For more on ice wines, which are made from juice pressed from frozen grapes, see page 174.) All the wines are very good; I'm especially impressed by the 1999 Pellegrini Vineyards Merlot, which Bob concurs is "showing" very well this afternoon. (The verb **to show** has, of course, a somewhat idiosyncratic meaning in Winespeak. Even in the bottle, a wine—any wine—is always changing: open it at one moment and it will be better or worse, more or less characterful, than it would be if opened a month, or a year, or several years later, or earlier, for that matter. When a Winespeaker says a wine is showing well, he or she means it's being drunk at a good time—a moment when it's realized its potential and is expressing itself especially eloquently.)

The wines, as I said, are terrific, but what's really fascinating to me is how frankly Bob talks to us about the ups and downs of the winemaking biz. He loves it—that's obvious—but it's anything but easy, especially for a small producer, and especially in an era increasingly glutted with wine, much of it very good, from all over the globe. Competition for consumers' attention isn't just ferocious; it's unimaginably intense, and many small producers, even makers of superior wines, find it nigh unto impossible to establish their brands in the larger marketplace.

But this aside makes it sound as if Bob Pellegrini is a carper. Far from it: he's warm, funny, and very enjoyable company—and, besides, I'm grateful for his willingness to discuss the tribulations that wine producers must endure. The conversation at most winery wine-tastings is strictly promotional, which, needless to say, can be a bit of a bore.

By now, it's going on three in the afternoon, the tasting's concluded, and it's time for my friend and me to think about heading back home to New York City. It's been a spectacularly informative day . . .

But Wait. (We're Not Quite Done.)

As thorough as our tour of the Pellegrini vineyards and winery was, it wasn't quite comprehensive. We didn't see *everything*, in part because not much was going on in certain areas of the winery, and in part because some of the steps in a wine's creation just wouldn't be very interesting—nor, indeed, visible—to the casual observer. Here's some of what we missed, as well as a few more winemaking terms with which you might want to be at least passing familiar:

Stabilization and Preservation. Besides the destemming, grape-crushing, and pressing operations, which were quiet during the hours we visited Pellegrini, we didn't witness or talk with Bob about some of the more technical procedures to which wines are commonly subjected in order to **stabilize** and **preserve** them—that is, to ensure their clarity and protect them against spoilage. These include **filtration, fining**, and—in almost all wines produced today—the addition of **sulfites** to prevent microbial growth and retard oxidation. Filtration, as you might guess, involves passing the wine through a filter or membrane to rid it of particles that might lead to haziness or sediments in the finished wine. (Filtration does have its diehard opponents in the winemaking world, who believe it deprives wine of some of its flavor—a topic we take up again in the following chapter.)

Fining serves a similar purpose, but here the removal of undesirable particles or other substances is achieved through the addition of a **fining agent** to the wine. This agent bonds with those particles or compounds, forming a precipitate that sinks to the bottom of the tank. The clarified wine is then racked off the sediment into another container. If you're beginning to feel that you should dust off your high school chemistry textbook, hold off: as a casual wine drinker, you don't *need* to understand this stuff. You might be interested to know, though, that **egg whites** are a common fining agent. (See? The term already sounds a little friendlier.) Because the protein in egg whites bonds so easily with tannins, egg whites have long been used to remove excess tannins from red wine—making it less harsh on the palate.

Sulfites might be of more concern to you, especially if you worry about preservatives and other additives in the food and beverages you consume. But most sources say that unless you have asthma, you probably shouldn't fret. Not only are these sulfur compounds added in miniscule amounts (regulated by law), but it's not as if wines *without* sulfites are sulfur-free; sulfur is a byproduct of fermentation, so there's some sulfur present in *any* wine. The warning "Contains Sulfites"—which, in the United States, must appear on the labels of all sulfited wines—is there to alert people who may suffer asthmatic symptoms if they ingest them. (Whether sulfited wines actually present a greater threat to asthma sufferers than nonsulfited wines is a question that has yet to be scientifically resolved.)

Bottling and After. The production process I most regret not having seen at Pellegrini is the **bottling** of the wines. In fact (and boo hoo), I've never seen wine being bottled at any of the wineries I've visited—I've always come at the wrong time of year. (At smaller wineries, bottling generally occurs in the spring.) No biggie, I guess: I'm not sure there's all that much for the layperson to learn by witnessing a bottling operation. But, hey, I love factories—who knows why?—and it's during bottling season that a winery is most factory-like.

Most white wines are **released**—made available for sale—after bottling, but for most fine red wines (and a few whites) the élevage phase continues after bottling. Red wines are typically **laid down** (that is, laid on their sides and stored) at the winery for some time before release, and, depending on the type and quality of the wine, this period can extend for two or three years or longer. This post-bottling, pre-release snooze enables a wine to at least begin its **bottle ageing** before leaving home—and prevents consumers from drinking wines still too young and undeveloped to be enjoyable. But, for many quality reds, pre-release bottle ageing constitutes a *minimum*; such wines can, and in many cases should, continue to age in the bottle for years after their release.

You'll sometimes see the word **reserve** on the label of an American wine, which *can* be an indication that this wine is of a higher quality than others produced by the same maker—that the grapes it was made from were especially good, and that it was treated to longer-than-usual ageing, both in the barrel and then in the bottle before release. But take heed: "Reserve" has no controlled, legal meaning in the American wine industry. Some producers, like Pellegrini (which occasionally makes a reserve wine), do take the word seriously, reserving it (yes, pun intended) for wines from great vintages that are given additional ageing. Some U.S. producers, however, simply slap the word on their labels, hoping to cash in on its cachet. To understand whether the presence of "reserve" on a label has any meaning, you've got to know something about the maker and its practices. (This unregulated situation differs from that in Spain, where the word *reserva* denotes a wine that has spent a greater-than-usual amount of time in barrel and in the bottle before release, and from that in Portugal, where *reserva* indicates a superior-vintage wine of higher-than-ordinary alcohol content. In Italy, the use of the word *riserva* is also regulated and generally connotes superior wines given additional barrel and bottle ageing, though its precise meaning differs according to the type of wine it's applied to.)

You can, by the way, learn more about Pellegrini Vineyards' wines by visiting the winery's website, at www.pellegrinivineyards.com. My experience tells me that the "tasting notes" you'll find there are to be trusted.

Hitting the Road (and the Bottle)

In most (populated) places in the United States, a winery visit is a very easy day trip to arrange. You don't have to live in or near one of the country's more famous wine-producing regions. In fact, there are now functioning wineries in every one of the fifty states—though the "wine" commercially produced in a few northerly states (Alaska, for example) is made from fruits—berries, apples—other than grapes or is **mead** (a winelike beverage made from honey).

The Internet has made it a snap to find wineries in your area: try Googling your state's name along with the word "wineries," and you're almost certain to find the website for the state or regional winegrowers' association. Alternately, check out www.allamericanwineries.com, which has a comprehensive state-by-state listing of U.S. wineries, with links to some growers' associations' websites as well as the sites of many individual wineries. In states with large numbers of wineries (New Jersey, Pennsylvania, and Texas are but three examples), growers' association sites usually include mapped itineraries—"wine trails," they're often called—for visiting a number of wineries within a given area.

In planning winery visits, note that some wine estates have onsite restaurants, and many are in the habit of holding weekend events (bluegrass or jazz festivals, classic car rallies, you name it) in an attempt to lasso in potential customers. At harvest time, some invite the public into the vineyard to help pick the grapes—which, frankly, strikes me as vaguely exploitive, but if you're the type who likes to pick his own

Halloween pumpkin or chop down her own Christmas tree, you may enjoy such unpaid labor. And there are even a few that hold harvest-time "grape stomps," inviting customers to take their shoes and socks off, roll up their trousers, and climb into the trough to squish the grapes the old-fashioned way.

Me, I think I'll pass—and meet you at the tasting bar. (Which reminds me: at some U.S. wineries, tastings are free, though some others do charge a nominal sum.)

You should not, by the way, necessarily trust the information on small wineries' websites to be accurate or complete. Call ahead to confirm the days and times when the winery is open and (especially) to ask whether it will be possible for you to tour the entire facility. Most smaller wineries are short on staff and don't have regularly scheduled tours, so you'll probably have to make a special appointment if you want to see more than just the tasting room and shop. Note, too, that it's more interesting to visit a winery at certain times of year—at harvest, for example, or during periods when wine is being bottled—than at others.

I'll meet you at the tasting bar

Besides visiting local wineries, there are lots of ways—an ever burgeoning number—of expanding your "hands-on" knowledge of wines and winemaking without having to travel too far from home. You might, for example, want to attend one of the hundreds of **wine festivals** that now take place in the United States each year. Although some so-called "festivals" are small events hosted by individual wineries, many are sponsored by state or regional winegrowers' associations or other industry organizations and bring together many different producers (and their wines) in one place, allowing you to sample a greater range of wines from a particular area, or wines of a particular type, than would otherwise be possible. Some of these affairs are huge: the annual San Francisco Zinfandel Festival, held in March, features hundreds of wines from hundreds of wineries. Not only that, but scores of local restaurants take part in the festivities, whipping up Zinfandel-friendly eats that teach you more about wine-and-food pairing—or at least "Zin"-and-food pairing—in an afternoon than you could otherwise learn in a lifetime. The San Francisco fête is sponsored by the Zinfandel Advocates and Producers association (ZAP); for more info, visit www.zinfandel.org. As with everything these days, the Internet is your best resource for learning about upcoming wine festivals in your vicinity: try Googling "wine festival[s]" and the name of your state.

If you're crowd-averse and in the mood for a formal wine-and-food pairing experience that's more intimately scaled, you might keep on the lookout for **winemaker's dinners** in your city. An increasing number of restaurants host these events, which feature multicourse meals in which each course is accompanied by one or another of a particular maker's wines—with the winemaker himself or herself emceeing the evening. Winemaker's dinners can be expensive, but aren't always outrageously so; you should be able to find one costing $50 to $70 per person. Your local wine shop or neighborhood wine bar might know about upcoming dinners; in fact, they're often cosponsored by such businesses. But another good resource is the website www.localwineevents.com, which has extensive listings of wine-related happenings around the country and world: it's also a great site to visit for information on festivals, wine classes, wine-shop tastings, and individual wineries' special events.

Wine Tours: Pleasures and Perils

Going on a **wine tour** in the United States or abroad—either an organized, group tour or one that you plan and execute yourself—seems the logical extension of visiting local wineries or attending the occasional wine festival. A wine tour can certainly provide an entertaining way of deepening your understanding of the wines of a given geographical area. But wine tours present certain perils, and it's salutary to keep these in mind when contemplating such a trip.

The most important question to ask yourself is, Just how compelling is my interest in wine? Accurately gauging your own level of interest is critical not just in deciding *whether* to do a wine tour, but also which kind of wine tour to join and which winemaking region you might want to visit. For example, will the tour be a wine *and food* tour? Will it include stops or stays at local farms or perhaps a series of lessons on how to cook dishes from the regional cuisine? (There are scads of agritourism/culinary tours on the market nowadays.) Will the tour include visits to non-wine-related points of interest (archaeological or historical sites, for example)?

As with visits to individual wineries, the time of year you schedule your tour for may also be important. If you're arranging your own tour, note that during the harvest season, some smaller wineries that put out the red carpet for visitors at other times of year may be unable to accommodate you—the staff may simply be too busy. (Of course, if you're going on a group tour, the scheduling exigencies will be handled for you.)

Regarding group tours, a few cautions are in order. First, you should be aware that most group tours are basically promotional in nature: the agencies that organize them, and the wineries with which they work, are in the business of selling you on the wines of a particular region—and, in fact, of selling you as many bottles of those wines as will fit in your carry-on and checked baggage. This isn't a bad thing, really; one of the lovely aspects of the wine business is that so much of it is conducted on a face-to-face, person-to-person level. Still, in many cases taking a wine tour is akin to living inside an extended infomercial.

Second caution: the sheer number of wine tours on the market nowadays makes selecting one a fraught task. Joel Zack, president of the New York City–based Heritage Tours agency (www.heritagetoursonline.com), which creates customized tours for high-end travelers, has a number of recommendations for anyone planning a wine tour abroad:

- Be as specific as possible about your own interests, wine-wise—especially if you're want to travel to a country (e.g., Spain) with highly diverse and widely scattered winemaking regions. For example, if your chief interest is in sparkling wines, you'll probably want to travel to the cava-producing region of Catalonia, in northeastern Spain; if fortified wines are your forte, you'll want to go to the Sherry-making centers of Andalusia, in the southwestern part of the country.

- Decide on the level of interaction with winemakers and participation in the winemaking process you desire. For some wine travelers, much of a journey's pleasure will hinge on meeting and talking with estate owners and winemakers; for others, comparatively anonymous group tours of wineries may suffice.

- Don't sign up for a tour until you've personally contacted the tour agency to ask some questions and

to request references from other North American travelers who've used the its services. (FAQs: Does the tour include stops at smaller, artisanal wineries as well as large commercial operations? Will the tastings be extensive, or will they be pro forma affairs in which you sample a wine or two before being shunted into the shop?) Being able to talk or exchange email with other American or Canadian clients is especially important; they'll be able to vouch personally for a tour's overall quality *and* its adherence to North American standards.

Third caution: Organized wine tours abroad are not for the strapped-for-cash set. A quick glance at several tour-agency websites reveals that a six-day motor-coach ramble through the vineyards of New Zealand will probably set you back about $3,000 (per person; airfare not included, natch). A trip of the same length in Bordeaux will run $5,000 or more. There are, to be sure, cheaper alternatives. You might, for example, choose to tour a winemaking region where the dollar is stronger. At the time of this writing, Argentina—still recovering from its financial meltdown of the late 1990s and early 2000s—was a relative bargain.

Alternately, you might adopt a strategy that allows you to plan your own itinerary, more or less, while freeing you of the responsibility of having to make all the winery arrangements yourself—and that will likely save you money to boot. In virtually every sizable city that's located in or adjacent to a major winemaking region—Santiago, Chile; Cape Town, South Africa; San Francisco, California; and so on—there are numerous agencies, easily found on the Internet, that offer inexpensive half-day and day-long trips to nearby wineries. Choose such a city, book a flight and hotel room, sign up for a few such tours—and spend the intervals between the tours engaged in other touristic pursuits.

CHAPTER THREE

Nose, Palate, Body

ANATOMY OF A WINE TASTING

W HEN YOU WERE LITTLE, YOU PROBABLY ENJOYED PLAYING WITH the things you were given to eat and drink. I know I did—and beverages were my forte, especially those drunk with a straw. I liked, for example, to blow bubbles in milkshakes and to make that annoying (to my mother) gurgling-slurping sound you can produce when you try to suck up whatever's left at the bottom of the cup. Gargling was fun, too—especially with viscous liquids. Of course, at some point socialization set in, and I ceased doing these tricks in company.

Well, wine tasting, properly performed, has something of the return of the repressed about it—as if it were a way for adults to play with beverages while feeling *très* respectable doing so. Yes, yes: I *know* that's not the *purpose* of tasting wine. I know that the odd little rituals of wine tasting—and all those socially discomfiting noises that wine tasters make—serve a more elevated function. I understand that one *tastes* a wine (as opposed to just slugging it down) in order to truly appreciate and to *learn* about it. But I can't help but feel that there's some rather more id-like motive smirking in the background. After all, now that chewing tobacco is passé, what other activity allows you to spit in public without shame or censure?

But let us bracket such psychoanalytic musings. Here, in all seriousness, is a step-by-step lesson in how to taste wine like the professionals do, with notes on the rationale behind each step. Tasting wine is a five-part procedure, and wine educators often describe the steps as **the five S's**: See, Swirl, Smell, Sip, and Spit (or Swallow). It's a useful mnemonic, and so I employ it here.

PRELIMINARIES

Before beginning, you've got to have the proper setup, which includes a bottle of wine (no kidding) and, if the bottle's stoppered with a cork, something to open it with. (The sidebar on pages 75–80 gives info and advice on wine-opener options.)

By the way, it's always more interesting to taste comparatively—that is, to sample two or more wines during a tasting. There's a Winespeak word for two or more wines tasted in tandem: a **flight**. (You're sure to encounter the word if you go to a wine bar.) If you do decide to do some comparative tastings, go through each of the steps outlined below with each wine before moving on to the next. It's also more interesting—*much* more interesting—to taste with others rather than all by yourself.

You'll learn more about wine's subtle and not-so-subtle variability if you sample wines of the same basic type for a given tasting: two or three Oregon Pinot Noirs, for example, or two or three white Bordeaux. You may even want to up the ante a bit by conducting what in Winespeak is called a **horizontal** tasting. In a horizontal tasting, all the wines are of the same type and the same vintage but are made by different producers: six different 2000 Cabernets from California's Sonoma Valley, for example, or six 2002 Rieslings from the Mosel region of Germany. (A **vertical tasting** is a snootier enterprise, and more difficult—and, usu-

The Worm Turns

For the three centuries that wine bottles have been stoppered with corks, the wine-drinking subset of the human race has been diligently searching for a cork-removal method that (a) doesn't wrench the back, neck, and/or arms of the person opening the bottle; (b) doesn't shred the cork in the process; and (c) is foolproof. This quest, as Ecclesiastes might say, long proved a "vanity of vanities, and a chasing after wind."

It's ironic that now, at just the historical moment when the cork may be passing out of fashion—perhaps to be replaced by the simple screw top—the diversity of devices for removing corks is proliferating. A glance at one Internet wine-accessories emporium revealed more than *fifty* different corkscrews and other cork-removing devices for sale—and that selection hardly covers the field. Some of the more recently invented devices do work well, but none is drawback-free.

Still the most commonly encountered type is what we might, with taxonomical exactitude, call the Good Old-Fashioned Corkscrew, of which there are numerous subspecies. The humblest is the kind you can find in virtually any liquor store, generally for about two bucks: the screw (which in Winespeak is called the **worm**) is enclosed in a plastic tube, which doubles as the corkscrew's handle. You pull the worm from the tube, insert the tube through a hole at the top of the worm, and—presto—you've got a functioning corkscrew of a simple screw-it-in-and-pull-it-out type. Very handy when you suddenly need a cork remover and have only a couple of dollars in your pocket, but this model definitely fails on the back-, neck-, or arm-wrenching score, since you must provide all the elbow grease yourself.

Slightly more sophisticated is the so-called **waiter's friend** corkscrew, which has a lever attached to one end of the handle that helps you lift the cork from the bottle. As the name indicates, it's the kind of corkscrew you're likeliest to see being used in restaurants. Besides the lever, the waiter's friend

WAITER'S FRIEND

has another advantage over the simpler screw-and-pull type: a little knife, which hinges out of a slot at the handle's opposite end, for cutting away the foil or plastic **capsule** encasing the wine bottle's neck and mouth. Less muscle-spasm-inducing than the screw-and-pull variety, the waiter's friend still isn't what you'd call *easy* to use. It's cheap, however: you can find a serviceable one for just a few dollars.

Equally familiar is the **wing corkscrew**. But, you know, let's not even go there. Wing corkscrews aren't, in fact, terrifically easy to use, and they have one distinct drawback: the arms, or wings, tend to break off after multiple uses. ('Fess up: you've got an old, amputated wing corkscrew that's perpetually convalescing at the back of the utensils drawer, don't you?)

Climbing up the ladder of inventiveness and ease of use, we come to the **Screwpull Table Model**.

WING CORKSCREW

"Screwpull" is a brand name: the device was invented by a Texas oil-driller and is manufactured by Le Creuset, the same company that makes that extraordinary (and extraordinarily heavy) enameled cast-iron cookware. Of the simpler, moderately priced, and readily available corkscrew types, this is definitely *Drinkology WINE*'s favorite. The two-piece machine is a wonder: you position the "guide frame" atop the mouth of the body, insert the extra-long worm through a hole at the top of the frame, screw it into the cork and just keep on turning the handle in the same direction. The cork, in seeming defiance of logic, rises up out of the

SCREWPULL TABLE MODEL

bottle and into the frame. Moreover, unlike the corkscrew types mentioned above, it securely guides the worm into the *center* of the cork, meaning there's almost no risk of splitting the cork or breaking it. At about ten dollars, the Screwpull isn't just a miracle—it's a *bargain* miracle.

Drawbacks? Well, though its maker dubs it "effortless," it isn't, or not quite. A more serious flaw is that it doesn't work at all well with synthetic "corks," which tend to get stuck—or to spin in place—once they're halfway out of the bottle.

Apparently, some users have also had the problem of natural corks getting jammed up in the top of the frame after removal. In mid-2004, Le Creuset introduced a newer version with a very similar name—the **Screwpull Table Corkscrew**—that's supposed to solve this problem. (A bright red plastic ball attached to the worm prevents the cork from moving too far up.) I'm sorry to report that I find this new model altogether less satisfactory than the old. Synthetic corks remain just as difficult to remove, and the more streamlined design of the

SCREWPULL
TABLE
CORKSCREW

new corkscrew actually feels *less* ergonomic. Let's hope Le Creuset doesn't discontinue the older, better version.

Before we leave the "good old-fashioned" corkscrew varieties behind, two notes: First, no matter which type of corkscrew you choose, *make sure* that the worm is an actual **helix** rather than a screw. The drawing at left shows the difference. A helix will penetrate the cork cleanly; a screw will tend to tear the cork apart as it makes its way through—and if the cork's on the dry side, it may break into fragments that you'll have to fish out of the wine. The best corkscrews of whatever type have helix-shaped worms that are coated in Teflon; they go in smoothly,

HELIX VS.
SCREW-TYPE
WORM

and there's even less chance that you'll destroy the cork. (The Teflon coating does tend to wear off over time, necessitating eventual replacement.)

FOIL CUTTER

Second, you'll do yourself a favor if, besides getting a good corkscrew, you also buy a functional **foil cutter**. Put the stress in the previous sentence on the word *functional*: there are loads of these little devices on the market, but I've only found one that works reliably. It's the foil cutter (pictured) made by our friends at Screwpull. You set it on the mouth of the wine bottle, squeeze the two prongs together, and twist—and four tiny circular blades concealed inside the prongs slice off the foil just below the bottle's lip, freeing it from the rest of the capsule. *Much* easier—and neater!—than scraping away at the foil with a knife.

The most popular of the newer-fangled cork-removal devices are the elaborate corkscrews known as **lever corkscrews**—the most famous being

LEVER CORKSCREW

the Rabbit, made by Metrokane. There are numerous variations on the market, but they all work in basically the same way: You rest the contraption atop the bottle's mouth and squeeze together the two, lower handles to grip the neck. Then you swing the lever over the top of the bottle, and a set of gears within the device instantly screws the worm into the cork; reverse the motion, and the cork is withdrawn, all in one fell and effort-free swoop. The lever corkscrews' major drawback, whatever the brand, is cost: they start at about $50 and go up from there. Of course, they're marketed partly as status symbols. If you're inclined, you can get yourself a chrome Rabbit with tasteful leather accents or even a sterling silver one. Me, I'm holding out for the diamond-encrusted model.

I failed miserably the first time I tried to use another of the newer cork-removal devices: a **pump "corkscrew,"** which isn't a cork*screw* at all—it's a hypodermic. Again, there a number of variations on the market; the one I haplessly purchased is a cylinder enclosing a needle and little cartridge of pressurized gas. You "telescope" the cylinder out, then place it over the wine bottle's neck. When you telescope it back down, the needle pokes through the cork; then you push a button at the top of the

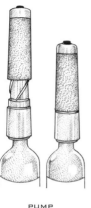

PUMP "CORKSCREW"

CONCERTINA CORKSCREW

cylinder, releasing a spurt of gas into the bottle—and the pressure drives out the cork. Well, once I'd figured this out (there were no instructions in the box), I performed the procedure and . . . *nada*. Turned out the gas cartridge that came with my newly purchased pump was empty. You may have better luck, but my experience nevertheless points to the major drawback of this type of device: even if it arrives full, the cartridge only holds enough gas for about eighty pops, and has to be periodically replaced. The replacement canisters aren't expensive—but who has the time to worry about this stuff?

Sadly, there's one marvelous kind of corkscrew that, so far as I know, isn't manufactured any more: the generic term for this type is **concertina corkscrew**, and the ones you see most often—the brand name is Zig Zag—were made by a French company and date, I believe, from the 1920s and '30s. After positioning the corkscrew atop the bottle and screwing in the worm, you pull on the handle and the accordion-like apparatus (see the drawing on the previous page) expands, withdrawing the cork. No, it's not effort-free, but it's *fun*, and, besides, these contraptions have an appealing retro look. Zig Zag and other concertina corkscrews can be found in antiques shops and other stores carrying wine paraphernalia, and they can be pricey: $200 and upwards. But, hey, I found my Zig Zag on eBay for twenty-five bucks. (Antique corkscrews, by the way, make great gifts for wine-loving friends.)

Whatever you do, *don't* choose a so-called **cork puller** as your everyday cork-removal gizmo. Cork pullers consist of two prongs, one slightly longer than the other, attached to a handle; you're supposed to insert the prongs on either side of the cork, then twist the handle and pull until the cork emerges. I guess there must be *somebody* who can operate these things successfully, but that somebody is not me. Whenever I've tried using one, the prongs have pushed the cork straight through *into* the bottle, which I suppose is one—though not the most satisfactory—way of getting to the wine inside. (My ineptness aside, I'm told cork pullers are useful for removing wet, crumbly, broken, or rotten corks, which may be a good enough reason to keep one on hand.)

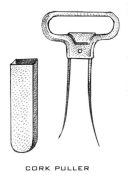

CORK PULLER

ally, expensive—to organize. The wines must all be of the same type and from the same producer, but represent different vintages. Unless you've been collecting wines for years and have a substantial cellar, it's unlikely you could put together a bona fide vertical tasting at home.)

Aside from the wine and an opener, there are just a few other essential components: bright, even lighting; a white surface on which to set your wineglass (if your table or counter is dark, a sheet of white copy paper will do fine); and, most important, the right kind of wineglass—a colorless, undecorated, thin-walled, stemmed wineglass whose sides taper slightly inward from the bowl to the mouth.

In other words, you need a *standard* sort of wineglass: one whose ovoid (rather than spherically shaped) bowl would hold, say, 11 to 13 ounces were it filled to the brim. You won't nearly be filling it to the brim, however. For tasting purposes, pour only about an inch of wine, or maybe even a little less, into the glass. If you're tasting a flight of wines, you may want to rinse the glass between wines or, better, to have several clean glasses ready; if your flight includes both whites and reds, you *must* rinse your glass thoroughly or change glasses before going from one color to the other. (*Drinkology WINE* isn't at all snooty about glassware; see the sidebar on pages 82–84.)

It's also a good idea to have a glass of water handy, to "cleanse your palate" between wines. A bland cracker may also help remove the previous wine's taste from your mouth; Bremner Wafers are especially good for this. It makes sense, too, to cut yourself a few slices or cubes of a bland cheese—I recommend Emmenthaler or a not-too-flavorful Gruyère—so that you can get some notion of what the wine you're sampling tastes like with food. (Granted, you'll only find out what the wine tastes like with that particular cheese, but the difference between the

SPEAKING OF TONGUES

How much difference does the kind of glass it's served in make to the taste of a wine?

This question is (like virtually everything else) a matter of some controversy in the wine world. The fortunes of one internationally famous wineglass manufacturer, the Austrian firm of Riedel Crystal, have over the past three-plus decades been built on the premise that the size and shape of a glass significantly and demonstrably affect how wine drunk from that glass will taste. It was in 1973 that Riedel's late president, Claus Josef Riedel (who died in 2004), introduced the company's Sommeliers glassware. This line of top-quality crystal now includes *twenty* different wineglasses (and the number keeps growing); each glass is purportedly scientifically designed to be the best possible vehicle for conveying a particular kind of wine—red Burgundy, white Burgundy, red Bordeaux, Zinfandel, Riesling, Sauternes, or whatever—to your nose and mouth.

Riedel's glasses are certainly beautiful, desirable objects, and there are lots of satisfied customers who believe its specially designed glasses are necessary to the full appreciation of this or that wine. The trouble is, scientists who actually study human sense-perception don't give much credence to the theory on which this differentiation among wineglasses is largely based. The theory's partly rooted in the outmoded notion that the human tongue is divided into more or less well-defined zones, each of which is responsible for perceiving a certain kind of taste: sweet, salty, sour, or bitter. Many's the introductory wine class, even today, that begins with a discussion of the so-called **tongue map**—a diagram that shows that the taste buds at the tip of the tongue register sweet flavors; those just behind taste salt; those farther back, along the sides of the tongue, perceive sour tastes; and those at the very back of the tongue register bitterness. Riedel's glasses (and similar lines by other glassmakers) are supposedly engineered to deliver each kind of wine to just the right place in your mouth—the place where you'll get the most out of that wine's particular combination of flavors.

The tongue map, unfortunately, is hokum. The current scientific consensus is that each of the thousands of taste buds in the mouth is sensitive to *all four* basic tastes. The implication is that a wine is going to taste pretty much the same no matter where in your mouth it "lands," and, in fact, a number of controlled studies have shown that even wine experts, when blindfolded, are unable to detect a difference between wine delivered in the "proper" glass and that same wine drunk from a jelly jar.

So does this mean that you shouldn't bother at all about the kind of wineglasses you use? Well, not quite. First, there's the aesthetic angle: any sensory experience is multidimensional, and drinking wine from what you think is a great-looking glass may enhance your pleasure in ways that aren't scientifically measurable. Beyond that, there are some functional considerations. Some of these are mentioned in the text: a wineglass should be clear, undecorated, and thin-walled so that you can easily *see* the wine inside; it should be stemmed so that the heat of your hand doesn't accelerate the warming of the wine; the sides of the (ovoid) bowl should be tapered so that you can swirl the wine without spilling it; and it should be large enough to hold several ounces of wine while still leaving plenty of room for the wine's aromas to accumulate in the bowl (and also to make swirling less hazardous).

It also makes sense to bow to a tradition that long predates Riedel's "scientific" breakthrough, and to serve red wines in glasses at least slightly

RED WINE
GLASS

WHITE WINE
GLASS

CHAMPAGNE FLUTE

larger than those you use for whites. Red wines' aromas are generally more powerful and complex than those of white wines, and the larger bowl helps capture and retain them, at least momentarily. For serving Champagnes and other sparkling wines, you should definitely have a set of the tall, narrow glasses called **flutes** or the slightly wider-bowled, more ovoid **tulip glasses**; both kinds prolong a sparkling wine's pleasure by controlling the rate at which the CO_2 can escape. (But use a standard wineglass rather than a flute or tulip glass if you're formally tasting sparkling wines, because a standard glass will capture their aroma better.)

TULIP GLASS

Beyond these basic types—red wine, white wine, and flute (or tulip glass)—what else do you need, glass-wise? Well, nothing, unless you're partial to Sherry or Port, in which case you'd be wise also to invest in a set of smaller stemmed glasses more appropriate to the smaller quantities in which these fortified wines are usually drunk. Out of the numberless small stemmed glasses available, *Drinkology WINE* likes the ones called **sipping glasses**, which look like narrow brandy snifters. They comfortably accommodate two ounces of wine—about the amount of Sherry or Port you'd want to pour for a single drink—while leaving plenty of room within the tapered bowl to capture the fragrance and allow for spill-free swirling.

Believe me, though: If you feel like springing for the specialized glasses in some top crystal-maker's line, ain't nobody gonna stop you. In fact, invite me over, so that we can conduct some scientific research of our own.

SIPPING GLASS

taste of the wine drunk by itself and drunk with something to eat can be enlightening.)

And you'll need a receptacle to spit into; if you're tasting with others, that receptacle should be opaque (a paper or Styrofoam cup, for instance). That others should have to watch and listen to you spit is icky enough; they shouldn't also be expected to have to stare at your abject effluvia.

There are two more pieces of *essential* wine-tasting equipment: paper and a pencil or pen for taking notes. The importance of taking notes while tasting can't be overemphasized. If you don't take notes, you'll forget—very quickly—what a wine looked like, smelled like, tasted like, and the tasting will have had little long-term value. To encourage yourself to take notes, don't think of your tastings as abstract exercises meant to "teach" you about wine. Think of them as *personal* explorations through which you'll discover which wines you like and which you don't—and which will help you feel a little less bewildered the next time you walk into a wine shop.

How casual or punctilious you want to be about note-taking is, of course, entirely up to you. You may want to keep a journal; you may want to transfer your notes to your computer after each tasting; or you may be satisfied with scrawling a few observations on stray pieces of paper and keeping them together in a file folder. Your degree of anal retentiveness isn't my concern. But it will be helpful if you make sure to write down some notes about each of the major tasting steps: as you *look* at a wine, immediately after you've *smelled* it, and then again after you've *tasted* it. (Should you also attempt to **score** the wine—to give it a letter grade or numeric rating? Personally, I think that would be a pretty useless exercise when you're just at the beginning of your wine-tasting adventures and have little basis for comparison. But for a note on wine-expert rating systems, see the sidebar that begins on the following page.)

SCORE BORED?

I'd heard that there are millions of people who base all their wine-purchasing decisions on wine critics' ratings, but I'd never met one until the summer of 2004. I was poking around the ill-stocked wine racks at the back of a really crummy liquor store somewhere in suburban New Jersey, hunting for something—anything—that I wouldn't feel too ashamed taking to a friend's house for dinner that evening. As I pursued what I was becoming convinced was a vain quest, I noticed I was being shadowed; my stalker was a fellow customer—a tall, gangly-looking old coot, wearing a very wrinkled orange shirt. He sidled up to me and suddenly declared, "You know, son, I never buy anything that got less than a 90 from Parker."

"Uh-huh. That so?" I responded. I hadn't been called "son" in decades, and I really didn't want to have this conversation.

"That's right," he said. "Nothing less than a 90—*at least.*" He stood there grinning at me—a *challenging* sort of grin. I felt like asking him what in the hell, if that was his rule of thumb, he was doing in this poor excuse for a liquor store. I thought better of it, however, muttered a quick, "Take care," and skedaddled, but not before grabbing an extremely dusty bottle of Riesling I'd been examining just before the interruption.

The Riesling, to my amazement, turned out to be delicious—but back to the matter at hand. There are a number of publications that rate, or score, wines, and there are a couple of different systems for doing so, but the best known and most widely followed are the scores handed down by the *Wine Spectator* magazine *(WS)* and by the *Wine Advocate (WA)*, the newsletter edited by Robert M. Parker, Jr.—the "Parker" referred to by my erstwhile chum in the Jersey liquor store. Both the *Wine Spectator* and the *Wine Advocate* taste wines blind and rate them against a 100-point scale—or what *appears* to be a 100-point scale. It's actually just 50 points: any wine that's rated automatically gets 50 points just for "showing up." There are subtle differences between the *Spectator*'s and Parker's systems, but, basically, the scores break down as follows:

> 90–100 points: Excellent to outstanding
>
> 80–89 points: Good to very good
>
> 70–79 points: Average
>
> 60–69 points: Below average
>
> 50–59 points: Poor (that is, undrinkable)

In both rating systems, wines are compared to others of their type and against the critics' own standards of what constitutes excellence for that type of wine. The same factors that you'll be weighing in your own wine tastings enter into the critics' judgment: the wine's appearance, its aroma, and its flavor. But for many red wines (and some whites), the critics tack on another criterion for evaluation: the wine's **ageworthiness**—that is, whether the wine possesses the balanced structure that will allow it to develop and improve in the bottle over time.

The *Spectator* and Parker are *very* important in the wine world—Parker being probably the more influential, though the *Spectator*, with a circulation of 400,000 or so (astonishing for a niche magazine), is probably responsible for getting more wine sold. (That I'd never met one of Parker's devotees before summer 2004 indicates only that I don't get out very much.) Poor *WS* or *WA* scores can threaten disaster for a winery—especially a small or startup winery without a large, long-established following. By the same token, if one or more of its wines should earn a *WS* or *WA* score in the mid- to high 90s, a wine producer nobody's ever heard of before might be catapulted to wine-world-wide fame (and suddenly be able to charge significantly higher prices for its products).

Score Bored?

Such power invites detractors, however, and Parker, especially, has come under a great deal of fire over the past several years. Parker's forte is French wines, especially those of Bordeaux. (His book *Bordeaux: A Consumer's Guide to the World's Finest Wines,* is a must-have reference for any would-be connoisseur.) On the one hand, Parker's been credited with reviving, even "saving," the Bordeaux wine industry because of his championing of the introduction of modern winemaking techniques there and his relentless push for higher quality. In 1993 he was even accorded the distinction—rare enough for foreigners and a first-time-ever achievement for a wine critic—of being inducted into the French Legion d'Honneur. On the other hand, he's frequently been slammed for what his critics view as his power to impose homogeneity—a sameness—on wines worldwide. To be successful, they claim, a wine has to be made to suit Parker's fairly narrow taste, and this has had the effect—or so they say—of radically reducing the diversity of wines produced in France and beyond.

As a wine newbie, you don't have to take sides in this contretemps. But how much attention should you pay to these or other rating systems? If you're just shopping for some wine and notice—either in a wine-store ad or one of those informational cards (they're called **shelf talkers**) clipped to a wine-store shelf—that a particular, not-too-expensive wine has won a high (85+) rating from *WS* or *WA,* you can be somewhat assured that you'll be getting good value. (Per usual, there's a caveat: Some retailers, whether inadvertently or intentionally, mislabel wines. The shelf-talker may claim that Château Qui Est-ce Que received a Parker score of 95; well, it did—in 2000—but the bottle on sale is a 2001, which only got a 78.)

If you intend to take the full plunge into winedom's depths—and even think you might be interested in starting a wine collection—you'd do well, probably, to subscribe to either the *Wine Spectator* or the *Wine Advocate*, or both, and to spend time perusing their buyer's guides before committing your hard-earned cash to any costly purchases. But no matter how casually or seriously you use the information provided by wine-scoring systems, there are a couple of things you should always keep in mind:

First, any score represents *one* taster's opinion—or perhaps the collective opinion of a small panel. It may be a deeply informed opinion, but it's still an opinion reflecting a single person's or (very) small group's taste—which your own preferences may or may not conform to. Second, the score awarded to a wine represents a "snapshot," at best, of that wine's character. Professional tasters like Parker and the *WS* staff critics taste *thousands* of wines annually, which means they're spending very little time (half a minute? a minute?) with any wine they're evaluating. (Among other things, that means they generally don't have the chance to see whether a wine might improve if given the chance to **breathe** for a while after being opened.) Third, the wines are being tasted and scored at a very young age—at the time of release and, in some cases, even before; the critic's prediction about a wine's potential is therefore a *guess* (albeit an educated one). And, finally, a rating represents a critic's assessment of a wine sampled all by itself—that is, *without food*. Since most wines are meant to be drunk with food, and since the experience of a wine can be dramatically different according to whether it's drunk by itself or accompanies a meal, this is a crucial caution. In fact, another common criticism leveled against wine critics, including Parker, is that they tend to give the highest ratings to powerhouse red wines—**"fruit bombs"**—that no dish could possibly stand up to.

So watch the scoreboard or be score bored. You're the only ump whose call finally matters.

Just a few more quick preparatory suggestions: Red wines should be tasted at or slightly below room temperature; whites should be chilled, but do yourself a favor and take the bottle(s) out of the fridge twenty minutes to half an hour before tasting, since a very cold temperature will dampen a wine's flavor. And if you're tasting reds that are likely to be relatively tannic (e.g., recent-vintage Cabernet Sauvignon or Zinfandel varietals; red Bordeaux or Bordeaux-style blends)—you should probably open the wines about an hour or so before tasting. Even the limited contact that the wine (still in the bottle) will have with the air during this period may help "soften" the tannins, making it less likely that they'll overwhelm the tasting experience. (In the—unlikely but possible, I guess—event that you're tasting a fine old Bordeaux, you'll want to go a step further and decant the wine ahead of time to rid it of any sediment. For advice on decanting, see pages 350–353.)

There. You're ready. Now on to the five S's.

STEP 1: SEE

You can learn quite a bit about a wine simply by eyeballing it as it rests inside a glass set on or held above a white surface. Without ever having seen the label, you might, for instance, be able to ascertain whether it's a younger or older wine and whether the grapes from which it was made were grown in a cooler or a hotter climate. A practiced eye might even be able to tell, within certain limits, what sort of grape or grapes it was (or wasn't) made from.

Examine the wine by looking down into the glass at about a 45-degree angle—or, better, pick up the glass by its stem and tilt it. The first thing you're checking for is any **visible fault**. Actually, visible faults—cloudiness, tartrate crystals (in white wines), or the presence of bubbles in wines that are supposed to be still—are fairly rare in this era of fastidious winemaking, but they do sometimes occur. (See the sidebar on **wine faults** at the end of this chapter.) In all probability, the wine will be **clear** or, in the case of an especially opaque young red, free of any fault detectable by the eye.

Next, focus on the wine's color and—if it's a red wine—on its transparency or opacity. Both reds and whites exhibit a fairly wide spectrum of hues. Whites can range from a pale, nearly colorless, greenish tint to a sunny yellow or a luscious amber; reds from a dense, inky purple to a deep ruby to a range of paler shades—garnet, brick red, even a semi-transparent tawny color that's hardly "red" at all. Now, a wine's color can be an indicator of any number of things, including the specific techniques used by the winemaker (for instance, how long a red wine was allowed to remain "on" the grape skins during fermentation and maceration), but here are the more important kinds of information that a wine's color may communicate:

The climate of the wine-growing region. Wines—both reds and whites—from hotter climates are usually more deeply colored than those from cooler places. For example, a Sauvignon Blanc–based wine from France's relatively cool Loire Valley (a white Sancerre, for instance) will *probably* be paler than a California Sauvignon Blanc varietal. (This is an inexact "science"; the hue will partly depend on where, exactly, in California the wine comes from.)

The age of the wine. White wines grow *darker* with age; they gradually oxidize and eventually turn brown. (There are a few "white" wines that are supposed to be brownish in color—Sherry, for example, is an intentionally oxidized "white" wine—but, for the most part, a brownish color indicates that a white is in need of a requiem mass.) Red wines, oppositely,

TASTING WINE

BEFORE TASTING
Fill the wine-tasting glass to a depth of about an inch.

STEP 1: SEE
Examine the wine by tilting the glass at a 45-degree angle.

STEP 3: SMELL
Poke your nose as deeply into the glass as it will comfortably go.

STEP 2: SWIRL
Grasp the glass firmly by the stem, and swirl vigorously.

STEP 4: SIP
Inhale, then take enough wine into your mouth to fully envelop your tongue.

STEP 5: SPIT
An opaque paper or Styrofoam cup makes an acceptable spittoon.

become *paler* as they grow older: over time, they **throw sediment** that's partly composed of pigments that have fallen out of suspension, thereby lightening the wine's color. Unlike darkness in a white wine, however, relative pallor in a red does not necessarily indicate that the wine has entered its dotage. Fine old red Bordeaux are, for example, often weakly colored (Bordeaux being well known for throwing lots of sediment as they age).

As you look down into the glass, you may also perceive a lessening of **color intensity** between the center, or **core**, of the wine (where it is deepest in the glass), and the edge, or **rim**. (Tilting the glass will help you discern this difference more clearly.) A white may be, for example, straw-colored at the core but watery—almost colorless—at the rim. A red that's boldly ruby-colored at the core might fade to a pinkish, fuchsia hue at the rim. The presence of a discernible rim may be an indication that the wine has spent some time in the bottle—that it's an older wine.

A caveat: You have to exercise a little caution in describing wines as "young" or "old," since a wine's seeming youth or maturity may have little to do with chronological age. Winespeakers prefer to talk about a

Not "age" but *stage*

wine's **stage of development**, or even its **evolution**, rather than its age, since different wines progress through their life cycles at very different rates. An eight-year-old Pinot Noir, to take just one possible example, might have sung its swan song, whereas an "ageworthy" Cabernet Sauvignon might just be reaching puberty eight years after vintage.

The kind of grape the wine was—or wasn't—*made from.* Guessing the grape by looking at the color of the wine is mostly the province of experts (who, in any case, can seldom infallibly do so, since color is affected by the winegrowing region's climate, winemaking methods, and the wine's age and because different grapes often produce wines of similar hue). But a wine's color, along with its degree of transparency/opacity, can provide telltale signs that it has *not* been made from a certain variety of grape, and quick-study novices can easily learn to interpret a few of these signals. If a red wine has a deep, impenetrable purplish-blackish color, it in all probability is *not* a Pinot Noir–based wine, since Pinot Noirs are typically lighter and redder in color. Some Pinot Noir–based wines—red Burgundies, for example—even have a semi-transparent quality under good light. (This wine that is definitely *not* a Pinot Noir could, however, be a Cabernet Sauvignon, or a Shiraz, or a Zinfandel, or something else.) The same, negative principle holds true for some whites. If the wine is brightly yellow—or, indeed, has much color at all—you can with reasonable safety bet the McMansion and SUV that it's *not* a dry Riesling, since dry Rieslings veer toward the pale-green end of the white-wine spectrum. By the same token, a pale green, nearly colorless wine is probably *not* a Gewürztraminer, because the Gewürztraminer grape's café au lait–colored skin usually imparts a slight pinkish-yellowish tint to the wine.

Oaking. A deeper color in a white wine might also indicate that the wine has spent some time in barrel—something, of course, that will be confirmed or disproved when the wine is smelled and tasted.

Note: If you're tasting a sparkling wine, you'll also want to note the size and quantity of the bubbles and the precise way in which the wine "sparkles." (Is it frothy and sudsy, or do the bubbles ascend through the wine in a more "civilized" manner—perhaps even in tight, military columns?) These characteristics provide clues to the quality of the wine and the method used in the wine's making. In general, the smaller the "beads" (i.e., the bubbles) and the more orderly their progression from the bottom of the glass to the wine's surface, the better the wine.

STEP 2: SWIRL

So far, you've been a passive observer. Now it's time to get actively involved by moving the wine around in the glass. The purpose of swirling is simple: as the Winespeakers say, swirling **opens** the wine, helping unleash its fragrance and flavor. The chemical compounds responsible for the wine's aroma and taste are **volatile organics**; by swirling, you're mixing them around, causing their molecules to collide and releasing some of them into the air. (Some wine-tasting strategies advise you to smell the wine before swirling and then again after; if the aroma remains the same—doesn't seem fuller and more complex after swirling—the wine's deficient and probably won't taste like much at all.)

For some professional wine-tasters, it's a point of pride to be able to swirl the wine energetically without setting the glass on the table or counter. The most athletically advanced tasters can even swirl while holding the glass by its foot rather than its stem—very posh! Wine newbies should *not* attempt such displays of prowess, however. Believe me, you'll wind up getting the wine all over the place, spattering yourself and annoying—if not actually splashing—the other tasters. Until you have a fair amount of practice under your cuff, swirl like the amateur you are: without lifting the glass from the table or counter surface, grasp the stem securely near the base, and begin moving the glass in a circular pattern. Don't be too ladylike about this: you really want to knock those volatile organic compounds around, so swirl rapidly, evenly, and firmly. If you're right-handed, you'll find it easier to swirl in a counterclockwise direction—a tendency that I, superstifious sod that I am, instantly trained myself out of when somebody told me that the French think that counterclockwise swirling is bad luck.

When you stop swirling, you may—depending on the wine—notice that some of the liquid adheres to the wall of the glass, forming rivulets that trail downward into the wine. These are the so-called **legs** (a.k.a. **tears**). Sometimes the legs are skinny; sometimes they're meaty; sometimes they straggle down the side of the glass; sometimes they form filmy sheets that descend smoothly and evenly. Now, there are people out there who make too much of a wine's legs— who think that "great legs" = great wine. "Get a load o' them legs!" is the kind of thing you hear bloviating guys proclaiming to their table companions in expense-account restaurants. Well, the gasbags are (per usual) *wrong*. A wine's legs are nothing other than any indicator of its alcoholic strength (and, if it's a sweet wine, of its residual sugar content, as well). That's *it*. They tell you nothing about a wine's quality.

Great legs ≠ great wine

Legs don't generally appear unless a wine is at least 12 percent alcohol. The higher the wine's alcohol content, the "stronger" (more developed, more viscous-looking) the legs. Because they signal alcoholic strength, the appearance of legs *is* an indication that the wine, when tasted, will probably turn out to be what Winespeakers call **medium-bodied** to **full-bodied** (alcohol being the prime constituent of a wine's "body"—but we'll get to that a little later).

STEP 3: SMELL

Now that you've roughed the wine up (so to speak), you're about to enter into a more intimate relation with it. You're going to smell it—and you're going to use your sense of smell in the deliberate, investigative way that you usually reserve for those moments when you're trying to determine whether the house might be on fire.

Pick the glass up, bring it to your face, and stick your nose inside it as far as it will comfortably go. Now *smell*. There's actually some controversy (wouldn't you know?) about *how* you should smell wine. Should you inhale long and deep, or is it better—more informative and revealing about the wine—to take a series of rapid, brief sniffs? One famous wine educator is an adamant proponent of the latter, pointing out that dogs (noted, you may recall, for the acuity of their sense of smell) typically utilize the lots-of-short-sniffs methodology. Personally, I don't much care: whatever works for you is just fine.

When smelling wine so intensively, you'll definitely notice just how *ephemeral* smells can be. A wine's aroma can be profoundly present when you first smell it, but smell it again an instant later and all that fragrance . . . disappears. (Or changes dramatically.) This is just the way the olfactory sense is engineered: the nose registers a scent, then forgets about it and goes looking, so to speak, for something else. When you're smelling a wine, the brevity of the perception can be frustrating. You detect something you recognize, you think you can almost identify it, and then—it's gone. You can compensate for this "now you smell it, now you don't" phenomenon by pausing briefly between sniffs. Set your glass down, wait a beat or two, then bring it back to your nose. The scent(s) you caught the first time will return, only to vanish again, of course. (To refresh your sense of smell between sniffs, you might employ a trick long used in perfume stores. Keep a small cup of coffee beans or ground coffee at hand; smell the wine, then the coffee, then the wine again.)

Winespeakers refer to a wine's aroma as its **nose**. They also refer to its taste as its **palate**—as if the organs of perception belonged to the wine, not the taster. Feel free to mock this lingo, if you want, but notice that it does evoke the *connectedness* of the wine-tasting experience—a breaking down of boundaries that can occur when your sensory attention is so meticulously focused. I won't pursue this mystical line of thinking, but let me say that even I—reverse wine snob that I used to be—have come to regard "nose" as a more useful term than "aroma" or "fragrance," since the things your nose detects when inhaling a wine aren't limited to smells per se. You may, for example, experience a sharp, tingling sensation in your nostrils—possibly an indication of high alcohol content, even though the ethyl alcohol in wine has no real odor. Or your nose may feel, rather than smell, a dusty sensation that may signal that the wine you're about to taste is rather high in tannins.

Some wines won't have much of a nose; they may—especially if they're simple, young wines—just smell clean, fresh, and fruity. Or a wine may smell of nothing much at all. A weak nose may be a mark of a lesser wine, but it ain't necessarily so. Some kinds of wine are simply less aromatic than others; a typical Chablis, for example, will be much less fragrant than a typical Riesling. And then there's a weird condition—which you should be aware of even if you're unlikely to experience it very often—that temporarily afflicts certain very good, ageworthy (and often expensive) wines. For a period of time that's unpredictable both in its onset and in its duration, some wines go through a kind of midlife crisis during which they "shut down"—they have almost no fragrance and almost no taste. The reasons for this temporary catatonia aren't well understood, scientifically; if you happen to open such a bottle at the wrong time, your pleasure will be limited to being able to brag that, yes indeed, you've had a quiescent or (as the Winespeakers say) **dumb** wine.

That condition's rare, though. You'll find that many, many wines present your nose with a complex concatenation of scents: some readily distinguishable and identifiable, others mere whiffs or "hints" hovering in the background, or "notes" that burst through very briefly, then immediately retreat. With some wines, this combination of aromas will seem well harmonized. Sometimes, though, the impression you'll get will be more like that delivered by atonal music; the various fragrances will compete, or conflict, or just seem not to hang together. What's important to point out, I think, is that *either* of these kinds of olfactory experience can be enjoyable (but then I happen to like atonal music).

Even more remarkable is that some smells that you might, in another context, find unpleasant can be tolerable or even enjoyable when you

This wine smells like a barnyard. Fabulous!

detect them while sniffing a glass of wine. Famously, Sauvignon Blanc–based wines from France's Loire Valley sometimes smell of **cat pee**—and nobody holds it against them. (In fact, *cat pee* is a technical wine-tasting term.) Some red wines have an odor commonly described as **barnyard**—and are relished by people who'd go all to pieces if confronted by an actual cow pie. During a *Drinkology WINE* tasting of red Bordeaux, one wine smelled like a dentist's office. Several of the tasters noticed it—and, to our surprise, we all found it sort of O.K.

Which is not to say that you won't occasionally come across a wine that just smells *nasty*. A truly off-putting odor is a sign that something's gone wrong, either during the winemaking process or after the wine was put in the bottle. A vinegary smell indicates—you guessed it—that the wine has soured. Don't drink it. A rotten-egg odor means there's something amiss with the wine's sulfur content. Don't drink it, either. But the offensive smell you're most likely to encounter is the musty, wet-cardboard odor associated with **cork taint**, or **"corkiness."** (For more on this wine fault, see the sidebar at the end of the chapter.) When you discover that a wine is corky, you'll probably want to end the tasting of that wine right then and there. (Cork taint doesn't present a health risk, but it ruins the pleasure of drinking the wine.)

But let's get back to the pleasant smells. Wine newbies are often intimidated by—or simply disbelieving of—the variety of fragrances (and flavors) that more experienced tasters say they can discern in a given wine. Your neighbor at the tasting table will be going on about how she smells bananas, or passion-fruit, or black cherries, or tangerines. Meanwhile all you smell is . . . wine. "How *can* a wine smell like bananas?" you ask yourself. "Isn't wine made from *grapes?*" Even more consternating are the *non*fruit scents and flavors that experienced tasters often claim to be perceiving: anything from mushrooms, to tobacco, to gasoline, to—I don't know—fine old saddle leather. No, you tell yourself. Nuh uh. You don't smell any of that stuff.

Or, wait a minute, maybe you *do*. Early on in any neo-oenophile's career, there comes a eureka moment when, suddenly, you *do* recognize a smell or flavor in the wine (other than "wine," that is). For many people, this first happens in a group setting: you're taking your first wine class, and the instructor, her nose immodestly burrowed deep in the tasting glass, is saying, "I'm getting Granny Smith apples." And so you pick your glass back up, and bring it to your nose, and . . . yes, there it *is*. You're briefly—but during that instant overwhelmingly—flooded with an unmistakable green-apple aroma. Pretty soon you find yourself getting rather good at this game. "Peaches," the teacher says, and you, too, smell peaches. "Earth," she says, "deep, rich earth, . . . and maybe some pine needles, too"—and, as far as your nose is concerned, you may as well be lying face-down on the forest floor.

Power of suggestion? Well, sure. In fact, honest wine professionals (there are some) admit that they often use a self-suggestion technique when trying to determine what, exactly, a wine smells and/or tastes like—quickly running through their own mental inventories of fragrances and flavors until they hit on a correspondence between what they're smelling or tasting now and the phantom of a previously experienced smell or taste that lives on in their sense-memory. (By the way, if you're worried about the limitations of your own sense-memory, there are some olfactory aids designed to acquaint you with the diversity of aromas you might encounter in wine. The best-known of these is a French product called Le Nez du Vin ["The Wine's Nose"], which consists of a set of vials containing fragrances ranging from quince, to linden, to cedar, to saffron, to toast—fifty-four aromas in all. Be forewarned, though: these little sets—available through a number of Internet emporia—are breathtakingly expensive.)

So suggestion is certainly involved, but recognizing scents and flavors in wine isn't just a matter of being susceptible to suggestion. For one thing,

Is it all just auto-hypnosis? even if you *are* susceptible, suggestion doesn't always work. Try as you might, you sometimes just won't be able to smell or taste what others insist they're perceiving in a given wine—even when you're very familiar with that aroma or flavor. The only lesson to draw from such an experience is that *everyone's* experience of wine is fundamentally subjective.

But does that mean that everybody's just engaging in a kind of auto-hypnosis—sometimes contagious, sometimes not—when they say things like, "Now I'm getting pineapples"? Not at all. In all probability, the person who smells a pineapple scent in a wine is *really* detecting an organic compound that is the same as a compound found in pineapples. Perhaps hundreds of such aroma- and flavor-generating compounds—created during fermentation and élevage and continuing to develop after bottling—may be present in a particular wine. The quantities are minute, measurable in parts per million or billion, but the human nose can be amazingly sensitive and discriminating. So if a fellow taster says he smells vinyl—but all you can smell is apricots—chances are that neither of you is making it up.

A caveat: You may have heard or read wine experts using the word **bouquet** in connection with a wine's aroma. Don't make the mistake of thinking that "bouquet" and "aroma" are the same thing, however. Winespeak reserves use of the term *bouquet* for the special kind of aroma that an ageworthy wine develops after years in the bottle. Every wine has an aroma (even if it's very attenuated); relatively few wines have a bouquet, which, by definition, is a smell that's profound, complex, and difficult to parse into constituent scents. As a matter of fact, one important distinction between younger and older (or more "developed") wines is that the smells and flavors of younger wines are easier to individually distinguish and describe than those of wines that have greater bottle age.

If you've followed me this far, you've probably noticed that, over the past several paragraphs, I've been using "smell" and "taste," "aroma" and "flavor" as if they were two sides of the same coin. Well, they are. The *Oxford Companion to Wine* even goes so far as to declare that a wine's aroma and its flavor are the *same thing*. Why? Because the olfactory apparatus (including the all-important *olfactory bulb*, a little organ that's lodged up near your sinuses) is so essentially involved in the sense of taste. In fact, without a sense of smell, you can't really taste much at all—as anyone who's ever suffered a bad cold knows.

Saying that aroma and flavor are one and the same, however, seems wrong to me—especially in a formal wine tasting, when this continuum of experience is somewhat artificially divided into separate steps. It might mislead you into thinking, for example, that you'll necessarily experience a continuity or harmony between the way a wine smells and the way it tastes. Though it's true that you will often notice such a coherence, you'll sometimes be surprised by how different a wine's aroma (in the nose) is from its flavor (in the mouth). This disjointedness—if that's the right word—can occasionally seem almost radical, but it has little if anything to do with a wine's quality. The fresh fruit aroma of a simple Italian Pinot Grigio will probably carry straight through into its taste, whereas the nose of a complex—and much more interesting—red Bordeaux may, depending on the wine, summon a range of impressions quite different from those that the wine delivers on the palate. And sometimes a wine has a powerful nose but a vague taste (or vice versa).

STEP 4: SIP

Now, finally, you get to put the wine in your mouth. As you might have guessed, there's again a specific way of doing it that's preferred by experts. Bring the glass to your lips, and, inhaling just before you do so, take just enough wine into your mouth that your tongue is enveloped—but not so much that you'll feel forced to swallow.

This is the point when a wine tasting—especially one where pros (or wine snobs) are present—gets noisy, and let me just say straight out that the sounds that professionals and/or snobs make with wine in their mouth are *gross*. According to the cognoscenti, you're supposed to sip the wine and then, without swallowing, open your mouth very slightly and inhale again—through your *mouth*, that is. This maneuver isn't just difficult to perform (you may want to practice in the privacy of your bathroom before attempting it in company), but it also inevitably creates a medley of sucking and gurgling noises that, frankly, I'd prefer not to hear. To my ear, the most objectionable are made by those who, to accomplish their goal, bite their lip (upper or lower) and draw the air in through their front teeth. Yuck.

Neither God nor evolution designed our oral cavities to work in this way, but even I—a reluctant mouth-breather—have got to say that the technique does produce the desired result. Taking in a small amount of air while holding the wine in your mouth wafts the volatile compounds escaping from the wine up into your nasal passages—and brings the ol' olfactory bulb into greater play, enhancing your experience of the wine's flavor.

The sensory experience of taking wine into your mouth isn't just about flavor, however; it has two other components: **body** and **mouthfeel**. In reality, of course, you'll be experiencing all these attributes of the wine simultaneously or in rapid and overlapping succession, but you should try to notice them independently.

Body. A wine's *body* is its perceived "weight" on your tongue. When a wine is described as full-bodied, or light-bodied, or medium-bodied, it means that it *feels* heavy, or light, or somewhere in between as it rests in your mouth. That may sound relatively simple, but inexperienced tasters sometimes have trouble discriminating between body and **intensity of flavor**. Intensity of flavor can add to the perception of body, but they're not the same. Think, for example, of cream: it feels heavy in the mouth, but the taste is relatively mild. Now compare cream, mentally, with Coca-Cola (or Pepsi; I don't care where your brand loyalties lie): in the mouth, the soda feels lighter than cream, but the flavor's more intense. Now compare cream and Coke/Pepsi with lemon juice. Body-wise, lemon juice is lightest of all; flavor-wise, it's most powerful.

Full-bodiedness in a wine is actually the result of several factors: not just concentration of flavor (sometimes referred to as **extract**), but also high alcohol content; the presence of residual sugar, if any; and possibly the presence of glycerol, or glycerin. (Glycerol is sometimes a byproduct of fermentation, but when it occurs it's present in such minute amounts that experts disagree about whether it makes any contribution whatsoever to a taster's perception of body.) Of all the factors, alcohol is the most important. It's unlikely that a dry wine that's low in alcohol would ever produce a full-bodied impression. Wines with high amounts of residual sugar—including, for example, dessert wines like Sauternes—often have a gooey quality that, along with their alcohol content, makes them feel very weighty on the tongue.

Mouthfeel: Tannins. In our appreciation of foods and beverages, *mouthfeel* can be almost as important as flavor. (We don't like potato chips just because they're salty, but also because they're crunchy.) Well, a given wine will also have a certain feel in your mouth—a sensation or set of sensations that can strongly influence your enjoyment of it. A wine's mouthfeel is partly dependent on its body, but there are other contributing factors. The most important of these, at least when tasting red wines, is **tannin content**. Most of the tannins present in a red wine originated in the grapes' skins and were extracted, along with pigment, during fermentation, although small amounts of wood tannins will also leach into wine if it is aged in an oak barrel. (You'll remember from the previous chapters that white wines, which are not fermented on the skins, have a tannin content that's so low as to be imperceptible—*unless,* that is, the white wine has been aged in wood.)

Tannins have no taste, but highly tannic wines produce a strong sensation in the mouth that most people find unpleasant. People vary in their sensitivity to tannins, but if you've ever drunk a tannic red wine, you probably know the feeling: it's that astringent, desiccating, prickly, gripping sensation that makes your tongue, the insides of your cheeks, and sometimes even your gums feel as if they've been attacked by an aggressive form of peachfuzz. Tannin molecules, you see, have what chemists call an affinity for proteins: when they latch onto the proteins in your saliva, the reaction causes this unmistakable sensation.

Does this mean that tannins are bad? Not at all—or, rather, not if they're present in the right proportion. Along with acid and alcohol, they're essential components of what Winespeakers call **structure**. They also help confer longevity on red wines. A low-tannin red is simply incapable of attaining any great age in bottle,

Most people find tannins unpleasant

but ageworthy reds, if drunk too young, can sometimes be too tannic—too "hard" or too "tight"—to be enjoyable to most drinkers. There are, granted, some macho types who think that a highly tannic wine is a good wine *because* it takes some courage and fortitude to drink; they should have their testosterone levels adjusted. That said, it *is* true that tannins can enhance the enjoyment of wine with certain foods: a thick, juicy steak is better accompanied by a fairly tannic red than by a "lighter" red with flimsier tannins.

Interestingly, as red wine ages, tannin molecules hook up; the molecular chains grow too heavy to remain in suspension; and the tannins fall out of the wine as sediment—which is why an ageworthy red will grow much **softer** as the years advance. And the slight oxidation that occurs when a red wine is opened an hour or two before tasting or serving can act as a kind of accelerated ageing: it can help take the edge off the tannins in a young red.

The key to deciding whether the tannin level of a particular red wine is right or wrong is **balance**. If the tannin in a wine is overwhelming—if it obliterates all other sensations and flavors—it's probably not a very good wine. But if the tannins, despite being unpleasantly strong, are counterbalanced by other sensations and flavors (alcohol, acidity, fruit), then there's a good chance that the wine is simply being drunk too young, and that it would have been much better (and its tannins much softer) had it been allowed to spend more time in the bottle.

It's worth noting here that encountering a truly, harshly tannic wine (whether balanced or unbalanced) is becoming a rarer and rarer event. That's because winemakers worldwide are increasingly "designing" their red wines to appeal to average drinkers, who tend to consume wines almost immediately after buying them. As wine connoisseurship becomes a middle-class hobby, the ranks of collectors who lay down fine red wines for drinking years hence are probably growing, but these consumers still account for only a fraction of the total market. The ordinary gal or guy wants a wine that's drinkable *now*, and that means a wine that's less tannic. There are various methods for buffering tannins or actually removing them from wine—including egg-white fining—and more and more winemakers customarily employ these techniques. As a member of the great unwashed, I have mixed feelings about this. I'm as impatient as the next person, and I, like many people, strongly dislike tannins' effects; but there are some kinds of red wine—Cabernet Sauvignon is the chief example—that just aren't themselves if deprived of too much of their tannic content, and the experience of drinking a too-soft Cabernet is . . . well, it's boring.

Mouthfeel: Other Components. Body and tannin-related effects aren't the only constituents of mouthfeel. Your experience of the **acid** in a wine and of its alcohol are matters more of mouthfeel than of taste (ethyl alcohol has, in fact, no taste). Acid's easy to recognize: you feel it as a familiar pinching, stinging, or "sharp" sensation, perhaps most strongly on the sides of your tongue, but note that this acidic "feel" may or may not be accompanied by a corresponding sour taste. (There are wines that are bracingly acidic but so powerfully, even "sweetly," fruity that they don't taste tart.)

Alcohol-related sensations may be a little harder for the wine new-comer to recognize, especially if you're not in the habit of drinking spirits. Alcohol can be experienced as a burning sensation at the back of your mouth or in your throat (if you swallow, that is). **"Hot" wine** Generally, this sensation is slight—and if the wine is low in **isn't so hot** alcohol you probably won't feel it at all. You're also less likely to notice it—even in high-alcohol wines—if it's counterbalanced by acid, tannins (if present), and flavor. If the burning sensation *is* strong, the wine's out of balance; it's **hot**, and that's a definite flaw.

Residual sugar—the sugar that remains in a sweet wine after fermentation—also affects mouthfeel. Of course, sweet wines *taste* sweet, but they also *feel* relatively heavy in the mouth (sugar magnifies a wine's body) *and* they may also have a viscous—a syrupy, or "thick"—quality. And now I'll go out on a limb and say that **dryness** is a constituent of mouthfeel, as well. How one perceives dryness is an interesting question, since it's not the presence but rather the *absence* of something (sweetness). But—without understanding (or caring) a whit about the physiology of the sensation—I think we *feel* dryness in our mouths, independent of acidity or tannins, which can heighten the impression.

Flavor. At long last we arrive at the most important of a wine's attributes: its flavor. But hold on a moment: in point of fact, we already began discussing flavor, back when we were talking about a wine's nose. Flavor, to repeat, is a combination of the tastes perceived by your taste buds and the sensory information communicated, while the wine is in your mouth (and even afterward), to your olfactory bulb. Flavors are often described, therefore, in terms very similar to those used to describe aroma. A wine may smell and/or taste "herbal," or "appley," or of this or that flower or fruit or spice. (If, by the way, this whole practice of describing wine's aromas/flavors by reference to other aromas/flavors bugs you, be sure to read the sidebar on pages 112–113.)

Needless to say, actually putting the wine in your mouth adds sensory dimensions that are inaccessible to the nose alone. For one thing, a wine's flavor changes in a definite, almost orderly progression as you take it into

Wine's flavor has a three-beat rhythm

your mouth, briefly hold it there, and then swallow it or spit it out. The experience of flavor has a three-beat rhythm, and (naturally) there's a Winespeak term for each of these "beats." The first is the **attack**—how the wine tastes immediately upon entering your mouth. The second is the **mid-palate**—what it tastes like during the moment that you allow it to hang out, intensifying (or not) its impression on your taste buds and olfactory apparatus. And the third is the **finish**—the persistence of flavor (or lack of it) after you've swallowed or spit. What you'll notice about a wine will change from beat to beat, but it's the mark of a good wine if flavor—not a particular flavor, but flavor's presence—is sustained throughout the experience. Wine pros put particular stock in a wine's finish. A **long** finish—and one in which the aftertaste remains pleasant and even complex—signals a superior wine; a **short** finish an inferior one. (Some wines have finishes so brief as to be nonexistent; some have finishes that extend for several minutes after the wine has left the mouth.)

Besides the wine's specific flavor characteristics—black pepper? green pepper? cinnamon? chocolate?—you'll want to pay attention, as it's in your mouth, to what Winespeakers call **fruit intensity**. Now, not all wines have a fruit flavor. (Some aren't supposed to.) But many, especially younger wines, *are* fruity, though the particular kinds of fruit they evoke differ. (Very few wines taste like *grapes*. Among fine wines, only those made from the Muscat family of grapes are generally regarded as "grapey" in flavor.) In a young red wine, a **pronounced** fruit intensity—a fruit flavor that's deep and also persistent—can be an indication that the wine may be ageworthy. For it to be so, though, the fruit has to be balanced by the "structural" constituents discussed earlier: alcohol, acid, and tannins. (Even if you never intend to lay down wines for consumption years hence, it can be fun to speculate about whether a wine you're tasting has ageing potential—and whether you're drinking it at the "right" or "wrong" time.)

Don't, by the way, make the mistake of confusing "fruit" with sweetness. Because fruit and sweetness are so deeply linked in our sense memories, a fruity wine can create the impression of sweetness even though it may be **bone dry**—containing only an imperceptible amount of sugar. How can you tell whether a fruity wine has some sugar in it? With very sweet wines, it'll be obvious, but with a dry or off-dry wine it might be difficult to tell. Try licking your lips after you've swallowed the wine or spit it out. Do you detect a sugary taste? If so, bingo. (Be suspicious, by the way, of wine-shop personnel who try to sell you a wine by describing it as "fruity"; oftentimes, what they really mean is that it's sweet. These deceivers are operating on the assumption that you're a typical American wine drinker who's prejudiced against sweet wines; hence the euphemism, which unfortunately tends to muddy the distinction between fruity and sweet.)

And now it's time to say goodbye to your mouthful of wine . . .

He-Man versus Girly Wines?

Today, wine aficionados (and wine writers) are in the habit of describing wines' aromas and flavors primarily by identifying them with *other* smells and tastes—often (though not always) the smells and tastes of other foods. It's such a universal way of articulating wines' differing characters that it seems self-evidently *right*. How better to describe a wine except by saying that it smells like scallions (for example) or tastes like strawberries (or whatever)? Or that it's "jammy" or "citrusy" (or possesses some other gustatory correspondence)?

The truth, however, is that this way of talking about wine is a very recent phenomenon—no more than a few decades old. It was largely the creation of American food and wine writers—and, like so many American habits, was rapidly adopted elsewhere. But it is, in fact, a *fashion* and was preceded, historically, by other conventional ways of describing and distinguishing wines.

If you look though wine books published before the early 1970s, you'll be hard-pressed to find many food-based descriptors in their pages. Wine writers of a generation and more ago tended to rely on a descriptive vocabulary based on metaphors of social station. Wines were typically lauded as "aristocratic," or "elegant," or they were snubbed as "rustic," or "low class." Go back a little further in time, and you'll still find this reliance on class distinctions, but the descriptive language will also be highly *gendered*. For hundreds of years (and well into the twentieth century) wines were often characterized as "masculine" or "feminine," and, yes, there was a definite hierarchy of value attached to the terms.

Something of both these tendencies survives in contemporary Winespeak. It still isn't unusual to hear wines described as "muscular" or as possessing or lacking "finesse"—or, indeed, as "masculine" or "elegant." But the wine writers who introduced the new aroma- and flavor-based vocabulary really meant to cast aside the old metaphors, not because they found them politically incorrect, but because they found them *imprecise*. A word like "feminine," applied to wine, has no fixed or agreed-upon meaning, whereas (or so the theory goes) if I say that a wine tastes like caramel, I'm saying something definite and verifiable about it.

Well, O.K. The reason this new way of talking about wine took off is that it *does* make good sense. But there are two limitations. One is that a given wine will seldom evoke exactly the same set of sense memories in the noses and mouths of two different tasters. But a bigger problem is that you just can't come close to fully describing a wine based just on "verifiable" aroma and flavor descriptors. It's impossible to convey what a good Chablis tastes like unless you use an (inexact) word like "austere"; and, for me, the flavor of a good Pinot Noir isn't so much marked by its resemblance to this or that berry but by a characteristic I'd call "incisiveness," or "poise." I *know* the terms are virtually meaningless (and maybe a tad pretentious, to boot); but they stand for a characteristic that's as unmistakable as it is inexpressible.

Face it: Complex, subtle smells and tastes are hard to put into words, and so on this level Winespeak will forever remain inexact. And that means, I guess, that Winespeak will forever have its poets and its b.s. artists—and that it may sometimes be hard to tell the difference.

Step 5: Spit (or Swallow)

I think it's safe to say that nobody really *enjoys* sipping a wine only to spit it out. In fact, your whole physiology militates against spitting: you put something in your mouth, and, if it tastes good, signals emanating from a very primitive part of your brain instruct you to *swallow* it. Assuming that the wine you're tasting isn't noxious, spitting it out serves one function only: to prevent you from becoming intoxicated.

Why is this important? Well, sometimes it isn't. If you're not driving anywhere after a tasting, or don't have any work to attend to, there's nothing morally wrong or practically inconvenient about swallowing. The trouble is, even a very low level of intoxication will tend to dull your senses and impair your judgment. That's why the pros—who are usually tasting several wines (sometimes many wines) in succession—spit. If you're tasting a flight of wines and want to retain your ability to finely discriminate among aromas and flavors, you'll follow their lead.

But only so far. For some professional tasters, spitting is an art: they spit with the bravura and long-distance accuracy of baseball players. They spit *grandiosely.* Unless you're a showoff with a very true aim, my advice is to behave more modestly: bring the spit cup to your lips and expel the fluid gently and as quietly as you can manage. If you're tasting in company, the others will appreciate your discretion.

The only trouble with spitting is that it does cut the experience of tasting a wine a bit short. There are taste buds at the back of your tongue—and even on your soft palate—so swallowing the wine brings more of your flavor receptors into play. That's why I tend to swallow at least a little bit of any wine I'm tasting. The tradeoff—enjoying a fuller flavor experience versus the risk of slightly dulling my senses—is, I find, worth it.

This Wine Stinks—Literally
(Cork Taint and Other Wine Faults)

A lot of things can go wrong with a bottle of wine, and, unfortunately, encountering wine that's been ruined by a biological or chemical process that took place in the bottle (or even before bottling) is not an extremely rare event. While sampling wines during the writing of this book, I encountered four of the following five problems—experts call them *wine faults*—at least once, some in wines I'd bought for home consumption, some in wines ordered in restaurants.

Knowing a little about wine faults is helpful, since being able to recognize these problems can reassure you that the problem is with the *wine*, not with your sense of vision, smell, or taste. It can also keep you from freaking out—as, for example, when you discover a dangerous-looking sediment at the bottom of your glass just as you're finishing off what seemed to be a perfectly good bottle.

Do take note, however. Just because a wine isn't a very good wine—or just because you don't happen to like it—does not mean that the wine is faulty. Saying that a bottle of wine has a fault means that there's something identifiably, *objectively* wrong with it—that it's not the wine it *should* be. Believe me, you'll be able to tell the difference between a wine that's merely poor-quality and one that's definitely flawed. (The British have a wonderful word for wine that, though it's free of technical faults, is dreadful—they call it **plonk**.)

Cork Taint. Probably the commonest fault is what's called *cork taint,* or *corkiness.* As may be obvious from the term, cork taint only afflicts wines stoppered with natural corks. The main culprit is a chemical called 2,4,6-trichloroanisole, or **TCA**, which is sometimes generated when molds infect a cork. (The blame doesn't always rest with the cork producer; some wineries have had problems with their cellars becoming infected with TCA-producing mold.) Cork taint produces an unmistakable and highly unpleasant odor that some compare to that of a wet dog or a dead mouse. To me, it's similar to the smell of a pile of old *National Geographic*s that have long been stored in a dank basement. The wine remains potable; you won't get sick if you drink it, but drinking it will not be an enjoyable experience.

When a wine is corky, the cork itself sometimes (not always) carries the telltale odor, which is why you should smell the cork after opening a bottle of wine—and why the waiter should give you the cork, or set it on the table beside you, when you order a bottle of wine in a restaurant. Reputable wine shops will allow you to return corky wines for replacement. (Note: If you want the wine replaced, don't throw away the evidence. Return the bottle with the offending cork and whatever wine remained unpoured when the problem was ascertained.)

Cork taint is a *big* problem—but just *how* big a problem is open to debate. The cork industry contends that only about 2 percent of cork-stoppered bottles are corked. But that's a low estimate; a recent *Wine Spectator* editorial claimed that, on some days, fully *15 percent* of the sample bottles evaluated in the magazine's offices are affected. (Is it possible that the *Spectator*'s sniffmeisters' sensitivity is just more acute than that of ordinary folk?) At any rate, the problem's magnitude—even if the low estimate is nearer the mark—becomes apparent when you consider that hundreds of millions of bottles of wine are produced, worldwide, each year, and that the vast majority of fine wines are still sealed with real-cork corks.

Alternative closures are fast catching up, however, as more and more makers seek to protect their wines against the trouble tainted corks can cause. Some industry prophets have predicted that within twenty years or so, most wines will be sealed with screw tops. (The other alternative, the synthetic "cork," is less satisfactory, since bottles sealed with synthetic stoppers can be difficult to open and because, at least in the opinion of some wine writers, the synthetics impart a chemical odor/flavor to wine and can lead to more rapid oxidation.) Whether you see this switchover as a good or a bad thing depends in part on how romantic an attachment you have to the process of uncorking a bottle of wine. But there's also scientific debate about the possible detriment to ageworthy wines sealed with absolutely airtight screw tops: it seems that corks, which because they're made from natural bark are ever so slightly porous, may permit a very slow "micro-oxidation" essential to fine wines' evolution in bottle. You can wager that the controversy over corks will continue for years to come.

Oxidation. Oxygen is the enemy of white wine, and oxidation is the reason that most white wines (there are important exceptions) don't age well and should be drunk within a few years of bottling. It's relatively easy to tell whether a white wine has oxidized past the point of drinkability. Oxidation causes white wine gradually to darken, first to amber and ultimately to brown—the chemical process is the same as the one that makes the flesh of a pear or apple turn brown once the fruit's been sliced. An oxidized white wine also loses its fruity aroma, becoming nearly odorless or perhaps slightly acrid—and it tastes unexciting and stale. (In comparatively rare cases where a certain bacteria is present in the bottle, oxidation can lead to the production of acetic acid, and the wine becomes vinegar.)

In most cases, an oxidized white wine is simply a wine that's over the hill: it should've been drunk earlier in its life. If served an oxidized wine in a restaurant, send it back and order something else, since another bottle of the same wine, of the same vintage, may be suffering a similar decrepitude. (It should be mentioned that red wines can also be injured by oxidation; though it will be more difficult to discern the problem visually, the flat, dead smell and taste are telltale signs.)

Refermentation. Champagne and other sparkling wines are supposed to bubble. *Frizzante* wines are supposed to be effervescent. And there are a few white table wines to which a tiny amount of carbon dioxide is deliberately added to liven them up. But, in general, still wines should be *still*. An ostensibly still wine that bubbles or fizzes when opened is a wine with a problem: it has **refermented** in the bottle, and that's a sign of sloppy, inconsistent winemaking. (All the yeast should have died but didn't, or some sort of bacteria has somehow made its way into the bottle.)

There's sometimes a signal that a (supposedly) still wine has inadvertently refermented: the gas produced by the fermentation process will sometimes push the cork partway out of the bottle. Be very suspicious if, when you go to open a bottle of wine, you notice that the cork protrudes beyond the bottle's lip—it might be a sign of refermentation, or perhaps an indication that the wine has suffered heat damage by being shipped in an unrefrigerated container. (In any case, *something* is wrong.) And be careful, too. The corks sealing bottles of Champagne and other sparkling wines are secured to the bottles' necks with a wire cage for a very good reason—to prevent them from shooting out. It's at least possible that the ordinary cork stoppering a wine that has wrongfully refermented in the bottle could fly out once the foil or plastic capsule has been removed.

Non-sparkling wines that unintentionally referment in the bottle taste *awful*. Think of the worst California "champagne" you ever drank (remember your trashy second cousin's wedding reception?), then imagine that sour, sudsy awfulness multiplied several-fold.

Tartrate crystals. Another wine fault that you're somewhat likely to encounter—especially in German or other white wines from cool climates—is one that doesn't affect the wine's smell or taste and poses absolutely no risk to your health. But if you see it without knowing what it is, it can be extremely disturbing.

It's called **tartrate precipitation**, and the little, whitish crystals that result—adhering to the cork or settling to the bottom of the bottle and, when the wine is poured, ending up in your wineglass—can look like fragments of glass. If you notice them after you've drunk some of the wine, you may be tempted to call 911. Calm down. The crystals won't hurt you (though you may want to strain what's left of the wine before drinking it).

Serendipitously, I first encountered this fault a few days after first reading about it. I was in a restaurant, drinking the last of a bottle of an otherwise excellent, dry Austrian Riesling, when I noticed a brownish-white, crystalline sediment at the bottom of my glass. "Aha!" I said to my *very* impressed companion. "Here we have an example of tartrate precipitation—perfectly harmless." I spooned a few of the crystals onto my fingers; they felt like very fragile fishscales, instantly disintegrating when I gently rubbed them together.

Again, you don't really need to know about the chemistry that causes these little crystals to form, but (just in case you're interested) they result when potassium present in the wine (or, more rarely, calcium from a container used to store the wine prior to bottling) combines with the wine's natural tartaric acid. (Since wines from cooler regions, like Germany and

THIS WINE STINKS—LITERALLY
(CORK TAINT AND OTHER WINE FAULTS)

Austria, generally have higher concentrations of tartaric acid, the problem is likelier to afflict these wines than others.) Usually, winemakers succeed in filtering or fining out these chemical salts before bottling, but the techniques for doing so aren't failsafe, and sometimes enough tartrates remain that crystals continue to form in the bottle.

One final note on tartrate crystallization: it can occur in red wines, too, but it's generally not noticeable because so many red wines—especially some older reds—are expected to "throw" at least a bit of sediment. When present in red wine sediment, tartrates aren't distinguishable from the rest of the muck, since they take on the color of the sediment's pigmented components.

Cloudiness. I've never personally encountered a wine that was **cloudy** or **hazy**. That's not so surprising, since contemporary winemakers, responding to consumers' expectation that wine should be crystal clear, go to great lengths to avoid this fault—filtering and fining their wines to rid them of anything that might cause cloudiness and scrupulously enforcing hygiene to prevent bacteria from making their way into bottled wine.

Cloudiness isn't necessarily a danger signal, but because it *might* be caused by bacteria, it's probably best not to drink a wine that looks cloudy or hazy. Do note, though, that some premier red wines are deliberately left unfiltered because their makers are convinced that filtration would rob them of flavor. **Unfiltered wines**—whose labels often trumpet the fact that they're unfiltered—may throw sediment, which, if shaken up, might give the wine a cloudy appearance, which in this case is not usually considered a fault.

CHAPTER FOUR

American Roots

AN EXTREMELY TRUNCATED WINE HISTORY

I F A CERTAIN LITTLE BUG HAD HAD ITS WAY, WE MIGHT NOT EVEN BE drinking wine today. If a certain bunch of killjoys had *not* had their way, the shelves in wine shops throughout the U.S. might nowadays be stocked with selections from Missouri as well as from California. And if a certain Parisian wine merchant hadn't pulled off a very neat trick, everybody might still think that no other wines in the world can possibly compete with those of Burgundy and Bordeaux.

I know you don't want me to give you a long lesson on the history of wine. (Not that that would be possible in a little book like this.) But I thought you might like to hear about three episodes in the recent history of wine (the past 150 years or so) that have unquestionably affected how we make, drink, and view wines today. The first two stories aren't pretty: one is about the worst epidemic ever to afflict the world's grapevines, and the other's about Prohibition and the depredations it caused the U.S. wine industry. I think you'll find the third a bit more light-hearted—though that may depend on your country of origin.

The Terminator

During the summer of 1863, a few winegrowers in the southern Rhône Valley, in southeastern France, noticed that something was wrong with their vines. The new growth was stunted, the leaves emerged sallow and unhealthy-looking, and the vines' productivity was weakened. Within a just a few years, the vines were dead—by which time this new disease, which no one had ever seen before, had spread elsewhere in the Rhône and begun to show up in other, geographically distant, winegrowing areas of France, as well.

The epidemic's cause wasn't discovered until 1868, when a French scientist identified the culprit as a tiny aphid to which he gave the Latin name ***Phylloxera vastatrix***, which translates, roughly, as "dry-leaf devastator." "Terminator" would be more like it, since this little yellow bug—

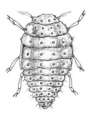

THE VARMINT

barely visible to the eye—almost caused the collapse of the wine industry worldwide. It would be nearly two decades before an effective way of controlling the epidemic was worked out and began to be widely implemented. By then, total wine production in France had been plummeted by more than *two-thirds*, and *Phylloxera* had traveled far and wide, infesting vineyards in Portugal, Turkey, Austria, California, Switzerland, Italy, Australia, and Spain.

Phylloxera, whose name is hard to say (fih-LOCKS-uh-ruh) but worth remembering, was an inadvertent American import—what today we'd call an *invasive species.* Hailing from eastern North America, *Phylloxera* had been infecting native American grapevines since the beginning of time, but American vine species had developed resistance to the parasite. The European wine grape varieties—all members of the *Vitis vinifera* species—had no such tolerance, and *Phylloxera*'s appearance in a vineyard was that vineyard's death warrant.

The precise route of *Phylloxera*'s migration is unknown, but it was probably the beneficiary, if that's the right word, of a European fad for American plants. Throughout the nineteenth century, thousands of American plant species—including vines—were shipped to Europe, mostly to serve as ornamentals in European gardens. *Phylloxera,* which usually infects grapevines' roots, hitched an easy trans-Atlantic ride. Once established, there was no stopping it, since the little critters can extend their domain by being blown around by the wind, by being transported from place to place on shoes or clothing or farm machinery carrying infected soil, or simply by taking a leisurely stroll over to the vineyard next door. (Aphids have legs; they can walk.) Early efforts to kill the pest—which included flooding vineyards and the application of pesticides—met with limited success. But, just as American vine species had been the inadvertent source of the epidemic, it was American vines that would provide the antidote.

You may remember from chapter 1 that grapevines are propagated *vegetatively*—new vines are made from cuttings from existing plants. Well, one way to do this is to **graft** a little branch (the technical term is *scion*) from one vine onto the root of another: the tissues of the scion and root grow together, and a new, complete plant is formed. By the early 1880s, a group of French scientists had become convinced that the only way to save Europe's *vinifera* varieties was to graft cuttings from them onto the roots of *Phylloxera*-resistant American species. At first, this idea was widely ridiculed by French wine producers, who feared that the character of their wines would be ruined by this marriage of *vinifera* and non-*vinifera* vines. Their concern wasn't just some early version of French anti-Americanism: it's a fact that most native American grapes make poor wines, whose aroma is often described as **foxy**—as smelling of animal fur—and the French winemakers reasonably thought that this undesirable characteristic might be transferred.

The fear turned out to be unjustified: grafted vines produced wines that were free of the foxy scent. In what was a model of Franco-American cooperation, the French scientists who proposed the "Americanist" solution teamed up with a scientist from Missouri. Together, they identified which American **rootstocks** possessed the greatest *Phylloxera* resistance, determined which were best suited to this or that soil or climate, and enlisted the aid of American nurseries to provide millions of rootstock cuttings for shipment to Europe. All over France, and then throughout Europe and the winegrowing world beyond, growers ripped the old vines from their vineyards and replaced them with new, grafted vines. Today, except in a few (geographically isolated) places that have managed to escape *Phylloxera* infestation, virtually all wine-grape vines, all over the world, have American roots.

Phylloxera is still very much with us. The rootstock solution didn't eradicate the pest; it simply helped ensure that vines would remain alive and productive even where *Phylloxera* is present. But there are still occasional outbreaks, with serious consequences. The worst in memory occurred in Napa and Sonoma counties in the late 1980s and early 1990s. How could that happen? Hadn't California's vineyards long since been replanted with grafted vines? Well, yes they had—but it turned out, to Napa and Sonoma growers' dismay, that the particular American rootstock widely used in that region wasn't as resistant to *Phylloxera* as everyone had believed. So the growers did the only thing they could do:

ripped out the dying vines and, at great expense, replaced them with new vines grafted onto different rootstocks.

THE PARTY POOPERS

Why in the world would the Frenchmen who were seeking a method for controlling *Phylloxera* have turned to a scientist from, of all places, *Missouri*? With apologies to friends in the Show Me State, it just doesn't seem—does it?—that there would've been anybody in late nineteenth-century Missouri who could've known very much about *wine*.

Well, that prejudicial view is just about as wrong, historically, as it could be. It may shock you to learn—it certainly surprised me—that for much of the nineteenth century, Missouri was the leading winemaking state in the United States. Though its share of the total market had dwindled by century's end, in 1869 Missouri accounted for 42 percent of this country's wine production. (That same year, California contributed 27 percent.) And despite California's gradual rise to prominence, Missouri winemaking remained strong until just after World War I, when it suddenly died.

Or, rather, was murdered. Terminators, you see, come in several varieties: some have six legs; some have just two. And what killed Missouri's wine industry was an affliction whose origins were all too human: an ailment known as **Prohibition**.

Imposed by the 18th Amendment to the Constitution and repealed by the 21st Amendment, national prohibition had long been pushed by a variety of well-meaning do-gooders concerned about alcoholism's destructive effects on American society, workplace productivity, family life, and spiritual health. Whatever one thinks of their intentions, Prohibition just didn't work very well. It was widely flouted, led to a massive wave of illegal liquor-trafficking controlled by organized crime, and did significant harm to the overall U.S. economy—an injury that was felt especially sharply after the stock market crash of 1929 and the onset of the Great Depression. It's probably no overstatement to say that Prohibition represents the single greatest failure ever by the U.S. government to achieve social goals through legislation. And it inflicted near-fatal damage on the American wine trade. Though national prohibition was in effect for only thirteen years, from 1920 through 1933, the wine industry in the United States did not really begin to fully recover until the 1960s and 1970s.

Some winegrowing regions weathered Prohibition better than others. The regulations through which Prohibition was implemented—which were spelled out in the Volstead Act, passed by Congress after the 18th Amendment had been ratified—did not amount to an outright, total ban on the manufacture or sale of alcoholic beverages. Home winemakers, for example, were allowed to produce a certain quantity of wine for personal consumption, and commercial wineries were permitted to continue making wine for religious use. These loopholes, which of course were widely exploited, enabled some winegrowers to earn a living by marketing fresh grapes for home winemaking and by creating a limited amount of wine for sale to churches. (How much of this homemade and communion wine ended up on the black market is an interesting question.) Under these constraints, California did relatively "well," meaning that a few vintners managed to survive and to recommence large-scale

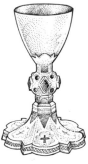

EXEMPTED

commercial winemaking operations after repeal. In Missouri and many other states, however, the industry simply succumbed.

Seven-plus decades after Prohibition's repeal, Missouri once again produces commercial wines. Beginning in the 1960s, a few Missourians got back into the winemaking business, some restoring and reactivating wineries abandoned forty years earlier. The industry has expanded greatly since then, and some Missouri wines—including reds made from the Norton grape (one of the few native American varieties suitable for creating fine table wines)—have earned critical praise and won national competitions. But it's nigh unto impossible to find a Missouri wine in a store or on a restaurant wine list outside the central Midwest. That's partly a direct result of Prohibition; however weakened, California had a leg up on other regions after Prohibition's repeal. But it's also partly an indirect result of America's experiment with national sobriety. Prohibition's repeal was accompanied by the enactment of numerous state statutes imposing a variety of regulations that hampered the interstate distribution of wine; many of those laws were in still in force more than seventy years later, though the situation may change dramatically following a 2005 Supreme Court decision declaring some restrictive wine-sale laws unconstitutional.

Like *Phylloxera*, the party-poopers are still with us. Though it's highly doubtful that we'll ever again see a sizable movement to ban alcohol nationally, there's many a county across the South and elsewhere that remains "dry" to this day, and many a municipality whose "blue laws" restrict where, when, and how alcohol can be sold, bought, and consumed. The prohibitionist impulse just seems deeply ingrained in the American character—or in the character of some Americans.

JUDGMENT OF PARIS

And speaking of American character: Is the character of American wines—no matter how good—inferior to that of the best French wines? Although there are (and will always be) partisans who respond to this question with a resounding "Oui!" the question sounds faintly ridiculous to the rest of us, who, without disparaging French wines in the least, enjoy a very wide variety of wines from all over the world without worrying overmuch about which are the "best" according to some universally applicable scale.

It wasn't always this way. Before the 1970s, few serious wine drinkers would have dared voice the heresy that French wines—especially the vaunted wines of Bordeaux and Burgundy—were not necessarily the best in the world. Sure, there were people who preferred other wines, but there was something close to consensus that red and white Bordeaux and Burgundies were wine's royal family. As the sentiment was put by British connoisseur George Saintsbury, whose 1920 memoir *Notes on a Cellar-Book* was an international bestseller, "If Claret [red Bordeaux] is the queen of . . . wines, Burgundy is the king." Other critics might've reversed the monarchial positions, but just about everybody paid homage to the court of France.

In 1976, the wine world's Bastille was stormed. There'd been stirrings of dissent before then, and the revolution continues to this day. But the defining event in the fall of the old order was a publicity stunt orchestrated by a Parisian wine merchant named Steven Spurrier. Whether Spurrier's stunt, which came to be known as the **Paris Tasting**, really *proved* anything would be argued about for years, but it certainly had the effect of changing people's perceptions. And in the wine world—where taste is everything—to alter perception is to change reality.

Spurrier's idea was an elegantly simple one: to celebrate the American Bicentennial—the two-hundredth anniversary of the American Revolution—he would organize a comparative tasting of French and California wines. Spurrier had recently toured California, and the wines he'd had there had convinced him that the best California Cabernet Sauvignon and Chardonnay varietals could hold their own against even the most celebrated of red Bordeaux and white Burgundies. He decided that the panel for his tasting should be composed of some of the French wine world's most influential figures, and so he invited the inspector-general of the government agency that administers the Appellation d'Origine Contrôlée system, editors of well-known French wine and food magazines, proprietors of world-famous Burgundy and Bordeaux estates, and other oeno-luminaries to participate. Though British, Spurrier was a well-connected figure in France; his wine shop was widely acknowledged as one of the best in Paris, and his invitations were eagerly accepted.

To grasp the magnitude of what Spurrier did, you've got to understand that an event like this had never really occurred before. Oh, there'd been lots of comparative public tastings of French and California wines, but never one held in France and in which only French judges participated. Not only that, but Spurrier decided that the tasting would be conducted blind: the bottles would be bagged and numbered, and the judges wouldn't know which wines they were sampling until after they'd rendered their verdicts.

Spurrier neglected to inform the panel of this detail beforehand, but not one of them balked when they arrived for the tasting, which was held on the patio at Paris's Hôtel Intercontinental on May 24, 1976. The presence of lots of press people didn't spook the judges either, so convinced were they, apparently, that the French wines—which included wines from some of Bordeaux' and Burgundy's most prestigious makers—would triumph. The panel members would have done themselves a favor by being more circumspect during the tasting, but, instead, several of them made no bones about loudly and adamantly declaring their preferences, lauding the wines that were "obviously" French and deriding those whose inferior nose and flavor were dead giveaways that they were from California.

How do you say "Pride goeth before the fall" *en français*? During the tasting, the judges had been asked to rate each of the wines sampled on a twenty-point scale. At the end, the bottles were unwrapped and the judges' scores tallied. And guess what? California wines took first place in both categories. A 1973 Cabernet Sauvignon made by Stag's Leap Wine Cellars, in Napa, won the reds. Among the whites, the highest point-total belonged to a 1973 Chardonnay from another Napa maker, Chateau Montelena. Not only that, but of the eleven wines with the highest scores, six were Californian.

And did an uproar ensue? But of course. The French wine industry cried foul and, if anything, made matters worse by claiming, for example, that the "delicate" French wines had performed poorly because they'd been jiggled about on their way to the hotel. Frankly, it wasn't as if the French wines had been *humiliated*: French entries had come in second, third, and fourth in the red wines category, and second and fourth among the whites. But apparently some found any challenge to France's supremacy intolerable.

The tasting and the fray that followed were covered by newspapers internationally. Wine writers opined on the competition's meaning for months—even years—after. *Time* magazine ran an article on the event headlined "Judgment of Paris"—though the ultimate fallout was a tad less earthshaking than the Trojan War.

Or was it? Chateau Montelena's website, even today, describes the Paris Tasting as the moment when California wines "came of age." But that's too narrow a view. The Californians' coup wasn't just a victory for American wines. The tasting and the media attention it engendered had the effect of leveling the playing field for *everyone, everywhere.* If American upstarts could beat the French at their own game, why then so could Australians, or South Africans, or Chileans—at least potentially. M. Spurrier had cut off the heads of the king and queen, and a new regime was ushered in: one of *liberté, égalité,* and . . . well, perhaps not *fraternité.*

CHAPTER FIVE

Cabs and Other "Vehicles"

(RED WINE VARIETIES)

W HEN IT COMES TO WINE, FEW PEOPLE ARE COLOR BLIND. SOME prefer reds, others whites. Some wine drinkers are such strong partisans of red or white that they refuse to drink wines of the other color—and, in my experience, this exclusivist tendency is more often found among red-wine lovers. I count at least two close friends who flatly declare, "I drink *only* red wine," and who look at you like you're nuts if you ask, "So what do you drink with fish?" (The answer: red wine, of course.)

My own taste pushes me more toward the white-wine camp, but I can certainly understand the "red heads." Red wines are, in general, so much more powerfully and complexly flavored—and, as compared to whites, make so assertive an impression on the nose and palate—that it's not hard to fathom someone's deciding that white wines are just too weak, too simple, too uninteresting to bother with. I think such conclusions are wrong, but at this level taste is not exactly arguable.

Individual preferences aside, it's clear that there are periodic shifts in allegiance by the American wine-drinking public as a whole. The 1970s were a white-wine era; reds gained ground during the 1980s and held sway throughout the '90s—their popularity bolstered by claims that drinking red wine is beneficial to your health (see the sidebar on pages 134–135). Now there are signs that the pendulum of fashion may have begun to swing back toward whites. Important? Well, to some extent, yes, since large-scale changes in taste can dictate which kinds of vines growers plant (and which they rip out) and can therefore have an effect on the kinds of wines most likely to appear on your local wine shop's shelves. And, as we'll see, shifts in fashion don't just have to do with red versus white. The wine public's taste for this or that variety also increases or wanes over time, and it can be dangerous for a particular kind of wine to become too popular, since this can lead to overproduction and, sometimes, to a general decline in quality, especially of the moderately priced wines that are most wine drinkers' staple fare.

But let's bracket such issues. This chapter's purpose is to acquaint you with the best-known varieties of red-wine grapes—the ones used to make the wines you're most likely to encounter in a typical wine shop, liquor store, or supermarket wine section. That list follows shortly, but first let's briefly review what you learned about red wine from the first several chapters of this book:

You learned that red wines' color comes from the *skins* of the dark-colored grapes from which it is made. You learned that the hues of these "red" grapes actually range, depending on the variety, from blue to an ebony-like black, and that color is *extracted* during *fermentation* and sometimes during pre-fermentation *cold soaking* or post-fermentation *maceration*. You learned that, besides color, *tannins* also leach into the

To Your Health?

Is drinking red wine good for you? Does it—as some claim—really lower your risk of coronary heart disease? And if so, how?

Since the early 1990s, a lot of ink's been shed by those arguing for and against the health benefits of red wine. The proponents have often pointed to the so-called **French paradox**—the fact that the French eat lots of fatty foods but have comparatively low rates of heart disease—as evidence that regularly drinking red wine (as the French do) is a healthy habit. Opponents find the connection unconvincing.

There are indications that moderate alcohol intake—one or two drinks per day—can help prevent cardiovascular disease. The problem is, this benefit doesn't appear to be specific to red wine: a daily shot or two of single malt scotch seems to work just as well. That is, *if* you believe the studies. The trouble with scientific research on the health effects of alcohol is that it's very difficult to organize rigorously controlled studies that could conclusively determine whether moderate drinking is, in fact, healthful. (Surveys aren't trustworthy because people *lie* about the amount they drink.) The one thing that researchers in the field do seem to agree on is that more is *not* better: any additional cardiovascular benefit you might derive from having more than two drinks a day is outweighed by an increased risk for ailments ranging from cancer to liver disease. Damn.

Some members of the "red wine is good for you" school argue, however, that it's not—or not just—the alcohol that's beneficial. They maintain that red wine's better for you than other alcoholic beverages because of the antioxidant properties of the **phenolics** it contains. (*Phenolics* is a catchall term for the pigments, tannins, and flavor compounds present in grape skins. The phenolic **resveratrol** is sometimes credited as the key antioxidant.) Because the skins of dark-colored grapes are especially rich in these substances, and because red wines are fermented on the skins, red wines contain much greater quantities of phenolics than do whites.

The thesis is that red wine's phenolics enhance your body's ability to produce "good" cholesterol (high-density lipoprotein, or HDL, cholesterol), thereby lowering the risk of heart attack or stroke. It's an attractive argument, but there's just one little problem: nobody's yet been able to scientifically demonstrate a correlation between red wine consumption and increased HDL. And even if such a correlation were established, it wouldn't necessarily constitute a rationale for drinking red wine as opposed to eating fresh dark-skinned grapes or drinking unfermented grape juice—the purple kind, that is—since these contain the same antioxidant compounds.

So it's a muddle. Unfortunately, it *is* clear that drinking even small amounts of red wine can be harmful to some individuals who suffer from what's known as **red wine headache syndrome**, or RWHS. Certain people just can't tolerate red wine: within fifteen minutes of drinking even half a glass, they get a pounding headache. (And, no, they don't have hangovers, which require a much greater intake of alcohol and whose onset doesn't usually occur until six or so hours after a drinking bout.) The syndrome is real, but the culprit—the substance in red wine that triggers RWHS—is unknown. Some researchers have blamed tannins; others the histamines present in red wine; and yet others have pointed to compounds called prostaglandins, which are associated with the inflammation that can cause headaches. (Partisans of this last theory say that you can prevent RWHS by taking ibuprofen fifteen or twenty minutes before you begin drinking.)

What's even more curious about RWHS is that some sufferers get a headache when they drink some kinds of red wine but not when they drink others. (A Bordeaux might set off the syndrome, but not a California Cabernet—or vice versa.) For such people, the advice might be to experiment with various reds, and then to stick to those that don't cause a headache. But that strategy makes drinking red wine a sort of school of hard knocks, doesn't it?

wine from the grape skins and seeds during fermentation and maceration, and that tannins help make red wines more long-lived than whites. You learned that red wines—far more often than whites—are *aged*, or matured, in oak barrels, and that red wines are generally *laid down* for a year or longer before being *released* by a winery. You learned that red wines, even when young, differ in color—they can be plummy purple, or ruby, or garnet—depending on grape variety, geographical origin, and even on the specific winemaking techniques used. And, finally, you learned that red wines grow lighter in color as they age.

Red wines, by the way, aren't all dry, still table wines. There are off-dry and sweet red wines, *frizzante* reds (the most familiar being Italian Lambruscos, which are also sweet), and reds whose alcohol content disqualifies them from the table wine category. Some of these, like Port (see pages 317–323), are deliberately fortified; others, like some super-potent California reds, have alcohol levels that naturally exceed 14 percent.

The listing of red-wine varieties that follows is divided into two chunks. First we meet the "Big Four" red-wine grapes: Cabernet Sauvignon, Merlot, Pinot Noir, and Syrah/Shiraz. Those descriptions are followed by briefer remarks on a number of other well-known red-wine grapes, listed alphabetically. The same kind of scheme is followed in the next chapter, on white-wine varieties. These little dictionaries are anything but comprehensive: across the world, literally thousands of different varieties of grapes are used to make wine; the vast majority are local varieties that remain largely unknown outside their home regions. Some varieties, though, have achieved worldwide fame despite being grown in only one or perhaps a few restricted locales. A few of these—Gamay and Nebbiolo, for example—are discussed below; others are mentioned elsewhere in the book.

THE BIG FOUR

Cabernet Sauvignon [cab-ur-NAY soh-vin-YAW^n]

Hail the Cab! It's probably no overstatement to say that of all the grape varieties used to make fine table wines, Cabernet Sauvignon is the single most important in the world. It's certainly one of the most widely planted. From its homeland in Bordeaux, Cabernet Sauvignon has traveled around the globe and is now grown not just in France, Australia, California, Chile, Italy, and other familiar winemaking countries and regions, but also in a variety of unexpected places, including (to name two) Lebanon and Russia.

The grape's cachet is such that the decision to grow and make wine from Cabernet Sauvignon is a signal that wine producers in a given region have "grown up"—that they consider themselves ready to compete with the big kids. As you learned in chapter 4, Cabernet varietals — along with white varietals made from the Chardonnay grape—played the leading role in establishing California's international fine wine–making reputation, and to this day Cabernet remains what many people think of first when they think of fine California red wines.

Given its near-omnipresence on the global wine scene, it's surprising to learn that Cabernet Sauvignon is, relatively speaking, a youngster among grape varieties. It probably originated in the seventeenth century as a spontaneous cross between a dark grape called Cabernet Franc (see page 147) and the white grape Sauvignon Blanc. (DNA tests have confirmed the parentage.) It appears not to have become important in the vineyards of Bordeaux until the late eighteenth century—another surprise, given how essential Cabernet Sauvignon is to so many of the red Bordeaux wines we know today. With Merlot (see below) and Cabernet Franc, it forms the triumvirate of grapes that are blended to create most (not all) red Bordeaux, and it's the major constituent in some of the most famous Bordeaux wines, including Château Latour and Château Mouton-Rothschild. (Two other grapes, Malbec and a variety called Petit Verdot, are sometimes used in red Bordeaux but usually play very minor roles.)

Cabernet Sauvignon is credited with providing the "backbone," or structure, of red Bordeaux and of blends, like the Meritage wines modeled on the traditional Bordeaux mix. (Highly aromatic Cabernet Franc enhances the nose; Merlot makes its major contribution to the palate.) And spine is something Cabernet has in spades. When given the long growing season it requires, this late-ripening, thick-skinned, blue-black grape produces wines that are deeply colored and intensely fruity and that can be highly tannic, "big" wines that may need to mellow for years in the bottle before reaching their peak.

Cabernet's tardy ripening is the variety's drawback, however. Not only can a cold fall or early frost ruin a Cabernet-dependent vintage, but if the grapes are harvested before they're sufficiently ripe, the resulting wine can have an unpleasantly **vegetal**, or **herbaceous**, character. It therefore performs most consistently in warmer climates with reliably temperate autumns: Australia, California, Chile, and Italy from Tuscany southward. In cooler Bordeaux, whose weather is less predictable, growing Cabernet is something of a crapshoot—one reason that knowing about the vintage is so important when buying Bordeaux wines. (Cabernet Sauvignon–dominated red Bordeaux remain the gold standard against which all other Cabs are judged, however.)

At their best, Cabernet Sauvignon–based wines are noted for their pronounced blackcurrant aroma and flavor (think of crème de cassis), often complemented by a cedar-like fragrance and taste. Tobacco is another descriptor commonly applied to Cabernet Sauvignon. (You'll even hear of its nose being compared to the smell of cigar boxes!) Some California Cabernet varietals are marked by a definite minty scent and flavor. But these are secondary attributes; Cabernet's **varietal character** (i.e., what makes it recognizable and sets it apart from other varieties) is dominated by black fruit and tannins. The power of good Cabernets demands that they be paired with powerfully flavored foods, such as roasted or grilled red meats.

Unfortunately, experts report that the quality of moderately priced California Cabernets—those in *Drinkology WINE*'s preferred price range of $30 a bottle and under—has generally diminished in recent years. That's probably the result of overproduction combined with many makers' desire to make their Cabernets less tannic and thus more accessible and acceptable to a generation of red-wine drinkers weaned on much softer, **"rounder"** Merlot varietals. That's a shame, because a Cabernet without its tannic architecture is like a tent without tent poles—flat. If you're looking for a Cabernet in the $10 to $30 range, you might do better choosing an Australian varietal (try to get one from the Coonawarra region of South Australia) or one from Chile. Of the moderately priced non-American Cabs sampled while researching *Drinkology WINE*, my favorite was a wine from Chile's Maipo Valley: the 2002 Antiguas Reservas Cabernet made by Cousiño-Macul, which retailed at less than $15.

> ## Cabernet without its tannic architecture is like a tent without tent poles

Merlot [mair-LOW]

Should one feel sorry for Merlot? Merlot varietals—especially from California—enjoyed skyrocketing popularity from the early 1990s on, as

Americans discovered that Merlot provided "pain free" red wine–drinking pleasure. The tannins in Merlot are silkier, less aggressive than those in Cabernet Sauvignon, which makes quaffing a typical young Merlot varietal a less punishing experience than drinking a similarly immature Cabernet. But Merlot's user-friendly nature may prove its undoing; many "serious" wine drinkers disparage the stuff *on account of* how easy it goes down, and this derisive (snooty?) attitude has begun to catch on. Poor Merlot: its fortunes may founder for the paradoxical reason that just about everybody thinks it's O.K.

Like Cabernet Sauvignon, Merlot hails from southwestern France; of "black" grape varieties (it's actually a very, very dark blue), Merlot is the most widely planted in Bordeaux. As mentioned above, it's one of the three grapes essential to most red Bordeaux; though it often plays second fiddle to Cabernet, it's the major ingredient in some of Bordeaux's most famous wines, including those from the appellations of St.-Émilion and Pomerol. (Château Petrus, a Pomerol wine that's one of the most highly regarded—and stratospherically priced—wines in the world, is 95 percent Merlot.) And Merlot is also like Cabernet in that it has traveled far and wide. Italy, Washington State, South Africa, Hungary, Bulgaria, and Moldova are among the many places it's landed and flourished. (You know where Moldova is, right?) Growers like Merlot because it doesn't demand as long a growing season as Cabernet and because it's much more tolerant, climate-wise, than the finicky Pinot Noir (see below).

Grown under the right conditions and properly vinified, Merlot is capable of ageing in the bottle—but ageworthiness isn't something that most drinkers of Merlot care much about. They want a wine that's *smooth* and immediately drinkable, and Merlot delivers. At their best,

Merlot varietals have a deep, rich, plummy and/or cherry-like flavor, with good acid and mild astringency. The sad truth, though, is that Merlot varietals are often *not* at their best. The craze for California Merlots has led, wouldn't you know, to overproduction, and too many of that state's makers are aiming their Merlots at the lowest-common-denominator consumer who *wants* a wine that's no trouble and doesn't really taste like much at all.

Deploring this trend, wine critics have turned their attention to Merlot varietals made elsewhere. Those from Washington State, in particular, have lately earned a good deal of praise. The best of the Merlots sampled while researching *Drinkology WINE,* however, came from points closer to (my) home: from Long Island—the Pellegrini Merlot mentioned in chapter 2—and, weirdly, from a small western New Jersey maker called Hopewell Valley Vineyards. (Both were under $20 a bottle.) My friends remain unconvinced that a New Jersey wine could deserve notice; I'm convinced they're just phobic.

Food-wise, Merlot varietals are versatile: they suit the full range of red meats just fine, and Merlot's plum and cherry flavors make it a good accompaniment to roast duck. Merlot's smoothness—and the unlikelihood that its taste will overpower that of other ingredients—make it a good choice for punches and mixed drinks that call for red wine.

Pinot Noir [PEE-noh NWAH^r]

If you've seen the 2004 film comedy *Sideways*—the only buddy movie/road movie ever to focus on wine—you already know two important things about Pinot Noir: that the grape is among the most difficult to grow and that the wines made from it can inspire a devotion bordering on fanaticism.

Some devotees of Pinot Noir like to say that it isn't so much a grape as it is a **vehicle** for conveying *terroir*: that is, that it doesn't impose its own character on a wine made from it so much as it reveals or expresses the vineyard where it was grown. But for me—someone who'd rather have a glass of Pinot Noir than any other red wine—the flavor of Pinot Noir is highly distinctive. "Raspberries" is a commonly applied descriptor, and, yes, Pinot Noir's flavor *is* reminiscent of raspberries. And Pinot Noir–based wines may also smell and taste of violets, or of earth. But I find, too, that Pinot Noir has a definite quality that goes beyond any set of easily nameable aromas and flavors. Pinot Noir tastes . . . well, it tastes *like Pinot Noir.* A good Pinot Noir has a sweetness that isn't sweet, a lightness that isn't light. To myself, I describe it as having a "bite" that hits me near the back of the tongue—but the trouble with that description, beyond its imprecision, is that it sounds pejorative. I don't mean it so. The bite I'm talking about is a love-bite.

The original home of this wonderful, obstreperous, thin-skinned black grape is Burgundy, in eastern France, where it's been grown since the Middle Ages (if not earlier). With the exception of the wines of Beaujolais—the southernmost part of Burgundy, which is sometimes treated as a separate region—virtually all red Burgundies are made entirely from Pinot Noir. We'll take a brief look at Burgundy later in the book, but I have to deliver a piece of sad and consternating news right here and now: for wine newbies with limited budgets, red Burgundies are mostly a bad bet. The most famous of Burgundy's Pinot Noir–based wines are unreachably expensive, at least for most people most of the time. Cheaper red Burgundies—ones costing $25 a bottle or under—are very likely to disappoint. And even if you've got the funds to occasionally swing for a pricey Burgundy, you've really got to know what you're buying. The Burgundy region's weather is so unpredictable, year to year, and Pinot Noir is so sensitive to meteorological offense, that even the most celebrated of Burgundy's vineyards are prone to unexciting vintages. So unless you do a lot of homework and/or have a knowledgeable adviser, you risk wasting your money if you plunk down $75 or $150 for a bottle of red Burgundy.

The good news for Pinot Noir–loving no-accounts like me and you is that there are alternatives. Pinot Noir may be persnickety—requiring a cool climate and flourishing only under a limited set of geological conditions—but there are places outside Burgundy where Pinot Noir is successfully grown, including the Willamette Valley of Oregon and a few cooler locales in California: the Russian River Valley of Sonoma County; the Carneros area, which straddles Sonoma and Napa counties; the Anderson Valley of Mendocino County; and a few spots along California's central coast. New Zealand has recently joined this smallish clique, with producers on that country's South Island creating Pinot Noir varietals that

Order a Pinot Noir; no one will be dissatisfied

balance fruit and acidity in the best Burgundian tradition. Pinot Noir varietals from Oregon, California, and New Zealand may not achieve the epiphanic heights of the best red Burgundies, but they can be extremely pleasurable wines—*and* they're less expensive and somewhat more consistent from vintage to vintage.

When it comes to being paired with food, Pinot Noir is remarkably welcoming. If, at a restaurant, you find yourself charged with choosing the wine for a group of friends all of whom are having very different dishes—sweetbreads, a pasta, a fish stew, a pork chop—order an Oregon or California Pinot Noir. It's very likely that no one will be dissatisfied. Among the many good west coast Pinot Noir varietals sampled while researching this book, I especially liked ones made by the BearBoat Winery of California's Russian River Valley (under $20) and by Oregon's Archery Summit (under $30). But even outside Burgundy, vintages do matter with this crankiest of grapes, so best consult with a trusted wine shop salesperson or, in a restaurant, with the waiter or sommelier before selecting a bottle.

Pinot Noir, by the way, is also an extremely important grape in Champagne. Most Champagnes incorporate at least some Pinot Noir in their blends. Pinot Noir's contribution to a Champagne's taste isn't necessarily discernible by a novice, except in the case of rosé Champagnes, which supply a nibble of that same lovely "bite" I noted above. To experience it, you might try the rosé Champagne made by the house of Gatinois (about $45, and well worth the cost).

Syrah/Shiraz [sih-RAH/shih-ROZ]

One word: *pepper*. Or maybe two words: *black pepper*.

Wines made from the Syrah grape very often taste like pepper—specifically, black pepper. They may taste like a lot of other things besides—blackberries, raspberries, chocolate—but pepper is very often a constituent of their flavor. With some Syrahs, the black pepper taste hovers in the background, becoming most noticeable on the finish, but a few Syrah-based wines

Why the two names? Who the heck knows?

have an overwhelmingly peppery taste: as if you've put your head back, opened your mouth, positioned the pepper grinder over it, and rotated the crank. (Whether you like this or not depends, I guess, on whether you're the sort of person who always answers, "Oh, yes, please!" when the waiter asks, "Would you like some fresh ground pepper on that?")

Syrah is one of those grapes that's inherently confusing to the neophyte because it goes by two different names: in Australia, South Africa, and (sometimes) elsewhere, it's called *Shiraz*. (In American English, that rhymes with "Oz," but Australians give the second syllable a longer, flatter vowel, as in "jazz.") Why the two names? Who knows? Shiraz is the name of a city in Iran, so some wine wags will tell you that the grape has a Persian origin. Untrue. In all probability, Syrah (a.k.a. Shiraz) is as French as French can be. It's been cultivated in the Rhône Valley of southeastern France since Roman times. Then, sometime in the early nineteenth century, Syrah vines made their way to South Africa, where the grape, for unknown reasons, was rechristened. From South Africa it was taken to Australia, where the new name stuck—and where Shiraz ultimately became that country's most famous red varietal. (To add to the wine novice's perplexity, there's another, different grape with a similar name: *Petite Sirah*—sometimes spelled *Petite Syrah*. Just remember that Shiraz = Syrah ≠ Petite Sirah, and you'll have a leg up on most people.)

Syrahs are *robust* reds. Even in France, whose finest wines are generally prized for their elegance and polish, the most highly regarded Syrah-based wines—those of the northern Rhône Valley—pack an earthy wallop. (Prices for the most famous appellation producing pure Syrah-based wines, Hermitage, are anything but down to earth, however.) The Syrah grape is relatively high in tannins, which means that many Syrahs/Shirazes age well. Its high tannin content is also the reason that Syrah is often blended with other varieties in order to give the resulting wines better structure. That's why Syrah typically appears, in greater or lesser proportion, in blended red wines of the southern Rhône, such as red Châteauneuf-du-Pape. The highly tannic fortitude of the most renowned *pure* Syrah French wines, however, carries a downside for the immediate-gratification inclined: in most cases, these powerful wines should not be drunk young.

Not to worry, however. There are oceans of good, affordable Syrah/Shiraz varietals for you to try right now: wines that don't require bottle ageing and that fit comfortably within the novice's abbreviated budget, as well. Given their generally low price (you can find scads of Australian Shirazes for $15 or less a bottle) you needn't be afraid to experiment with various labels until you find one (or two, or three) that suit your taste. American Syrah varietals range greatly in price, but it is possible to find better-than-acceptable ones at less than $20 a bottle. (Francis Ford Coppola's "Diamond Series, Green Label" Syrah, like all the moderately priced wines from this director-turned-vintner, is a damned good buy; it retails for about $15.) But of all the Shiraz varietals sampled for this book, I preferred a South African wine from a maker called Rust en Vrede. That bottle, however, was a gift from a South African friend; Rust en Vrede wines are, unfortunately, hard to find in the U.S. If you do happen across one, buy it—no, buy two, and send one to me.

Don't neglect, either, the many blended wines in which Syrah/Shiraz plays a part. You're likely to find Australian Shiraz/Cabernet/Merlot blends at price points low enough to justify kangarooing from maker to maker until you find one you like.

There's a consensus among wine writers regarding the kind of food that pairs best with Syrahs/Shirazes: *meat*. That's *red* meat—especially steak. Count me in, though I'm also of the mind that some pasta dishes—those with hearty red sauces, especially if there's ground meat or sausage involved—make grand matches with Syrah-based wines. To my taste, Syrahs are among the least satisfactory reds to drink as aperitifs. No, they're definitely made for combat—beautiful, glorious, *inspiring* combat—with succulent, dark, rich, greasy, even gamey meats. Syrah's poetry is bloody, carnivorous. Venison, anyone?

A Few Other Reds You Ought to Know

Cabernet Franc [cab-ur-NAY FRAH^n; cab-ur-NAY FRAHNK]
The third member of the Bordeaux "triumvirate," Cabernet Franc is less well known than Cabernet Sauvignon or Merlot. Usually a supporting actor, it does a star turn in a very few red Bordeaux, including, most notably, the famous wine called Château Cheval Blanc. Earlier to ripen than its offspring Cabernet Sauvignon, Cabernet Franc is more widely planted in Bordeaux than its relatively minor role might lead you to expect; that's because many growers hedge their bets with it: if a cold or rainy fall diminishes the Cabernet Sauvignon harvest, they may make up the difference with Franc.

Cab Franc is also important outside Bordeaux. A major variety of the middle Loire Valley, it's the primary component in the red wines of the Chinon appellation—whose cherry and raspberry flavors can be deliciously candylike (without being sweet). Makers in California and Long Island have been experimenting with Cabernet Franc varietals; though these have recently become fashionable, the ones I've sampled have left me unwowed. Franc is known for its powerful aroma—that's why it's prized in Bordeaux blends—but these American wines often seem *all nose*, with disappointingly evanescent flavor and a guillotined finish.

Gamay [gaa-MAY]
Gamay is *the* grape of Beaujolais—the only region of Burgundy whose red wines are not made from Pinot Noir. American wine drinkers have

become familiar with the grape through the relentlessly promoted Beaujolais Nouveau wines that appear in shops near the end of November each year. Though these infant wines, made from grapes harvested a mere two months earlier, are hardly the best that Beaujolais produces, they do convey Gamay wines' essential character: a bluish-red color, low alcohol and high acidity, and a smell and taste that are fresh and exuberantly fruit-juicy. If you've never had one, do try a Beaujolais Nouveau this coming holiday season; in a good year, it can be an extremely refreshing, lively wine whose lightness makes it a good accompaniment to the Thanksgiving turkey or Christmas capon. But then do yourself another favor and expand your acquaintance with Gamay to include some of the more "adult" Beaujolais—a Beaujolais-Villages for starters, and then perhaps one or more wines from the smaller, more prestigious appellations within Beaujolais. (For more on these wines, whose labels, annoyingly, sometimes do not tell you that they're from Beaujolais, see pages 276–277.) Gamay's an underrated and unfashionable grape, which means that no Beaujolais, no matter how high its caliber, will shoot holes in your credit card.

Grenache [gruh-NOSH]

Here's a puzzle: How can it be that you may never have heard of this grape, which is one of the most widely planted red-wine varieties in the world? For the simple reason that it's primarily a blending grape and is seldom used to create varietal wines. It's such a vital component of the red wines of France's southern Rhône Valley and of many Spanish reds, however, that it's worth the wine newbie's attention.

In the Rhône, Grenache plays a major part in the reds of Châteauneuf-du-Pape, but it's also a prime ingredient in wines from the nearby appellations of Gigondas and Vacqueyras, easier to find than they are to pronounce (zhee-GAW^n-dah, vah-keh-RAHSS). Like Châteauneuf, they're dependable choices if you're looking for a reasonably powerful red; Vacqueyras, generally less expensive than Gigondas, is also easier to drink young.

The grape's homeland is Spain, where it's called Garnacha. It's often part of the blend of the red wines of Spain's Rioja region (which are dominated by the variety called Tempranillo; see below). In the Catalonian district of Priorat (a.k.a. Priorato), it's often the foundation of a new generation of blended reds that have captivated critics—but whose comparative rarity makes most of them too pricey for *Drinkology WINE*'s pocketbook.

Relatively low in tannin and relatively weak in color, Grenache is often used in rosés. (If you can find a bottle, you might try a rosé from the Lirac appellation, also in the southern Rhône.) Grenache loves hot climates, which led to its long exploitation by California and Australian jug-wine makers. The poor reputation it thereby gained has been countered, in recent years, by a number of American (and Aussie) producers intent on making fine reds in the classic southern Rhône style. One of these so-called **Rhône Rangers**, California's quirky Bonny Doon Vineyards, actually produces an all-Grenache wine under the brand name Clos de Gilroy. (It retails for under fifteen bucks and cryptically sports a portrait of Marcel Proust on the label.)

Malbec [MAHL-beck]

Malbec is an international variety that didn't just travel—it up and left home, resettling elsewhere. Native to France, it once dominated the vineyards of Bordeaux, from which it has all but disappeared. (Its importance elsewhere in France has likewise declined.) In the late nineteenth century, however, it was brought by immigrants to Argentina, where it staked its claim in the area surrounding the city of Mendoza in the foothills of the Andes Mountains. The change of scenery suited the grape, which is now virtually synonymous with fine Argentine red wine.

Take it from me: Argentine Malbecs and Malbec blends (it's often partnered with Syrah) are *fantastic* wines—and, with so many going for $20 a bottle or less, are fantastic *values,* as well. If you don't go below eight bucks (imagine!), you'll have trouble finding an Argentine Malbec that isn't at least acceptable. Venture into the $15 to $20 range, though, and you'll be astonished at how aromatic, deep, rich, and velvety wines made from this errant grape can be. Alamos, Cateña, and Trumpeter are three reliable producers, though Argentine Malbecs are such cheap (and accommodating) dates that, hey, why not play the field?

Nebbiolo [neh-BYOL-loh]
Nebbiolo-based wines, like those made from Pinot Noir, inspire an almost cultish devotion. Like Pinot Noir, Nebbiolo is lauded for its ability to express *terroir*—the *terroir* in this case being that of the world-famous vineyards surrounding the hilltowns of Barolo and Barbaresco in the Piedmont (It., Piemonte) region of northwestern Italy. Though Nebbiolo is grown elsewhere in Italy (where it is known by a variety of regional names), you'd be hard-pressed to find other Nebbiolo-based wines in your local wine shop. No, in America, Nebbiolo *means* Barolo and Barbaresco—highly tannic, acidic, deeply colored, ageworthy wines with a decidedly floral scent. (Others detect roses and violets; I've usually smelled—been almost overwhelmed by—the fragrance of hyacinths in these wines.) They're also frighteningly expensive. You're unlikely to

happen across a Barolo or Barbaresco costing less than $40 or $50, but if you do, don't think, "Wow! What a bargain!" Think, "This is so cheap that it can't be any good." The high price of these wines results from a simple supply/demand equation: the output of the Barolo and Barbaresco vineyards is tiny, while the desire for them—fueled, in part, by how fashionable they are—is enormous.

Petite Sirah [peh-TEET sih-RAH]

This is the grape that is *not* Syrah, despite the names' similarity. DNA analysis has shown that the grapes are indeed related, but don't make the mistake of believing that a Petite Sirah varietal will provide the same kind of taste experience as a Syrah or Shiraz. And don't imagine, either, that the "petite" in Petite Syrah's name connotes a fine-boned delicacy. Petite Sirahs are darkly colored and sometimes profoundly tannic—many shouldn't be drunk before they've spent significant time in the bottle.

First planted in California in the 1880s, Petite Sirah was long used mostly as a blending wine, adding color and oomph to Cabernet or Pinot Noir varietals that would otherwise have been unacceptably pale or weak. (Remember: U.S. law permits up to 25 percent of a varietal to be composed of wine from grapes other than the one after which it's named.) Despite its utility, however, Petite Syrah was in serious decline in California until rescued by growers impressed by its ability to create wines that achieve a muscular balance between tannins, acidity, and fruit. (Petite Sirah is also noted for its powerful blackberry and blueberry flavors.) In 2002, these growers banded together in an association wittily dubbed P.S. I Love You, whose membership continues to grow.

A number of California makers—Bogle, Foppiano, Parducci—turn out moderately priced ($11–$14/bottle) Petite Sirah varietals that, though potently flavored, aren't so tannic that they can't be drunk on release. In my opinion, though, neo-oenophytes will be wise to think of Petite Sirah as a collector's wine. If you do find yourself in possession of a bottle of young-ish Petite Sirah and simply cannot wait a decade or so to open it (I know the feeling), make sure to accompany your impatient indulgence with a hefty, strongly flavored meal. This ain't no sippin' wine.

Sangiovese [sahn-joh-VAY-zeh]
Its very name—which translates as "blood of Jove [i.e., Jupiter]"— bespeaks Sangiovese's ancient lineage. Now the most widely planted red-wine grape in Italy, Sangiovese has been around since . . . , well, no one really knows when. (But it may even have been cultivated by the pre-Roman Etruscans of central Italy.) Though it's grown up and down Italy's boot—and, in fact, in California and elsewhere—Sangiovese is most closely associated with the wines of Tuscany, including Brunello de Montalcino, Chianti, Chianti Classico, and Vino Nobile di Montepulciano. (Brunello is 100 percent Sangiovese; Chianti, Chianti Classico, and Vino Nobile di Montepulciano are usually blends, though a few wines of each type are made entirely of this one grape.)

Sangiovese has an odd set of characteristics for such a famous and beloved grape. Though Sangiovese is fairly tannic, most wines based on it have limited life spans (generally not longer than ten years, though there are exceptions). Sangiovese-based wines—especially those made from grapes grown at higher altitudes—are also high in acidity. And, compared with other reds, they're rather weakly colored and not terrifically fruity. High tannins, high acid, weak color, low fruit intensity:

given what you've learned about red wines, this doesn't exactly sound like a menu for success, does it? Obviously, there's something missing from this list, and that something is *finesse*. When made well—as many are, nowadays—Sangiovese-based wines more than make up for what they lack with a serious, understated elegance: the vinous equivalent of a little black dress and a string of pearls. (Ordinary Chiantis, though they're generally much better than they were several decades back, can still be a little pedestrian, but to see what I mean, try one of the numerous Chianti Classico Riservas on the market. The latter wines, made in the Chianti Classico zone of the larger Chianti district, are typically made from top-quality grapes and are given additional wood ageing.)

Tempranillo [tem-prah-NEE-yoh]
Tempranillo has *structure* in spades, and that's what makes it one of Spain's most important and widely grown red-wine varieties. Its assertive tannins and indelible color make it the armature upon which many of Spain's blended red wines—including Rioja and the reds of the Ribera del Duero and Penedès regions—are built. (In Ribera del Duero, it's known by the name of its local strain, Tinto Fino; in the Penedès, as Ull de Llebre.) Tempranillo's worth including on your list of must-know varieties because it's nearly a constant in Spain's blended reds, giving them their sometimes mouth-puckering astringency and deep red hue—and conferring longevity on blends that, without it, would not survive so long in the bottle.

Nowadays, you can also find Spanish Tempranillo varietals virtually everywhere—their near-ubiquity tracking the growing popularity of Spanish wines generally. The quality of these varietals is terrifically uneven. It's not necessarily that they're too tannic—it's been obvious from the Tempranillos I've sampled that the winemakers had gone to great lengths to create softer, less-tannic wines that ordinary drinkers might readily accept. It's that many aren't any great shakes—either empty of flavor or possessing a fruitiness that, frankly, seemed forced. I'll keep tasting, hoping to be proved wrong—not too forbidding a task, since so many Tempranillo varietals are *so* reasonably priced ($8 to $15 a bottle).

Zinfandel [ZIN-fin-dell]

For a long, long time, many wine experts thought that Zinfandel was America's lone native *vinifera* variety. Its presence in California dates back so far—all the way to the years following the Gold Rush of 1849— that people believed it had always been there. DNA analysis, however, has lately robbed Zin of that distinction. It turns out that it's the same grape as an Italian variety called Primitivo, and was doubtless carried to California by a sentimental, enterprising immigrant who (a) couldn't imagine life in the New World without a vineyard to remind him of home and (b) figured he could rake in a nugget or two by selling a little *vino* to thirsty prospectors. But no matter: though it originated elsewhere, Zinfandel now *belongs* to California, and the wines that are made from it there resemble no others in the world.

Frankly, I'm not a lover of Zinfandel, though I can grok why others are. It can be so doggoned powerful—not just alcohol-wise but also in its fruit intensity and rugged earthiness—that I regret being too sissified to appreciate it. It certainly packs a wallop: Zinfandel varietals average 15 percent alcohol, and some fly as high as 18 percent—a potency otherwise unheard-of among non-fortified wines.

California red Zinfandel varietals are made in two different styles: the lighter-bodied of these is sometimes called the "claret" style. "Lighter-bodied" is a relative term, however: even these lighter Zinfandels are anything but light when set alongside truly lighter-bodied wines. Still, they virtually levitate when compared with Zinfandels made in the so-called "port" style, which are deeply extracted wines whose residual sugar and off-the-charts

"Old vine" Zinfandels have a definite cachet

alcohol make them resemble Port. Unfortunately, the label of a Zinfandel variety won't tell you which style the maker follows—but if the alcohol level is inching toward 18 percent, it's more than likely the wine will be in the port style.

Zinfandel vines can be extremely hardy and long-lived. There are some in California that are well over a hundred years old. These vines survived abandonment during Prohibition and remain productive well into their second century. (I'd like to know where I could get myself a gene splice from one of these codgers.) **Old vine** Zinfandels have a definite cachet; they're touted as especially vigorously flavored wines; since I, wuss that I am, don't especially go for Zinfandel at its most rough-hewn, I'm not too enthralled. A milder, claret-style Zinfandel that I do find drinkable is that produced by the Amador Foothill winery of California's Shenandoah Valley; it's widely available, retailing for less than $15.

The Zinfandel grape is also the basis for a popular off-dry blush wine called White Zinfandel. It—and the uncountable thousands who enjoy it—are disdained by "serious" wine drinkers. Though I don't like it, either (I find it cloying and empty), I am not about to put you down for keeping a bottle in your fridge. Everyone should have a shameful secret.

Impress Your Friends—
Without Breaking the Bank

In the late 1960s and 1970s, a few well-established but maverick-minded winemakers in the Italian region of Tuscany began creating red wines that didn't fit into any familiar category. In fact, these newfangled wines defied the regulations of the Italian appellation system—the Denominazione di Origine Controllata (DOC) system—which, like its French counterpart, strictly specifies which grape varieties can be used in wines named for specific geographic locales. The mavericks' innovation was to grow the classic Bordeaux varieties—Cabernet Sauvignon and/or Merlot—in their Tuscan vineyards and then either to blend these with the local Sangiovese or to create wines made entirely from the homegrown French grapes. The Italian wine bureaucracy had a conniption, refusing to grant these "foreign" wines DOC status and consigning them to the *vino da tavola* ("table wine") category usually reserved for the most ordinary wines.

The thing was, these Franco-Italian hybrid wines were anything *but* ordinary. Word quickly spread that these powerfully extracted, deeply complex wines were among the best reds being produced in Italy. Dubbed **Super Tuscans**, they soon took their place among the world's most desired and costliest wines. The first and most famous of the Super Tuscans—Ornellaia, Sassicaia, and Tignanello—remain firmly ensconced in the wine pantheon, as sought-after and as expensive as the most renowned Bordeaux and Burgundies. Except, perhaps, for the most special occasions, they're out of your and my reach. (I may spring for a case of each when I'm appointed King of the World.)

But recall: this section is titled "Impress Your Friends—*Without Breaking the Bank*," so I'm about to let you in on a little secret. Other

Italian winemakers, in Tuscany and elsewhere, were quick to note Sassicaia's and Tignanello's success, and—guess what?—they imitated them. Turns out that French grapes can perform extremely well in Italian climes from Veneto (in the north) to Sicily (in the south), and so there are now scads of other Super Tuscan and Super Tuscan–like Italian reds on the market. Some are pricey, but lots aren't, and even some of the least expensive are marvelous wines. Three sampled during the research for this book that I heartily recommend are Villa Puccini Red, a Tuscan Sangiovese-and-Merlot combo (about $11!); the Brentino Cabernet Sauvignon–Merlot blend made by the Veneto maker Maculan (about $17); and a Cab-Merlot blend, called Camelot, made by the Sicilian producer Firriato (sampled in Sicily, where it retailed for under $30). The wine-shop proprietor who introduced me to the non-Tuscan Cab-Merlot blends calls them "faux Super Tuscans," but there's nothing faux about these delicious wines.

(A footnote: The Super Tuscans' success had the eventual effect of altering DOC regulations: Sassicaia was ultimately granted its own DOC status, and rules regarding which grapes could be used in the Chianti district were relaxed, allowing the French varieties to play a role in those blends.)

CHAPTER SIX

Chardonnay and Its Discontents

WHITE WINE VARIETIES

SOME YEARS AGO—I'M NOT SAYING HOW MANY—I HAD OCCASION to accompany a friend to several gatherings of a wine club on Manhattan's Upper West Side. I was a very dutiful friend: these events were not enjoyable in the least. Presiding over the meetings was a truly demonic individual, and all the members of the club were in his thrall. He was one of those hyper-bright, supremely glib, but fundamentally deranged people who manage through sheer force of will to collect a circle of yes-men. His judgment was Law.

Now, I'm not a joiner—and I was so repelled by the wine club's rituals of obedience that I began refusing my friend's invitations to attend— but I've got to say that this Wine Lucifer's fiats had an effect even on me. His personality had nothing of the live-and-let-live about it, and he took his preference for red wine to a fascistic extreme I've never witnessed in any other red-wine aficionado. White wine drinkers, according to this guy, weren't just misguided, or ill-informed, or gustatory cowards. They were *stupid*. They were barely human. They were beneath contempt.

And so, despite the fact that I despised this fellow and stopped attending his masques of the red death, his opinions worked their black-grape magic on me. I began to distrust my liking for white wine. I told myself that I—like any self-respecting adult—preferred reds. I began to look down on white-wine drinkers. (I didn't go so far as to tell them what I thought of them—just silently comforted myself with my conviction of superiority.) It took years of therapy to undo the damage. (O.K., I admit I had some other problems, as well.) But now I can say it. I'd holler it from the rooftops if I weren't so terrified of heights:

I was deluded. When it comes down to it, I'm awfully partial to white wines.

So there. Pour yourself a glass of Chardonnay, or Pinot Grigio, or Riesling, or Sauvignon Blanc, and join me in the coming-out party. Or, hell, I don't care: have a glass of your favorite red—or even rosé. No matter what your political leanings, wine drinking should inspire a multi-culti kind of attitude. The more diverse, the merrier. (Or so I say. As you read on, you'll see that I haven't completely freed myself of biases. Oh, well.)

Before going on to the listings of white-wine varieties, let's again take a moment to review some information from previous chapters.

First, white wines aren't really white (i.e., colorless). Some are indeed very pale, having only the slightest green or straw-colored tinge, but others are golden, or bright yellow, or even amber in hue. More intense color sometimes indicates that the grapes used in the wine were grown in a relatively warm climate; whites from cooler regions tend toward the paler end of the spectrum. White wines also tend to darken as they age—a browning effect resulting from the wine's gradual oxidation in bottle. Though a few white wines are supposed to be brownish—as with Sherry, which is intentionally oxidized (see pages 309–315)—oxygen is the foe of most white wines, and a dark color often indicates that a white wine is well past its prime.

You learned that the grape juice used to make whites is separated from the grape skins before fermentation, and that—because virtually all the pigment in a grape berry resides in its skin—this means that even dark-colored grapes (most notably, Pinot Noir) can be used to make white wines. And you learned that, in general, better white wines are made only from the free-run juice that flows from the grapes during crushing. You'll also recall that, because of the separation of skins from juice, white wines are vastly lower in tannins and phenolics than reds.

Remember, too, that comparatively few types of white wine are fermented or matured in oak. (Besides Chardonnay, which is often oaked, this chapter will introduce you to a few other varieties that are sometimes—or even usually—barrel-matured.) Generally, white wines are not as capable of evolving in the bottle as are reds—and are therefore best drunk within a few years of bottling—though there are important exceptions: oaked Chardonnays can be long-lived; superior Rieslings are capable of great bottle age; and some sweet white wines are among the most ageworthy wines of all.

You learned, as well, that many whites are prized for their bracing acidity, and that therefore winemakers sometimes suppress the secondary, malolactic fermentation that can cause a wine to lose its crisp edge. Grapes' acidity, by the way, generally declines as they ripen and their sugar content rises; since grapes ripen more fully in warmer climates with longer growing seasons, the whites most renowned for their acidity tend to come from the northernmost, coolest winegrowing regions.

In the warmest winegrowing regions, white grapes' acidity can simply fizzle: the unbalanced wines that result aren't just flabby—they're extremely short-lived, since acid has an important preservative function.

Whites, like reds, come in every conceivable style: still, fizzy, and bubbly; dry, off-dry, and sweet; table wines and fortified wines. Since many of the world's most highly regarded sweet wines are white, a side-bar providing sweet-wine basics is included in this chapter (see page 170). And, lest we overlook them, I'm including a brief introduction to those in-between wines—rosés—in this chapter, as well (page 198).

As you sample white wines, keep in mind that generally—there are exceptions to every wine rule—they are best drunk chilled, but also that removing a bottle of white wine from the refrigerator twenty minutes or so before serving and allowing it to warm just a bit will enhance its nose and flavor.

THE BIG FOUR

Chardonnay [shar-duh-NAY]

"I'll have a glass of Chardonnay." Or is it, "I'll have a glass of *anything but* Chardonnay"? Two camps. At war.

For a long, long time, the first was in the ascendant. In fact, it seemed to be the *only* camp. But more recently the tide may have begun to turn, as the **ABC** ("anything but Chardonnay") crowd has shed its closet and begun to trumpet its opposition noisily—vindictively, even.

All this uproar about a *grape*? How come?

Because for years, heavily oaked California Chardonnay varietals—under a legion of labels—dominated the American white wine market. For most casual American wine drinkers, and indeed for many who style themselves connoisseurs, these wines came to define Chardonnay. What's more, this style of Chardonnay varietal spread far and wide around the globe—and not just to New World regions like Chile and Australia. Why, even some Italian winemakers, in defiance of local traditions and in some cases of DOC stipulations, began ripping other vines out of their vineyards, replacing them with Chardonnay, and fermenting and/or seasoning the wine in new oak barrels. At some point, this juggernaut just had to inspire a counter-reaction.

Just *why* oaky Chardonnays got to be so overwhelmingly popular is a little hard to figure. For one thing, they don't strike me as particularly *easy* wines to like. In and of itself, the Chardonnay grape isn't particularly distinctive (it doesn't have the immediately identifiable flavor of, say, a Riesling or of many Sauvignon Blancs). But it does take very well to oak.

Oaked Chards' success is hard to understand

Aficionados of heavily oaked Chardonnays praise these wines' notes of vanilla, their toastiness, their butteriness, and so on. But what they're lauding, finally, are the *oak's* flavors—flavors that originated in a forest, not a vineyard.

Even more baffling is the astounding success that heavily oaked Chardonnays continue to enjoy as aperitif wines. Many of these varietals are big-shouldered wines that demand to be drunk with a meal—a *substantial* meal. (Think of a nice, huge, fatty, grilled veal chop.) But drink an oaked California "Chard" by itself? Whyever would you, when there are so many other, lighter and much more refreshing, white wines to choose from?

I was discussing this puzzler with a restaurateur friend—the owner of a place whose small but well-selected wine list includes half a dozen Chardonnay varietals among the dozen or so whites offered. "We have lots of Chardonnay because it's what people ask for," he said. "And, frankly, I think they ask for Chardonnay because it's easy for Americans to *pronounce*."(As he and I sat at his restaurant's bar mulling the question over, a good-looking blonde sat down beside us and said to the bartender, "Oh, I don't know. I guess I'll just have a glass of Chardonnay.")

Huh? I'm telling you that a worldwide wine revolution occurred because many Americans—as unschooled in foreign languages as they are in grape varieties—find it too difficult to say "Sauvignon Blanc" or "Gewürztraminer"? Hmm. When you think about it, it's a neat answer to the riddle, especially when you consider that *shar-duh-NAY* isn't just easy to say, but also sounds French, which until the Franco-American political squabbles of the past few years, was pretty much universally considered an attractive quality.

The name *sounds* French, of course, because the name *is* French. And if we take a look at some of the wines produced from the Chardonnay grape in its original homeland, we can see that the pro- versus anti-Chardonnay "war" isn't a battle about a grape but rather a skirmish over a particular style of wine. It's more than possible—in fact, it's all but guaranteed—that even if you dislike oaked California-style Chardonnays, you'll love one or more of the French wines made, in whole or in part, from the Chardonnay grape. As I note above, Chardonnay is not by itself a very distinctively flavored grape, but it compensates for that lack by excelling, as the Winespeakers say, at expressing *terroir*. And because the grape is so good at communicating gustatory information about the soils and climates of the places it's grown, French Chardonnay-based wines taste very different from one another depending on where they come from.

The grape's homeland is Burgundy, where it's the second most widely planted variety (after Pinot Noir). If you make a killing at the poker table and can afford to buy one of the grand Chardonnay-based wines from the heartland of Burgundy, the Côte d'Or, you'll immediately recognize the style that California makers of oaked Chardonnay have sought—sometimes with great success, sometimes not—to emulate. The classic Côte d'Or whites (Corton, Meursault, Le Montrachet, Chassagne-Montrachet, and Puligny-Montrachet are among the most famous appellations) are also aged in oak, and, in fact, wood-induced flavors can dominate these wines when they are young. But there's a difference: even when the oak influence is profound, Côte d'Or whites seldom have the lumberlike quality of ordinary, oak-clobbered California Chards. And when, after a few years in bottle, the oak flavors diminish, these wines exhibit a nuanced complexity that only a few other white wines on the planet can rival.

That, and the fact that they're produced in comparatively tiny amounts, are what make the Côte d'Or whites so dear. There are alternatives. The Chardonnay-based wines of the Mâconnais district of Burgundy, though also often matured in wood, are generally fruitier and more approachable (to the palate and the pocketbook) than those from the Côte d'Or. The most famous Mâconnais wine is Pouilly-Fuissé; though its stateside popularity has waned somewhat since its heyday in the 1980s, the price of a bottle of Pouilly-Fuissé remains steeper than it ought to be. Instead, try something from the Mâconnais appellation of St.-Véran; though St.-Véran surrounds the smaller Pouilly-Fuissé appellation, its wines are more reasonably priced, and they offer something close to the pleasure of the Côte d'Or whites at a fraction of the cost.

Venture afield from Burgundy proper, and you'll deepen your appreciation of Chardonnay's diversity. For example, Chardonnay is also the grape used in the beautifully austere, almost ascetic, white wines of the Chablis appellation, northeast of Burgundy. And it's the major white variety of Champagne, where it's harvested early, while the grapes are highly acidic and before their fruit flavors fully develop—perfect for the racy quality that Champagne lovers adore in these most famous of sparkling wines. Taste a *blanc de blancs* ("white from whites") Champagne—made entirely from Chardonnay—in tandem with an oaked California Chard, and you'll be astonished that the same grape could be used to create such vastly different wines.

O.K., I've hammered so long and hard on oaky California Chardonnays that your head would have to be made of wood for you not to get that these aren't my favorite whites. But let me give the devil his due by mentioning that among California Chards, those that come from the Edna Valley—near the city of San Luis Obispo on California's central coast—consistently offer good value for the price. You should be able to find an Edna Valley Chardonnay—

Edna Valley Chards provide good value

there are numerous makers—in the $20 to $30 range. And I'll even go so far as to confess that there is an Italian Chardonnay, made in something akin to the oaked California style, that I greatly admire. Made by a Tuscan winery, Ruffino, it's called Libaio Chardonnay. I've had it with dishes ranging from penne putanesca, to lamb chops, to a spinach, pear, and pine nut salad, and it's acquitted itself gamely each time. And here's the kicker: it retails for less than ten bucks a bottle.

Finally, I'll let you in on a not-so-secret secret. The reaction against oaked Chardonnays has begun to influence the way that even some California makers handle the grape. For more details on a brand-new generation of *unwooded* California Chards, see pages 229–230.

Pinot Gris/Pinot Grigio [PEE-noh GREE/PEE-noh GREE-joh]
From the mid-1990s on, oaked California Chardonnay started to suffer some stiff competition—at least when drunk as an aperitif—from another white wine: Italian Pinot Grigio. Across America, "I guess I'll have a glass of Pinot Grigio" began to be heard nearly as often as the formerly hegemonic "I guess I'll have a glass of Chardonnay." Which goes to show how inexplicable changes in wine fashion can be, since Italian Pinot Grigios—at least the ones they're likely to pour at an ordinary restaurant bar—are about as different from California-style Chardonnays as a bikini is from a suit of armor.

At their best, the mass-produced Italian Pinot Grigios with which American drinkers are most familiar are clean, crisp, bone-dry whites that don't show much at all in the way of fragrance or flavor, except perhaps a citrusy, mineral brightness. That they're nearly free of distinguishing characteristics may not matter much when what you want is to have your thirst quenched quickly, and at a very manageable price. They're white wine's answer to run-of-the-mill Merlots: immediately likable wines you don't have to work to acquire a taste for—which, of course, is why they're disparaged by the snobs.

So let's acknowledge the reason for these inconsequential wines' popularity while admitting that the snobs, per usual, do have a point. Or, rather, several points. First: mass-market P.G.'s vary greatly in quality; too often, they're slightly sour nullities whose only advantage over lemon water is that they get you high. Second (and more important): even at their most refreshing, these wines reveal few of the wonders that the grape they're made from is capable of working.

That grape is called Pinot Gris ("gray Pinot") in its country of origin, France. (*Grigio* means "gray" in Italian, hence the different names.) The variety—whose berries actually exhibit a wide range of colors, from silver-blue to dirty pink—came into being in the vineyards of Burgundy, probably in the Middle Ages and probably as a natural mutation of Burgundy's great black grape, Pinot Noir. Though in the past Pinot Gris played a minor role in some red Burgundies—smoothing the edges of the sometimes angular Pinot Noir—it has now all but disappeared from its birthplace. To achieve its potential, it had to move out from under the parental thumb, and so it traveled about Europe, eventually landing in the sliver of winemaking territory at France's northeastern corner: Alsace.

Alsatian Pinot Gris varietals (remember, Alsace is the one region of France allowed to give its wines varietal names under the AC system) certainly number among the most remarkable white wines on earth. And one of the things that's so remarkable about them is that they're so diverse. Usually dry, they can also be off-dry or sweet; they can be keen and light or have an unctuous viscosity; they can be pale, nearly colorless, or descend to a coppery hue that tilts toward amber. (Deeper color in a Pinot Gris isn't necessarily an indication of age; the grapes' comparatively dark skins can tinge the juice when the grapes are crushed.)

Their diversity can make Alsatian Pinot Gris–based wines rather frustrating to the wine newbie, and even to the experienced connoisseur, because there's not necessarily any telling what kind of wine you're buying when you pluck a bottle from the shelf. That said, a sweet Alsatian Pinot Gris might (emphasis on the *might*) carry one of the following two legends on its label: *vendange tardive* (VT) or *sélection des grains nobles* (SGN). The former means **late harvest**—made from ultra-ripe, sugar-laden grapes. (Note that not all VT wines are sweet; some are super-concentrated dry wines.) *SGN* indicates an even later harvest, when some of the berries *(grains)* are infected with "noble rot," a fungus that further concentrates the sugar in the grapes. (For more on noble rot, see page 172.)

Because of their unpredictability of style, exploring Alsatian Pinot Gris varietals can be fun, though your spirit of adventure may be dampened by the cost of these wines, many of which tend go for $40 and up per bottle. There are, however, exceptions. Look for those produced by a maker called F. E. Trimbach, which produces reliably good, dry Pinot Gris varietals retailing at under $30.

Before reaching Alsace, Pinot Gris had made its peripatetic way around German-speaking Europe, including the regions of northern Italy that were long controlled by the Austro-Hungarian Empire. The grape remains popular in Germany today, where it is used to create both dry wines (called Grauburgunders) and sweet wines (called Ruländers)—though both types are difficult to impossible to find in the United States.

Luckily, we do have a very wide range of Italian Pinot Grigios available to us, including many from the northeastern Italian regions of Trentino–Alto Adige and Friuli–Venezia Giulia. Many makers in these two regions—part of the German cultural sphere until comparatively recent times—produce Pinot Grigios that are much more robust and fuller-flavored than the ubiquitous mass-market Italian P.G.'s described earlier. No, they're not as complex or as divergent in style as their Alsatian cousins, but they can be simply scrumptious. Three that I've especially liked are those from the Alto Adige makers Tiefenbrunner (under $20) and Kris (under $12) and—best of all—from a Friulian maker called Livio Felluga (under $20). These wines skillfully couple a nutty flavor with a lively acidity—making them excellent partners for a midday meal, especially if the menu includes bacon, sausage, ham, or other smoked or cured meats.

And American Pinot Gris admirers have another option, as well. Over the past three decades, California and Oregon growers have had great success with the variety (usually calling it by its French rather than its Italian name). Pinot Gris varietals from Oregon's Willamette Valley are especially notable.

One caution: The labels of many Italian Pinot Grigios of both the mass-produced and the more finely crafted types carry the words *Pinot Grigio delle Venezie*. This phrase indicating place of origin tells you almost nothing, because the Venezie ("the Venices") comprises three adjoining regions historically associated with the city of Venice: the aforementioned Trentino–Alto Adige and Friuli–Venezia Giulia, as well as the Veneto, a larger region, sandwiched between the others, that is home to Venice itself. You may not be able to tell by reading a label whether a Pinot Grigio comes from Alto Adige or Friuli (and therefore stands a chance of being a better-quality wine) or from the Veneto —the source of much of the insipid, mass-produced P.G. on the market.

Riesling [REES-ling]
If you've never drunk a German, Austrian, or Alsatian Riesling, I pity you and I envy you. Pity, because you've so far missed out on one of the most extraordinary experiences wine can offer. Envy, because one day you *will* drink one of these Rieslings; it'll be—I promise —as revelatory as falling in love for the first time; and the fact that you've still got that sublime moment in your future is . . . well, it's just plain enviable.

Not that one grows inured to Riesling's charms. The worship it inspires in Riesling enthusiasts matches the passion that Pinot Noir fanatics feel for their grape. Or even exceeds it: "Riesling is the single greatest grape variety in the world," is a conviction one hears voiced again and again.

Quick: The world's single most celebrated wine—is it red or white? Dry or sweet? What's your guess?

If you guessed red and dry, it's time to examine your prejudices. The wine in question is Château d'Yquem [SHAH-toh dee-KEHM]. Widely considered the greatest wine on the planet, it's made on an age-old estate in the Sauternes appellation of Bordeaux. Yquem (ee-KEHM, for short) is created from a combination of Sémillon and Sauvignon Blanc grapes; barrel ageing helps give the wine its trademark brilliant yellow color. That golden hue is appropriate, given how expensive the stuff is. (Don't think stratosphere; think orbit of Pluto.) And, boy, is it sweet: a "dessert" wine, it's guaranteed to overpower virtually any dessert you can think of. It's also one of the world's longest-lived wines; it can survive—and continue to evolve—so long in bottle that the *Oxford Companion to Wine* describes it as "almost immortal."

So how come you guessed wrong? Assuming that you're an ordinary American wine drinker (nothing wrong with that), there are probably several factors at work. The first is fashion: not only are reds held in more esteem than whites among the wine-drinking public at large, but sweet wines aren't nearly as popular as wines that are dry. The fashion for dry wines has been developing over a very long time. Four and more centuries ago, most wines were sweet. That wasn't necessarily due to any preference for sweet wines on our ancestors' part; it was largely a matter of practicality. In those days, before glass wine bottles (and corks for stoppering them) came into widespread use, it was difficult to transport dry wines without their oxidizing and spoiling. Since sugar's a natural preservative, sweet wines had a better chance of surviving the long haul from winery to market than did dry wines. Bottling changed all that, and dry wines began their long, slow climb to dominion.

American wine drinkers' all-too-common disparagement of sweet wines is probably also rooted in our personal histories. Most of us didn't grow up drinking wine. We grew up drinking Kool-Aid, Pepsi, Dr Pepper. (O.K., *your* parents made you drink cranberry juice, but my argument still holds.) If you're like me, your first acquaintance with wine was via some cough-syrup-sweet horror that, oh yeah, resembled soda pop or fruit juice. As adulthood advanced and your taste became more discriminating, you put away childish things— and decided that sweet wines just don't meet your standards of decency.

Well, you need to grow up a little more—and to forget about the sickening-sweet concoctions you guzzled during your dissipated youth. The world's great sweet wines are immensely sophisticated and provide complex, revelatory pleasures of a different order than those delivered by dry wines. Here are just a few of the basics. (If you want to learn more, there's an entertaining and comprehensive recent book on the subject: James Peterson's *Sweet Wines*, published in 2002.)

I assume it's no great revelation that sweet wines are sweet because they contain sugar. But the methods by which the world's great sweet wines are created are surprisingly various. Yes, some wines are sweet because the grapes they're made from are, all by themselves, so naturally ripe—so bursting with sugar—that yeast cannot convert all that sugar into alcohol during fermentation. Remember: once the alcohol in fermenting must reaches a level of 14 percent or so (sometimes a few percentage points higher), the yeast die; if a significant amount of **residual sugar** remains, the wine will be sweet.

Interestingly, though, this is *not* how most sweet wines are made. Some depend on something happening to—or being done to—the grapes that alters their sugar content. Others rely on fermentation's being intentionally, prematurely interrupted before dryness is achieved. And yet others are made from dry wines that are sweetened after fermentation has ended.

Something Happens to the Grapes. What happens is that they're allowed to rot on the vine before they're picked. This sounds icky, and, in fact, rotting

WHAT ROT!

grape clusters aren't very appetizing to look at, but there's a particular kind of rot—a fungal infection that certain grapes, in certain vineyards, are prone to—that can be extremely desirable and that's essential to the creation of some of the world's most famous sweet wines, Château d'Yquem included. The fungus is called ***Botrytis cinerea*** (boh-TRI-tiss sin-UH-ree-uh), and wines made from *Botrytis*-infected grapes are called **botrytized** (BOH-trih-tized) wines.

A BOTRYTIS-INFECTED
CLUSTER

A *Botrytis* outbreak isn't always a good thing. The fungus is mightily temperamental, and takes the weather *very* personally. If the weeks leading up to the harvest are rainy, *Botrytis*'s mood can turn grim and vindictive; it will spread quickly through a vineyard, attacking the flesh of the waterlogged grapes and ruining the vintage with what's called **gray rot**. But if the pre-harvest weeks are sunny—the days' warmth offset by early-morning fogs—*Botrytis*'s disposition is much more relaxed. It makes its lackadaisical way around the vineyard, debonairely defiling a few clusters here, a few clusters there—and the "disease" it produces is of a much kindlier nature. In this form, known as **noble rot**, *Botrytis* attacks the grape skins, delicately insinuating itself into the berries' flesh. As the fungus grows, it siphons water from within the infected berries, shriveling them and greatly concentrating their sugars.

By the time these shrunken, raisinlike grapes are hand-picked—cluster by cluster, sometimes berry by berry—their sugars are so concentrated that the juice pressed from them can't possibly be fermented to dryness. (The sugar content may be so high that fermentation is actually inhibited.) The resulting wines—depending on how long the infection is allowed to progress and the ratio of botrytized to non-botrytized grapes used—range from sweet to exceedingly sweet.

Besides Sauternes, botrytized wines include those from Barsac, Sauternes' neighboring appellation in Bordeaux; the Auslese, Beerenauslese, and Trockenbeerenauslese wines of Germany (see the section on Riesling, pages 179–180); and the Hungarian wine known as **Tokaji** (toh-KYE[yeh]). The beneficial effects of noble rot were actually discovered in Hungary in the mid-seventeenth century. During the 1800s, "Tokays" were greatly prized: the Russian royal family made a particular fetish of them. But as the fashion for sweet wines dwindled, Tokaji's fame began to recede. Then, with the communist takeover of Hungary after World War II, Tokaji suffered further indignities: not only did quality decline, but shipments to the West were almost completely cut off. Within just a few generations, what had once been one of the world's most sought-after wines was all but forgotten outside Eastern Europe. Tokaji's reputation is, however, being resuscitated: it's not so unusual, now, for a good U.S. wine shop to carry one or two of these redoubtable wines. They're expensive, yes, but not as compared with the great French and German sweet wines. You may pay $40 for a 500-ml bottle but that's a trifling amount to fork over for a taste of the wine of the czars.

Botrytized wines aren't just sweet; their rich, sometimes labyrinthinely complex flavors are due in large measure to the biochemical changes that noble rot induces within the grapes it infects. Once you've had one, you'll forever after recognize the idiosyncratic aroma/flavor shared by all botrytized wines. Some have described it as butterscotch-like, and others as being reminiscent of petroleum or even rubber cement (!). But, really, it's so distinctive that analogies fail. A caveat: Some people, try as they might, just don't like this taste. If you don't care for it, you needn't give up on sweet wines altogether; there are plenty of superb, non-botrytized sweet wines for you to try.

Something Happens—or Is Done—to the Grapes. They're allowed to freeze on the vine, or they're harvested before the frost and then frozen in commercial freezers. Wine made from juice pressed from frozen grapes is called, appropriately, **ice wine**. It's extremely sweet, because when the grapes are pressed before they've thawed, much of the water remains behind as ice crystals, and the sugars in the extracted liquid are therefore extraordinarily concentrated. Traditionalists sneer at the ever more widespread practice of artificially freezing the grapes after harvest, believing that the resulting ice wines have nowhere near the complexity of flavor of those made from grapes frozen naturally. But post-harvest freezing dramatically lowers the cost of producing ice wine, since grapes frozen on the vine must be hand-picked, sometimes berry by berry, in the dead of winter.

The making of ice wines originated in Germany (our term is a literal translation of the German **Eiswein**). German Eisweins can be doubly complex, since the vine-frozen grapes are sometimes infected by noble rot before winter sets in. Canada—which has a larger and healthier wine industry than one might guess, given its climate—has become the world's largest producer of traditionally made ice wine (which the Canadians, truer to the term's German-language origin, spell "icewine"). The icewines made by the Ontario vintner Inniskillin are delectable—their honeylike viscosity balanced by a piercing acidity. Because they're created in the old-fashioned, labor-intensive way, Canadian icewines are expensive; Inniskillin's can run $60 or more for a 375-ml bottle. (One of Inniskillin's icewines, like some by other Canadian makers, is based on an unusual white grape called Vidal Blanc, a so-called **French hybrid**—meaning a cross between a native American grape and a *vinifera* variety. Its tropical-fruit lusciousness is wondrous.)

Something Is Done to the Grapes. They're dried or partially dried before being pressed. That is, they're turned into raisins, or almost-raisins. Drying wine grapes before pressing and fermentation is an ancient practice—the Greeks and Romans did it—and the original rationale, once again, was to stabilize the resulting (sweet) wine, making it longer-lived and easier to transport during the millennia before the invention of the glass wine bottle. As may be obvious, drying *desiccates* grapes: as water content diminishes, sugar concentration intensifies.

Several methods are traditionally employed for drying wine grapes. The oldest (now extremely rare) is to twist the grape cluster's stem, interrupting the flow of sap to the berries, and to leave it on the vine until the grapes have shriveled. More commonly, ripe grapes are harvested, then spread on straw mats to dry—either in the sun or inside, in attics or in "lofts" specially built for the purpose. Sweet wines made from sun-dried grapes include the Passito di Pantelleria discussed in the section on the Muscat family of grapes (page 194). Much better known, however, are several northern Italian sweet wines made from the juice of grapes dried indoors. These include **Recioto di Soave** (white), **Recioto della Valpolicella** (red), both from the Veneto region, and the Tuscan sweet white wine **Vin Santo**. (Almost all wines made from dried grapes are sweet, but there is one *very* notable exception: the magnificently concentrated dry Italian red known as Amarone; see page 294.)

Fermentation Is Interrupted. Any wine can, at least theoretically, be made sweet by interrupting the fermentation process before it's completed, that is, by killing the yeast before they've finished converting the grape sugars to alcohol. The commonest way to accomplish this is to add distilled spirits to the fermenting must, raising the total alcohol level above that at which yeast can survive. This is how Port becomes sweet, but it's also the method used to create the French fortified wines known as **Vins Doux Naturels**—"natural sweet wines" that result not from nature but from human intervention! (Another kind of French fortified wine, **Vin de Liqueur**, takes the intervention a step

What Rot!

further: the grape juice is dosed with spirits before fermentation has even begun—meaning that these potent and tooth-achingly sweet wines aren't technically *wines* at all.)

Sweetness Is Added after Fermentation. Some sweet wines—including most sweet Sherries (see pages 314–315)—begin their vinous lives as dry wines. They're sweetened after fermentation by being blended with a sweet wine.

Does this cover the field? Well, not quite. The sweetness of sweet Champagnes largely derives from the addition of sugar syrup to the wine at the end of the winemaking process—but that's a subject we'll take up in the following chapter.

Serving notes: Most sweet white wines should be served chilled—but remember the injunction, repeated throughout this book, against serving white wines immediately upon removing them from the fridge. (Give the wine twenty or so minutes to warm up a bit.) Extremely sweet wines— Sauternes, Barsac, Tokaji, Passito di Pantelleria, the ultra-sweet German whites, and so on—don't partner well with a wide range of foods. Though they're often termed "dessert wines," don't make the mistake of serving them with complicated desserts (the flavors will wage war); stick to plain, unadorned cakes; simple custards; or perhaps fresh- or stewed-fruit desserts. Better yet, serve such wines with a fresh fruit–and–cheese course, or even all by themselves. Because very sweet wines are so lush, it's unlikely you'll want to drink a great quantity in a single sitting, which is why so many are sold in 375-ml bottles. If refrigerated, very sweet wines—at least those whose sugar content is balanced by high acidity—survive for a goodly time, so don't feel pressured to polish off a Canadian icewine (for example) within a few days of opening; it'll probably keep for weeks.

Though I'm not quite a card-carrying member of the cult, don't expect any irreverence from me when it comes to Riesling. That's because Rieslings, at their best, provide a kind of pleasure no other wine seems capable of delivering: one that's sensually immensely satisfying and that simultaneously feels spiritually purifying. (O.K., maybe that's a bit cultish, but stay with me.) A good Riesling—and there are *many* good Rieslings—so nimbly balances fruit intensity with cleansing acidity that you don't feel sullied or corrupted by the enjoyment. That goes for sweet Rieslings as well as for dry, since in a well-made sweet Riesling the acid is always there to cut any cloying effect the sugar might otherwise produce. Rieslings are paradoxical wines: the dry ones' fruitiness can give the impression of sweetness even when there's little or no sugar present; and because of the countervailing acidity, the sweet ones don't muddle your palate. (Acid and sugar both have preservative effects, and a side benefit of sweet Rieslings' acid-sugar balance is that it confers great longevity on these wines; the greatest sweet Rieslings can mature in bottle for sixty or seventy years, or longer.)

Of the Big Eight varieties, Riesling is the only one that isn't French in origin. Though it's now grown in many far-flung places—Australia, New Zealand, Chile, South Africa, Washington and New York states— Riesling's native land is Germany. And I'm of the strong opinion that German Rieslings, along with those from adjacent Alsace and Austria, are the best in the world. Riesling is a cool-climate grape, or rather it's a grape that manages, against the odds, to achieve its pinnacle at the northernmost fringes of winedom—places with harsh winters and short growing seasons, where the grape's chance of fully ripening is always at issue. In other words, it likes a challenge, and to my taste the only other

Rieslings that come close to those of Germany, Alsace, and Austria are the ones produced in the Finger Lakes region of New York State, whose climate resembles that of Riesling's homeland.

Riesling is the most important fine-wine grape throughout Germany, but the German Rieslings you're most likely to find in U.S. wine shops are those from the Mosel-Saar-Ruwer region of southwestern Germany. (The Mosel River is a tributary of the Rhine; the Saar and the Ruwer are smaller rivers feeding into the Mosel.) Despite that limited choice, we're not so bad off, because Mosel (pronounced MOH-zuhl, not moh-ZELL) wines are widely regarded as Riesling's apogee. Mightily floral, bursting with peach and pear flavors, and undergirded by a mineral solidity conferred by the Mosel's slatey soils, they also have what Winespeakers call a **transparency**—a crystalline depth—that surpasses all others. (If the meaning of "transparency" eludes you, try a Mosel Riesling, and you'll get it.)

German wine labels are notoriously difficult to interpret, and the German system for classifying wines is both unique and complicated. You only need to know a little bit about this; unfortunately, though, the terms can be forbidding to the Deutsch-less wine newbie. First, be aware that the best-quality German wines carry the phrase **Qualitätswein mit Prädikat** on their labels. "QmP" wines (the full phrase means "quality wines with special attributes") are categorized according to the **level of ripeness** the grapes had achieved when harvested. There are six such categories, and since you'll see these terms on many German Rieslings' labels, you should have at least a passing familiarity with them. Here they are, with (possibly helpful) pronunciation keys and brief explanations:

- **Kabinett** (kah-bee-NET). Kabinett Rieslings are made from grapes picked during the main harvest—the least ripe in this six-level scheme. That doesn't mean these wines taste "green" or unripe (they can, in fact, be wonderfully fruity), but they are generally dry or off-dry and haven't the concentration of flavor of wines made from riper grapes. If you've never had a German Riesling, you should probably introduce yourself to the genre with a Kabinett, since Kabinetts are, as Rieslings go, rather understated.

- **Spätlese** (SHPET-lay-zuh). Spätleses are made from grapes allowed to develop a week or so longer on the vine. (The name means "late harvest.") Some Spätleses are dry; others are slightly sweet; but the flavor is almost always fuller and deeper than that of a Kabinett. Produced in smaller quantities than Kabinetts, Spätleses are about half again as expensive. They're generally my favorite Rieslings, since I relish the battle that occurs in my mouth between their keen, tingling acidity and their potent fruit. (Note: Spätleses need not be sweet, though many are slightly so.)

- **Auslese** (AOWZ-lay-zuh). Profoundly aromatic and almost always noticeably sweet, Rieslings of the Auslese ("select harvest") category go a step beyond Spätleses. In most years, German Riesling growers will pass over some clusters when doing the Spätlese harvest—in the hope that the weather will remain warm and sunny long enough for these grapes to continue to develop. It's a risk, but if the weather holds, the left-behind clusters will produce sweet wines of exceptional lushness. Because of their comparative rarity, Ausleses are usually at least three times as costly as Kabinetts.

- **Beerenauslese** (BEAR-en-AOWZ-lay-zuh) The process of selection is protracted even further for Beerenausleses. In warm years when the Auslese harvest is successfully accomplished, a grower may choose to leave a very few bunches behind on the slender chance that the frost will hold off a little while longer. At this very late stage, the berries are exploding with sugar, and some will have become infected with the *Botrytis* fungus, making them so fragile that—assuming the weather doesn't turn before they can be picked—they must be harvested berry by berry. The great rarity of these honeylike "berry select harvest" wines and the intensive labor required to produce them makes them expensive.

- **Trockenbeerenauslese** (TRAH-ken-BEAR-en-AOWZ-lay-zuh— no kidding!). These Rieslings are the *ne plus ultra* of German white wines. By now, you can guess what this term implies: that, in truly exceptional vintages when the frost is very, very delayed, some clusters are left to hang on the vine even past the Beerenauslese harvest. If the frost continues to hold off—a big if—the *Botrytis*-infected berries will shrivel (the name means "dry-berry select harvest"). The syrupy juice from these raisinlike berries, picked individually, will be fermented to produce sweet wines of unparalleled richness. Trockenbeerenausleses can be hard to find, and the best go for hundreds of dollars a bottle.

- **Eiswein** (ICE-vine). As you learned earlier, Eiswein means what it sounds like it means: ice wine. Though Riesling-based Eisweins from Germany aren't particularly uncommon, they're costly. The frozen berries are harvested by hand in the dead of January (this painstaking labor adds to Eisweins' cost) and then pressed before they have a chance to thaw. Because much of the grapes' water is left behind as ice, the juice is extremely concentrated, and the dessert wines that result are powerfully flavored (while lacking the complexity of Beerenausleses and Trockenbeerenausleses).

So, how's your German coming along? If you're feeling a little dummkopf-ish, don't worry. It's not likely you'll encounter a Beeren- or Trockenbeerenauslese very often. (If you're offered one, don't bother trying to pronounce the name; just enjoy.) Note, though, that German Rieslings, despite a recent upswing in popularity, are seriously undervalued given their outstanding quality. There are lots of Kabinetts available in the $10 to $20 range. If you're comfortable paying up to $30 a bottle, there's no reason you can't occasionally enjoy a Spätlese. And even Ausleses aren't utterly unaffordable; the spectacular Auslese produced by the Mosel vintners Joh. Jos. Prüm, for example, might run $60 a bottle. I know that's well outside *Drinkology WINE*'s ordinary price range, but it's not an exorbitant amount to pay for a truly exquisite wine.

Of all the wines sampled during the research for this book, no other category performed as consistently well as Mosel Rieslings. That doesn't mean you won't occasionally be disappointed, but it does mean you're highly unlikely to get an undrinkable bottle. The best Spätlese sampled came from a Mosel maker called Milz (about $25), but you'll no doubt find others just as good. When choosing a Riesling, you might want to check the back label for the name of the importer. I've found that the Rieslings imported by a Syosset, New York, firm called Michael Skurnik Wines (and selected by Terry Thiese) are almost always exceptional. It should be mentioned, too, that there are lots of German Rieslings out there that don't rate the QmP imprimatur but that, nevertheless, are refreshing and even interesting wines. A house favorite is the ***trocken*** ("dry") Riesling made by Fürst Löwenstein, of Germany's Rheingau district. Though it hasn't the depth of a typical Mosel Kabinett and it isn't a QmP wine, it's immensely drinkable—and it retails for about $14.

About non-German Rieslings: The little lineup of Alsatian wines you're likely to find in your local wine shop will doubtless contain one or more Rieslings. Be fearless here, as well. Alsatian wines of whatever label and whatever varietal are phenomenally dependable, and it's almost certain you'll enjoy whichever Alsatian Riesling you choose. Austrian Rieslings are harder to come by in this country; going to a Viennese restaurant may offer your best chance of getting acquainted with these wines, which are generally dry and higher in alcohol than their German counterparts. (Choose one, if possible, from Austria's Wachau district.) As I indicated earlier, I'm not much of a fan of non-European Rieslings, although those made by the German-born vintner Hermann J. Wiemer at his Dundee, New York, winery come very close indeed to the Mosel model. In New York, Washington State, and elsewhere in the United States, the Riesling grape is sometimes called *Johannisberg* Riesling (the name comes from a town in Germany). Washington Johannisberg Riesling varietals can be refreshing wines, no question, but *Drinkology WINE* considers their virtues to be but dim reflections of German Rieslings' glories.

When it comes to food, Riesling is chameleon-like in its adaptability. As you might guess, German Kabinetts and Spätleses and (dry) Austrian and Alsatian Rieslings are natural partners of "Middle" European dishes—anything from sauerbraten, to Wiener schnitzel, to humble bratwurst. But the impression of sweetness delivered by even the driest Rieslings makes them good choices for spicy Asian fare, as well. The pleasures of Auslese Rieslings are a tad sybaritic, so don't force a meal to compete with an Auslese. Instead, serve an Auslese with a cheese course that includes at least one creamy, vigorously flavored blue (a Stilton or Gorgonzola, maybe).

Now go ahead: fall in love.

Sauvignon Blanc [soh-veen-YAWn BLAHn]

Wines made from the Sauvignon Blanc grape can give the concept of varietal character a run for its money. Sauvignon Blanc wines are usually described as being **grassy** or **herbal** (when this character is too pronounced, they're criticized as **vegetal**), and they're also generally known for their high acidity. But while it's true that many top Sauvignon Blanc–based wines do have an herbal or grassy component to their scent and taste, this quality is mostly or wholly absent from other Sauvignon Blancs, which, though less interesting, can be pleasant and drinkable. And when the grapes are grown in warmer climates, they can lose the keen acidity for which great S.B.-based wines are treasured—or disliked, depending on your taste.

I've discovered that I love citrusy, acidic white wines—when, that is, the wine's acidity is counterbalanced by other qualities, as it is in what I consider the best of the wines made from Sauvignon Blanc grapes. I equally relish the herbal character for which S.B. wines are famed, and my recommendations are rooted in these preferences.

Sauvignon Blanc–based wines rank among the three most popular kinds of white wine (after Chardonnay and neck-and-neck with Pinot Grigio), and the grape is now grown throughout the wine-producing world. But France is S.B.'s home base—as should be obvious from the grape's name, which in French means "wild [or savage] white." (Interestingly, this white grape is indeed related to the famous red-wine grape whose name it partly shares: Cabernet Sauvignon.) In France, Sauvignon Blanc is used, all by itself, to create several of the most famous wines of the Loire Valley, including white Sancerre and Pouilly-Fumé, and it is an important component of blended white Bordeaux, including both the dry white wines of the Graves and Pessac-Léognan appellations and the sweet dessert wines of Sauternes. But its French origins are only the beginning of the Sauvignon Blanc story; the variety has flourished in California and elsewhere throughout the New World, including Australia, Chile, and (especially in the past few decades) New Zealand and South Africa.

To gain an immediate grasp of the unmistakable character of a classic-style S.B., though, you should go back to the source: Try a medium-priced Sancerre (about $15 bottle). (Moderately priced Sancerres are reliably good; I happen to like Henri Bourgeois's Le MD de Bourgeois Sancerre.) Then use the Sancerre as a benchmark for comparing the other Sauvignon Blanc–based wines you try.

Which should you sample? If I'm right, the Sancerre will have given you a fairly complex smell-and-taste experience: a nose both fruity and herbal, a powerful middle dominated (at least for me, with most of the Sancerres I've drunk) by a grapefruitlike taste, and a long, delectable finish commingling acid, fruit, and a pleasant, mineral sharpness that's also characteristic of many S.B.-based wines. If this complex combo pleases you, try measuring it against the following wines, all in the $10 to $30 price range:

> Grgich Hills Fumé Blanc (Napa Valley, California)
>
> Santa Rita Sauvignon Blanc Reserva (Chile)
>
> Thabani Sauvignon Blanc (South Africa)

Notice that the California wine is called **Fumé Blanc** (FOO-may BLAHⁿ), not Sauvignon Blanc. We've seen instances where one grape goes by two or more different names (Pinot Grigio/Pinot Gris), but the tendency of some California vintners to call their S.B.-based wine Fumé Blanc has a unique origin: the renaming of the varietal was a marketing scheme dreamed up by the savvy California winemaker Robert Mondavi several decades back. These varietals were then new to the American market, and Mondavi reasoned that the average American wine-drinker might have difficulty pronouncing *Sauvignon*—and might well forego ever buying a bottle in order to spare him- or herself the embarrassment of stumbling over the name. (Sound familiar?) Mondavi chose to replace it with *Fumé* not just because it's comparatively easier on the American tongue and ear, but also because it conjures the grape's French heritage: Pouilly-*Fumé* is, as I say above, a well-known S.B.-based Loire wine, and the French word *fumé* means "smoky," evoking the smoky, "gunflint-y" flavor that Sauvignon Blancs are sometimes said to possess. Anyway, Mondavi's brainstorm made rain, and a number of California producers got under the same umbrella.

You'll notice something different, too, when you taste the California wine. Unlike most S.B.-based wines from the Loire, some California Sauvignon Blancs are oaked—*briefly* oaked—and you'll detect a hint of wood in the smell and flavor of the Grgich Hills I'm recommending. As you know from the section on Chardonnay, I'm not generally a fan of white wines aged in oak, but this is one of the exceptions that proves my rule. In the Grgich wine, the oaking augments and enriches the grape's natural depth and complexity; it's nice.

The Chilean Sauvignon Blanc isn't as good, but I suggest it because I think it's easier, with this particular wine, to discern the separate components of S.B.'s classic smell and taste: it's as if the wine "falls apart" in the nose and on the tongue, allowing you to distinguish and separately enjoy the fruit, the grassiness, and the lemony acidity. That the flavors *aren't* well married makes each more noticeable, and you can learn a lot about Sauvignon Blanc by drinking a glass of Santa Rita. On the other hand, I recommend the Thabani wine—from a South African producer that's only been in the wine biz for a few years—just because it's so delicious (granted, the S.B. character is more muted in this wine).

Once a winemaking backwater, South Africa has risen to global prominence over the past decade—in large measure because of how good the country's Sauvignon Blancs can be. In this regard, the winemakers of the Western Cape Province have trod the same path to renown as their counterparts in another distant, southern hemisphere land: New Zealand. Critically lauded New Zealand Sauvignon Blancs are now as common as, well, grass.

If your taste differs from mine—if the mere thought of a sour-ish, grassy wine makes you scrunch up your face unpleasantly—that doesn't mean you won't like *any* Sauvignon Blanc. If the white wines you tend to prefer are light but fruity and relatively low-acid, you'll be able to find Sauvignon Blancs that suit you: you might limit your sampling to a few bottles each of Sauvignon Blancs from California and Australia. My bet is that though some of these will show Sauvignon Blanc's distinctive characteristics, others—more to your liking—will not. You might, for example, include a bottle of Sauvignon Blanc by a California winery called Mirassou in your taste-test. Although I don't much enjoy this maker's take on Sauvignon Blanc—simple and light, but immensely fruity on the tongue, with little in the way of nose or finish—I can well imagine that others might, and this style does strike me as extremely versatile when it comes to pairing with food.

Speaking of food: Sauvignon Blancs—especially the unoaked S.B.-based wines of the Loire—tend to go well with seafood, especially oysters, other shellfish, and white-fleshed fish (in dishes where the taste of the seafood, not of the sauce, predominates). As an aperitif, a typical Sauvignon Blanc makes for an interesting alternative to the typical Pinot Grigio; the incisively mineral, mouth-puckering tanginess of a Sancerre can be terrifically thirst quenching on a hot summer evening. Note, however, that you have to be careful when pairing S.B.-based wines with cheese. They're an absolute disaster with blues—as I know from having tried to couple the Grgich wine with a chunk of Stilton. (The citrus flavors of the wine underlined the sharpness of the Stilton's mold and machete'd the cheese's creaminess.) Sauvignon Blancs do work well enough with milder, hard cheeses (Manchego, Gruyère), and they can be very good with soft goat cheeses—a classic combo.

A Few Other Whites You Ought to Know

Chenin Blanc [SHEH-nen BLAH^n]

Pity the poor immigrant. Chenin Blanc, a small-berried, tightly clustered, light green grape, is responsible for some of the celebrated white wines of the middle Loire Valley, especially those from the Vouvray appellation. Exported to New World winemaking regions, however, its reputation tanked, even as the grape itself flourished.

How can that be? It's a simple matter of *yield*. New World producers of mass-market wines—especially in California and South Africa (where Chenin Blanc was introduced by Dutch settlers as early as the mid-1600s, and where it's often called by its Afrikaner name, **Steen**)—took advantage of the variety's ability, when planted in relatively warm climates, to produce enormous yields, sometimes four times as high as the grape achieves in the less gentle climate of the middle Loire. Like a downtrodden migrant whose true talents go unrecognized, Chenin Blanc became a workhorse variety, used to manufacture oceans of down-the-hatch jug wine—this from a grape that, in France, has for centuries been employed to create remarkable wines that couple a tingling acidity with a deep, honeylike fruitiness.

Luckily, this is changing. A small but growing number of wine producers in both California and South Africa are returning Chenin Blanc to its roots, so to speak—planting C.B. vines in cooler areas to maximize acidity, limiting yields, and in some cases using time-honored Loire Valley techniques to create crisp, delicious, and even relatively complex varietals that easily vie with moderately priced Vouvrays. (Let me say that moderately priced dry or off-dry Vouvrays—I'm talking about wines that can retail for as little as $9 a bottle!—can be pretty darned good.)

To quickly school yourself in Chenin Blanc, you might try the following selections. (Do your shopping at a larger wine store; American and South African Chenin Blancs remain relative rarities.) Your experimentation won't set you back much: the most expensive of these wines, the South African, cost me about $16; the other two can each be gotten for $10 or less.

> Château de Montfort Vouvray (France), or any Vouvray costing between $9 and $15 a bottle (They're quite reliable.)
>
> Dry Creek Chenin Blanc (Sonoma County, California)
>
> Mulderbosch Chenin Blanc (Stellenbosch, South Africa)

You'll certainly note the profoundly citrusy acidity in all three. (Vouvrays may also have a distinctly apple-like flavor.) The California and South African wines may seem a tiny bit spritzy—a desirable characteristic. The Mulderbosch is slightly, almost imperceptibly, oaked—something that would never be done in Vouvray but that adds some gravity here. And even though all these wines are dry, their fruit flavor is so powerful and full that it masquerades as sweetness. If your taste tends in that direction, you'll probably appreciate any of these as a summertime aperitif. But even if you prefer whites that are more "austere," you'd do well to try a Chenin Blanc with food. Oysters make for a traditional pairing with C.B.-based wines. And off-dry or dry-but-somehow-sweet-tasting Vouvrays and C.B. varietals seem made for spicy-and-sweet Chinese dishes (think cold sesame noodles).

A few California producers, led by a Napa winery called Pine Ridge, are blending Chenin Blanc with Viognier, a highly perfumed variety (see below). Smart move. Pine Ridge's piercingly aromatic but solidly grounded blend of 80 percent Chenin Blanc and 20 percent Viognier is a favorite.

Gewürztraminer [geh-VERTZ-trah-mee-ner]
The first time I ever had a Gewürztraminer, I *hated* it. The second time, the meeting was a little—a *little*—more amicable. The third time, I began to find the wine interesting. By now, Gewürztraminer varietals are among my favorite white wines. But, boy, are they an acquired taste.

Or, rather, an acquired *smell*. Because of all white-wine varieties, Gewürztraminer produces the most aromatic wines. Head-spinningly aromatic. The fragrance, usually, is that of roses. And we're not talking the neutered, attenuated smell of the long-stemmed hybrids you buy for your sweetie on Valentine's Day. We're talking the aggressive, respiratory system–challenging "old rose" scent that I associate, from boyhood, with my Great Aunt Lena's perfume. Now, Lena was a nice old lady, but I believe she *bathed* in rosewater. Even blindfolded and wearing earplugs, you'd have known that she was in the house. Same with Gewürztraminer: its scent is so distinctive that even wine novices readily learn to recognize it.

Gewürztraminer, like some other renowned grapes, originated in one place and came to fame in quite another, but the route it pursued traveled in the opposite direction from that of many varieties. It's the descendant of a northern Italian grape called Traminer (after Tramin, the German name of the Alto Adige town of Termeno). By the 1600s, it was ensconced in Germany, where it eventually mutated into the form we know today: a grape whose brownish-pink berries result in highly colored, highly fragrant wines. (*Gewürztraminer* means "perfumed Traminer.") And from Germany it made its way to Alsace, in whose vineyards it has done its greatest work.

Though Gewürztraminer is nowadays grown elsewhere around the world (you saw it in Bob Pellegrini's Long Island vineyards in chapter 2), there's general agreement that Alsatian Gewurztraminers (the name is usually spelled without the umlaut in Alsace) are the best. I concur. For a taste—or whiff—of Gewurztraminer at its most exceptionally floral, you might try the varietal produced by the Alsatian maker Willm (less than $15 a bottle) or—if you can find it—by Haag (less than $20). If you, too, had a Great Aunt Lena and the prospect of summoning her ghost in its full-flowered odiferousness is a bit too much to contemplate, begin instead with a Gewürz from California (Sonoma Valley), Oregon, or New York State. (The Lenz winery, of Long Island's North Fork, makes an excellent Gewürztraminer, retailing at about $15, that's less overwhelmingly fragrant than its Alsatian relatives.)

The experience of a Gewürz doesn't end with the nose. These wines can be potently fruity—rather like Rieslings on the palate. They're very good partnered with foie gras, with greasy smoked meats (sausages!), and—because of the impression of sweetness delivered even by dry Gewürztraminers—with spicy foods.

Grüner Veltliner [GROO-ner FELT-lih-ner]
Wines made from this Austrian variety—it's Austria's most important white-wine grape—have begun showing up in force on the wine lists of fashionable restaurants. For Riesling fans, Grüner Veltliners have an automatic appeal, since they share Rieslings' aromatic nose and potent fruit. ("Peaches" is a commonly applied descriptor.) Grüner Veltliners differ from Rieslings, though, in being spicier—a characteristic that's especially noticcable on the finish. The combination of fruit and pepperiness makes G.V.'s compatible with a considerable range of foods, from gravy-laden stews, to grilled pork chops, to chicken dishes. (Austrians drink them with everything.) Despite their fashionability, Grüner Veltliners remain hard to find in most American wine shops: you'll probably be limited to one or perhaps two choices. The crisp, dry, and fairly commonly available Berger Grüner Veltliner imported by Michael Skurnik Wines provides a good-enough introduction to the grape at a comfortable price: less than $15 for a one-liter bottle. If you're able to spend morc, try the G.V. by a maker called Schloss Gobelsburg; it's appreciably more characterful, and, at less than $25, still within *Drinkology WINE*'s preferred price range.

Müller-Thurgau [MYOO-ler TOOR-gow]
Best known for its use in cheap German wine such as Liebfraumilch, this hybrid vine variety was developed in the late nineteenth century by

a Herr Doktor Müller in the Swiss canton of Thurgau, hence the hyphenated name. Wines made from M.-T. are widely dismissed by critics as mediocre and **flabby** (that is, lacking the acid needed to balance the fruit), and the variety would hardly rate a mention in this book were it not for the sensational results achieved with the grape by some growers in Oregon's Willamette Valley.

You won't find Oregon Müller-Thurgaus everywhere; the number of acres planted with the vine remains very small (probably still under a hundred, divvied up among more than a dozen growers). But if you do happen upon a bottle, buy it. (You won't pay very much for your experiment—maybe eight to eleven dollars.) Oregon Müller-Thurgaus aren't complex wines; they don't show much in the way of nose or finish; but they're crisply delicious in the mouth, and they make for very respectable summertime aperitifs.

The Muscat Family [MUSS-kat]

Here comes a term—Muscat—that seems designed to make wine novices want to pull out their hair. (Since I have very little left, I'm mercifully spared the ability for such self-injury, but I would if I could.) *Muscat,* you see, isn't the name of a grape; it's the name of a *huge extended family* of grapes—hundreds of varieties, of every color a grape can come in, and used to make virtually every possible kind of wine (dry, sweet, fizzy, still, white, red, you name it). As befits such a large and geographically dispersed clan, the Muscat family of grapes has a long lineage: its ancestors grew in the vineyards of ancient Greece and Rome, where these highly perfumed grapes were noted for their propensity to attract insects. (The name may derive either from the Greek word for bees or the Latin for flies.) That aromatic quality is imparted to the wines made from the various Muscat grapes, and these wines also share another family trait that's unique among *vinifera*-based wines: they actually taste like grapes.

Starting from the doubtless correct assumption that none of us will ever memorize the Muscat family vine, let's focus on just two of the most famous Muscat varieties. The first is best known by one of its French names: **Muscat Blanc à Petits Grains** ("white Muscat with little berries"). I say *one* of its French names, because it's known by a dozen different names in France alone. (And dozens more elsewhere. Makes you want to stick to Chardonnay, doesn't it?) Muscat Blanc is grown just about everywhere—France (including Alsace), Germany, Spain, Australia, South Africa, Uzbekistan (yes, Uzbekistan). But the Muscat Blanc–based wines you're likeliest to see in American wine shops come from Italy, where the grape, there called Moscato, is the basis for the sparkling wine known as Asti (named for the town of Asti in the Piedmont region).

Run-of-the-mill Astis don't appeal to me, however, so I'm going to recommend that you make your acquaintance with this grape via a different, more serious sort of wine from the same place in Italy. This other wine has a deceptively similar name: Moscato d'Asti. Ordinary Asti is frothy, sugary, and light, but Moscato d'Asti is just slightly fizzy, and its flavor and texture are honeylike. It's a dessert wine, no question, but one whose minimal carbonation gives it a surprising and very enjoyable edge. The first time I had it, it accompanied a pumpkin custard, and it was *scrumptious*. (So was the custard.) The maker was Batasiolo; the cost about $13—an interesting and affordable alternative to other, much higher priced, dessert wines.

The other Muscat variety you may want to befriend is called **Muscat of Alexandria**. Like Muscat Blanc, this is a very ancient grape (its origin, as the name implies, is probably Egyptian), and it's now grown throughout the Mediterranean and elsewhere. Wine critics don't much like Muscat of Alexandria, considering most M.O.A.–based wines vastly inferior to those made from Muscat Blanc. But everyone seems to agree that there is *one* wine made from Muscat of Alexandria that's worth paying attention to: the dessert wine called Passito di Pantelleria. Made from dried grapes—that is, raisins—on the little island of Pantelleria (which though part of Italy is just off the North African coast), this dark-hued, ultra-rich wine is a treasure.

I've just got to mention another sweet Muscat-based wine, despite the fact—forgive me!—that you may have trouble finding it. That's because it's from Romania, of all places, and so you're unlikely to encounter it except in wine shops with a predominantly Eastern European clientele. It's called Tămîioasă (tuh-moi-WASS-ah), and it's made from a strain of Muscat Blanc that's been grown in Romania since antiquity. Only a few labels—maybe only two—are imported into the United States; the Tămîioasă I've had is called Golden Valley, and its pleasures approached those of a good Sauternes, which ain't bad for a wine that costs about $7 a bottle.

Pinot Blanc [PEE-noh BLAHⁿ]

Flirtation tip: You and a new-ish "friend" have just sat down at a bar that has a fairly extensive selection of by-the-glass wines. Your companion—whom you know to be a Chardonnay fan—says, "Gee, I don't know what I want. I'd like to get something different. What should I have?" Take it from me: if there's an Alsatian Pinot Blanc on the list, suggest that he or she have the Pinot Blanc. Your friend will be impressed by how well you understand his/her taste, and the friendship will begin to blossom.

Historically, this grape has followed an itinerary similar to that of Pinot Gris. Born in the vineyards of Burgundy (probably as a lighter-skinned mutation of Pinot Gris, itself a mutation of Pinot Noir), the variety moved on to Alsace—and, again like Pinot Gris, eventually disappeared from its birthplace. From Alsace, it spread to Germany and then to Austria. German and Austrian Pinot Blanc–based wines, called Weisser Burgunder and Weissburgunder, respectively, are critically acclaimed but difficult to find in the U.S. So let's stick with the Alsatian P.B.:

Your friend will love it because Alsatian Pinot Blancs have a full-bodied fruitiness similar to that of many Chardonnays—substantial but not terrifically distinctive—while being more acidic, hence a lot crisper, than most garden-variety Chards. (They're also not generally oaked.) Tired of laboring under the weight of oaked California Chardonnays, your friend's palate will experience an epiphany: finally, a white wine that jibes with his or her taste buds' desire but one that's more comfortable to drink as an aperitif.

Now, let's take this seduction a bit further. You and your friend proceed to dinner. Assuming, again, that the restaurant you choose has a somewhat sizable, well-rounded wine list, order a bottle of California Pinot Blanc to accompany your meal. (Have the roast chicken, or maybe a pork chop.) Believe me, the flowers of friendship will bloom all the more extravagantly. The style of the California P.B. will differ from that of the Alsatian: it'll probably be oaked, and its fruit flavors will be sultrier (more tropical, less "northern"). Again, your friend will recognize a flavor that he/she adores, but in a guise that's lighter-hearted, more fun, than the Chards he or she has begun to tire of. Hmm, he or she will think, this person really has an insight into my soul.

What you do after dinner is your concern. Don't sue me if the strategy doesn't work. But you owe it to your love life to give it a shot.

Sémillon [say-mee-YAW^n]

By itself, the Sémillon grape isn't all that noteworthy. Among Sémillon-based varietals only those from Australia (especially from the Hunter Valley in the state of New South Wales) and from Washington State have earned much critical attention. No, for the most part Sémillon is like a dullish, inconspicuous, nondescript single person who suddenly becomes a lot more interesting and vibrant when he or she meets the perfect mate. Sémillon's ideal partner is Sauvignon Blanc, and together they create some of the greatest white wines of France: the dry whites of the Graves and Pessac-Léognan appellations of Bordeaux and the sweet whites of Bordeaux' Sauternes and Barsac appellations. As in a great marriage, the partners complement one another; they're each other's "better half."

The gifts that Sémillon brings to the partnership are several. It takes well to oak. (Both the dry whites of Graves/Pessac-Léognan and the sweet wines of Sauternes/Barsac are barrel matured.) It ages well. (White Graves/Pessac-Léognan wines are among the highly select group of dry whites that are long-lived in the bottle; great Sauternes can continue to evolve in the bottle for *hundreds* of years.) Its golden color is intensified by oak maturation. (It's responsible for the trademark bright banana-oil yellow of the most famous Sauternes.) And it's highly susceptible to that desirable disease called noble rot, making it essential to Bordeaux' botrytized dessert wines. Without Sémillon, the world wouldn't have Château d'Yquem—and that contribution's enough to justify Sémillon's inclusion on your must-know list of white-wine grapes.

Viognier [vee-ahn-YAY]

Sometimes prevailing fashion just doesn't suit you. You prefer narrow neckties, but fashionable cravats are as wide as bibs. You like miniskirts, but hemlines are plunging. Everybody's wearing Nikes, but you and your penny loafers just don't do it. That's how I feel about Viognier: it's so fashionable it's phat—but I'm stuck back in the era of groovy and far-out. I could, I guess, just leave Viognier off this list (this *is* my book), but fashion commands that I put it in.

And so I do—but I'm gonna diss it. Or, rather, I'm gonna diss its American, off-the-rack incarnation. Viognier is the sole grape composing several "couture" whites from France's Rhône Valley (Condrieu, Château-Grillet), and it's sometimes added to one of France's most celebrated reds, Côte-Rôtie (otherwise pure Syrah). But I'm exempting them and directing all my venom toward California Viognier varietals. I know it's unfair, but, hey, I'm entitled to my opinion, and my opinion is that these are among the most overdone, overblown, over-hyped wines on earth. They're not perfumed; they're *perfumy*. They're as fruity as a fruit basket. (This is not a compliment.) They're alcoholic—not something I'm constitutionally opposed to, but there are better ways of getting soused. All in all, they're just too much for me.

Before you grow to dislike me too much, do notice that I'm not just a nabob of negativism when it comes to Viognier California-style. I think it makes a fabulous accessory—as in the Chenin Blanc–Viognier blends mentioned in the section on Chenin Blanc, above. I just don't think it rates an entire outfit. Feel free to feel differently about Viognier varietals. And to make fun of my shoes.

AND WHAT ABOUT ROSÉS?

Is pink the new red? Is it the new white?

Over the past couple of years, rosé wines—long off the radar of serious American wine drinkers—have been enjoying an extended moment in the sun. (I think it's perfectly appropriate to mix metaphors when talking about rosés, the best of which so accommodatingly combine attributes of both red and white wines.) Especially during the summer months, good wine shops are carrying a much wider selection of rosés—French, Italian, Greek, American, and even some Australian wines—than previously, and newspaper wine writers are devoting more column inches to rosés than ever before. These are welcome trends, for good rosés can be terrifically companionable wines. *Refreshment* is rosé's keyword, so summer's definitely the time to enjoy these wines, both as aperitifs and with meals.

A rosé is not a rosé is not a rosé, however. (Sorry: the pun was inevitable.) There are two basic methods for creating rosés, and, in general, only one of these produces acceptable wines. The first, not-so-good method involves blending finished red and white wines; mass-produced rosés are often created in this manner, and the resulting wines are usually sorely lacking in integrity. (Rosé Champagnes are the exception; almost always blends of white and red wines, "pink" Champagnes can be masterworks of the Champagne maker's art—but see the following chapter for more.) The second, more "holistic" way of creating a rosé wine begins with red-wine grapes, which are macerated on the skins for a brief period to extract moderate amounts of color, tannins, and phenolics. The juice is then racked off the skins and fermented—and the rest of the winemaking process is the same as that followed for most white wines (basically, a few months of stabilization in steel tanks followed by bottling and immediate release).

Despite their color—which can range from coral to cranberry, depending on the kind of grape(s) used and the length of the maceration—rosés are more like white wines than reds: they should be drunk within a year or two of bottling, and they're best served chilled. Yes, some rosés pack a red wine–like punch, but this isn't a virtue in itself; rather, it serves to underscore and enliven their refreshing character. (The depth of a rosé's color, by the way, provides little clue as to the wine's intensity of flavor.)

Rosé wine–making traditions run deepest in Spain, Greece, and parts of France (especially the Loire Valley and the southern Rhône and other areas of southern France), and you'd do well to commence your exploration of rosés with a few Spanish, French, and—if you can find them—Greek examples. Be forewarned, though: place of origin is no guarantee of a rosé's quality. I've had marvelous Loire rosés, berrylike and crisp, and I've had Loire rosés that tasted like Robitussin (no kidding—*just like* Robitussin). I've had Spanish rosés that were indistinct and watery, and others whose complexity rivals that of some superior red wines—while retaining the palate-brightening cleanness of a good, acidic white. (The half-Cabernet, half-Garnacha [Grenache] rosé made by Vega Sindoa, of Spain's Navarra *denominación*, is a winner, with a lively finish that just doesn't quit.)

Rosés can theoretically be made from any red-wine grape (or combination of varieties), but certain varieties seem better suited to rosés than others. These include Pinot Noir (used in pink Sancerre, it's also the basis for many California rosés), Grenache, and, in Spain, Tempranillo. Greek rosés are often based on an indigenous variety called Xynomavro (Xinomavro); the Xynomavro-based, Akakias-brand rosé by a Greek maker called Kir-Yianni has a delicately floral nose and a protracted rosehips–and–pink grapefruit finish. Rosés from France's southern Rhône, like the region's reds, are usually based on a complicated blend of red varieties, including Grenache, Syrah, Cinsault (SAA^n-soh) and others; you might try one from the Tavel appellation, famous for rosés whose evanescent scent belies their hefty impact on the taste buds. Cost-wise, there's not much of an impediment to sampling a wide variety of rosés, since quality rosés rarely exceed $20 per bottle and there are plenty enough in the $10 to $15 range to keep you busy all summer long.

Rosés, though themselves neither fish nor fowl, go well with both—and with lots of other foods, besides. In fact, there's virtually no summertime supper—including burgers on the grill—that doesn't lend itself to a good rosé.

IMPRESS YOUR FRIENDS—
WITHOUT BREAKING THE BANK (PART 2)

And speaking of summertime . . .

It was a warm late-June evening. My birthday. One of my dearest and oldest chums, Betsy, had come to my house to fix dinner for me and a small group of friends. The centerpiece of the meal was one of my favorite dishes, crab imperial (simple, rich, and tangy). I supplied the wines: a couple of white Burgundies and a couple of bottles of a white wine I'd never drunk before: Muscadet.

The Burgundies—a Pouilly-Fuissé and a St.-Véran—were disappointing. Maybe they were just the wrong wines for that evening, but everyone thought they were duds: heavy, dull, dispiriting. Luckily, I'd reserved the Muscadet to serve with the meal itself. Though I hadn't much thought about what I was doing, this turned out to be a genius move. The crab was out of this world—and the Muscadet its perfect mate.

Muscadet with crab. Muscadet with fish. Muscadet with virtually any seafood dish you can imagine. Muscadet as an aperitif. Muscadet *in summer*. To my mind, no other white wine suits a summer evening quite as well—it became my household's default white during that July, August, and well into September. This is not an "intellectual" wine; it takes absolutely no effort to understand or appreciate it. But it's one of the most refreshing, most sheerly enjoyable wines in existence.

Muscadet [moose-kah-DAY] comes from the westernmost part of France's Loire River Valley, the area surrounding the city of Nantes, very near where the Loire empties into the Atlantic. Maybe it's the vineyards' proximity to the sea that makes Muscadets such natural partners with seafood. (I tend to distrust such "mystical" connections, but in this case the complementarity is so exact that . . . who knows?) The wine is based on a single grape, called Muscadet locally but better known as Melon de Bourgogne. There are four appellations, but the best—and, happily, the ones you're likeliest to find represented in your neighborhood wine shop—are Muscadet de Sèvre-et-Maine and Muscadet Côtes de Grandlieu. Some Muscadet labels carry the phrase *sur lie* ("on the lees"); these are the ones you want. When allowed to rest on its lees between autumn fermentation and spring bottling, Muscadet develops a gentle creaminess without losing its citrusy punch. (Think lemon sherbet without the sugar.) The on-the-lees nap also confers a slight (very slight) fizziness—a welcome shiver on a midsummer's night.

Muscadets are low in alcohol (French regulations limit them to 12.3 percent alcohol, max), and they're low in price: the one I've liked best, a Côtes de Grandlieu from the Clos de la Sénaigerie vineyard, retails for less than $12. Nearly as good (and about as inexpensive) is the Muscadet Sèvre-et-Maine made by Château du Cléray. Both are *sur lie* wines.

CHAPTER SEVEN

Fluted Columns

(SPARKLING WINES)

L ET US ALL NOW PRAISE COMMON DUST. THAT'S RIGHT, BECAUSE IF there weren't any dust in the world, we wouldn't have sparkling wine. (And wouldn't that be tedious.)

All sparkling wine, you see, contains dissolved carbon dioxide gas. It's long been understood that to form bubbles, the CO_2 molecules have to encounter some friction—have to be rubbed the right way, so to speak. Until very recently, it was thought that the necessary resistance was provided by tiny imperfections in the interior surface of a wineglass—a belief that led many a connoisseur to take a knife to his favorite Champagne flute, scratching the bottom of the bowl to get those columns of bubbles marching double-time. But it turns out there's no need to abuse your fine crystal; the bubbles actually result from the interaction of the dissolved CO_2 with microscopic particles of dust. So unless you live in a perfectly dust-free environment (not *Drinkology WINE*'s house, I can assure you), if you pour it, they will come. (The discovery of dust's role in producing sparkling wine's bubbles, by the way, was made by French scientist Gérard Liger-Belair—whom one newspaper wag dubbed "the fizzicist.")

Having resolved the troubling bubble issue, it's time to ask the prior question: How did the CO_2 get into the wine in the first place? Well, it depends. There are several different methods for making sparkling wine. The most important—in terms of the quality if not the quantity of the wine produced—is the *méthode champenoise*, the traditional, or classic, method developed by the makers of the world's most renowned sparkling wine: Champagne. So let's first focus our attention there.

THE BOTTLE OF THE MARNE

First off, you've just got to get over your predilection for calling all sparkling wine *Champagne*. It isn't. Properly speaking, the name belongs solely to the wine produced in the Champagne appellation of France, centered in the valley of the Marne River about a hundred miles (give or take) northeast of Paris. The French have thrown a decades-long fit about the propensity of other sparkling wine makers, elsewhere in the world, to co-opt the name for their products. The tantrum is justified; not only did the vintners of Champagne invent the classic method for creating sparkling wine, but the name, by historical, geographical right, belongs to them alone. Also, the sparkling wines of Champagne are unlike any others—even those that, like the best California sparklers, are based on the same grapes and are created using the very same technique originally developed in France. Sparkling wines made elsewhere than Champagne can be excellent—you might even prefer them—but Champagne they are not, by definition.

The development of the *méthode champenoise* is a textbook case of making the best of a bum deal. Champagne is one of the northernmost, chilliest winegrowing regions in Europe. Although wine's been made in Champagne ever since the Romans conquered Gaul, winemaking there

KEEP IT MUMM. DON'T POP!

Unless you're in the locker room celebrating your World Series victory—in which case the bottle should be shaken vigorously before you pop the cork and spray your half-undressed teammates with the ejaculate—the idea is to open a sparkling wine as *gently* as possible. A loud POP! signals that precious bubble-making gas is being wasted.

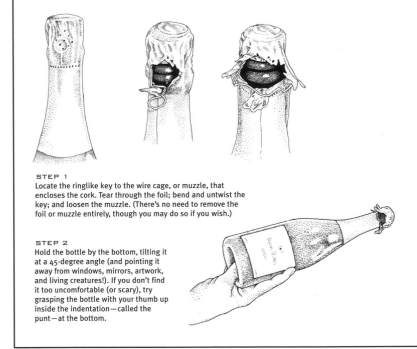

STEP 1
Locate the ringlike key to the wire cage, or muzzle, that encloses the cork. Tear through the foil; bend and untwist the key; and loosen the muzzle. (There's no need to remove the foil or muzzle entirely, though you may do so if you wish.)

STEP 2
Hold the bottle by the bottom, tilting it at a 45-degree angle (and pointing it away from windows, mirrors, artwork, and living creatures!). If you don't find it too uncomfortable (or scary), try grasping the bottle with your thumb up inside the indentation—called the punt—at the bottom.

STEP 3

Grip the cork with your other hand, and slowly twist the bottle (*not* the cork). This gentle twisting motion, aided by the pressure within the bottle, should be enough to release the cork. If the wine's been chilled and the bottle hasn't been shaken, the cork should emerge with only the subtlest of popping sounds.

STEP 4

To prevent the wine from foaming up and spilling over, tilt each flute as you pour the wine into it. Pour only an inch or two into each glass, then top up all the glasses.

has always been a fraught endeavor. The soils are extremely poor (Champagne's vineyards today are among the most heavily fertilized on earth) and are underlain by white chalk that can impart a decidedly mineral flavor to the region's wine. Champagne is prone to late-spring frosts (we're talking *June*) that can kill the grapevines' buds, and the growing season is brief, impeding the grapes' ability to fully ripen—climatic conditions that make for inconsistent vintages and that, even in the best years, lead to wines that are high in acid and relatively low in fruit. And the area often suffers harsh, cold winters that, in the millennia before temperature-controlled winemaking, were responsible for an especially odd characteristic that afflicted Champagne's wines: they fizzed. I say "afflicted" because this was mostly considered a fault, not a virtue.

Now we know why Champagne's wines tended to bubble. In late autumn, it would often grow so cold in the winemaking chambers that fermentation would simply shut down, only to recommence when temperatures warmed in the spring. But the biology of fermentation has only been understood since the mid-1800s, and in the preceding centuries the fizziness of their wines befuddled and consternated Champagne's winemakers. Of course, there were a few people who *liked* these strange, fizzy wines, but even this posed a problem, since it could never be predicted whether a given batch of wine *would* referment and because wines stored in porous wooden casks (as virtually all wines were before the late seventeenth century) tended to lose their sparkle during transport.

Operating on a Gallic version of the principle, "When life gives you lemons, make lemonade," Champagne's winemakers ultimately overcame all the hurdles that nature had tossed their way. They developed markets for their bizarre wines. (Novelty has always attracted the fashionable set, and so it's no surprise that sparkling Champagnes were first taken up, in the late seventeenth century, by London café society and trendsetters at the French court at Versailles.) They improved consistency by blending together wines from different vineyards and, eventually, from different vintages. And, with the advent of glass wine bottles and cork stoppers, they invented ways to ensure that their wines would always bubble and that the effervescence wouldn't dissipate before the wines were opened.

All this took a long time. Crucial advances in winemaking were introduced by the monk **Dom Pérignon,** who from 1668 until his death in 1715 was the head winemaker at the Abbey of Hautvillers, near the Champagne town of Épernay. (Before the Revolution, French wine-making was largely a monastic pursuit.) Often credited with the "invention" of Champagne, Brother Pérignon actually devoted himself to perfecting blending techniques and to the creation of (still) white wines from black grapes. Other *champenois* winemakers—their names largely lost to history—contributed other innovations, including the specification of thick-walled glass bottles capable of resisting the pressure exerted by the dissolved gas within. (That bottled-up force is equal to five or six times atmospheric pressure at sea level; the thinner-walled bottles used for Champagne during the eighteenth century regularly exploded.) It wasn't until the early nineteenth century, however, that Champagne as we know it today was born: crystalline straw- or pink-hued wine whose millions of tiny bubbles rise to the wine's surface in captivating, almost orderly progression.

Champagne is made from only three grapes: the white grape Chardonnay and the black grapes Pinot Noir and Pinot Meunier (PEE-noh muh-NYAY). Pinot Noir accounts for 75 percent of the grapes grown in the region, and it's the major constituent in most Champagnes. (It's absent, however, from **blanc de blancs** Champagnes; these "white from whites" wines are based solely on Chardonnay.) The vast majority of Champagnes are blends—not just of the three grapes, but of wines made from grapes from different vineyards and of wines from different vintages. Refermentation is no longer an accidental process. For the past couple of centuries, all Champagnes have been made from still wines that are *deliberately* refermented in the bottle. That's the key to the *méthode champenoise*, which—in brief summary—works like this:

To make a **nonvintage** (NV) Champagne, the winemaker begins with a selection of still **base wines**—some from the current vintage and some **reserve wines** from previous years. The combination will vary from year to year, but with NV Champagnes the aim is always to recreate, as closely as possible, the particular style for which a Champagne house is known. Blending—which may bring together scores of different base wines—is a tricky business, since the winemaker has to make an educated guess about how the mix of wines will be affected by the rest of the process, and it's the rest of the process that will largely determine how the finished wine will taste and behave.

Blending is followed by **tirage** (tih-RAHZH): the wine is bottled, but before the bottles are (temporarily) capped and laid on their sides, a mixture of yeast and sugar syrup is added to each. And what do yeast do when they find themselves swimming in a lovely sugary solution? Right: they gobble up the sugar, converting it to alcohol and CO_2. In the closed environment of the bottle, the CO_2 has nowhere to go—and so it remains dissolved in the wine.

This second, in-bottle fermentation takes four to eight weeks, after which the Champagne ages on the lees—the dead yeast cells, which form a sediment along the bottom side of the bottle—for an extended period of time (at least fifteen months, though many NV Champagnes are aged for up to three years). It's during this *sur lie* bottle ageing that Champagne acquires much of its distinctive character: the bready, biscuity, sometimes haylike flavors that Winespeakers call **autolytic**, because they're transferred by the chemical process of autolysis from the lees to the wine. (The longer the ageing, the finer the bubbles, or **beads**—and small bubbles are considered a mark of a better wine.)

Before the early nineteenth century, the *méthode* more or less stopped here. It took a very clever woman to come up with a way of removing the lees sediment from the Champagne bottle—thereby ensuring that

---

HOUSES OF REPUTE

The Champagne appellation has more than fifteen thousand growers, but the wine's manufacture is mostly controlled by 110 or so major makers, or **houses**. Oddly, some of the most famous houses—Krug, G. H. Mumm, Louis Roederer, Charles Heidsieck—have German-sounding names; that's because they were founded by German immigrants who came to the area in the nineteenth century and wound up taking over a large share of the industry. Until a few decades ago, most Champagne houses were family-run businesses, but many have since been bought by large liquor companies and luxury-goods conglomerates.

At the same time that this consolidation has been going on, an increasing number of individual growers—people who used to sell all their grapes to the major houses—have struck out on their own, making hand-crafted **grower Champagnes** that have spurred critical excitement and that offer extraordinary quality for the price (sometimes significantly lower than the big-name Champagnes). Ask your local wine merchants if they carry any "grower Champagnes." If they do, experiment ebulliently!

---

the wine wouldn't be cloudy—without also allowing the gas to escape. The woman was **la Veuve Clicquot** ("the Widow Clicquot"; her full name was Nicole Barbe Clicquot-Ponsardin), who inherited the Champagne house of Clicquot on the death of her husband in 1806. Whether the legend that she herself invented the process called **riddling** (Fr., *remuage* [reh-MWAHZH]) is accurate or not, it remains true that

RIDDLING BOARD

the house of Clicquot, which she renamed Veuve Clicquot-Ponsardin, pioneered the method, revolutionizing Champagne-making.

Riddling, which literally means "shaking," involves the very gradual repositioning of the Champagne bottle from the horizontal position (in which it has lain during ageing) until the bottle is upside down. Each time the bottle is moved an increment closer to being totally inverted, it is shaken and turned to detach the gluey lees from the side of the bottle and cause them to slowly sink into the neck. When done manually, the whole operation takes about six weeks, and is performed on a **riddling board** (Fr., *pupitre* [poo-PEET^r]), which resembles a sandwich board with holes for holding the bottles. (Today, only about 25 percent of Champagne is hand-riddled; the rest is riddled by a machine called a gyropalette, which completes the process in three days—but the principle remains the same.)

So now you've got an upside-down bottle with all the lees settled in the neck. How—you might well ask—does that help matters? Easy.

(Well, sort of.) You dip the bottle's neck in a freezing solution, which turns the lees into a solid, icy mass. Then you turn the bottle right side up and uncap it—and the pressure from the gas in the wine **disgorges** the frozen plug of lees, shooting it out of the neck.

We're not yet quite done with the *méthode champenoise*. Before the bottle is permanently stoppered, the wine is topped up with what's called the **dosage** (pronounced in the French manner: doh-SAHZH). The dosage—a mixture of sugar syrup and still reserve wine—doesn't just fill the space vacated by the lees; it also determines the level of sweetness of the finished Champagne. In line with Americans' preference for dry wine, most Champagne (and other sparkling wine) sold here is **brut** [BROOT] or **extra brut**—meaning dry or very dry. But Champagnes are actually made in six different levels of sweetness, some of which have deceptive names:

Extra brut The driest Champagne; contains no more than 0.6 percent sugar.

Brut Dry; contains less than 1.5 percent sugar. Some brut Champagnes can, however, taste ever-so-slightly sweet, so you've got to know the maker's style.

Extra sec Slightly sweet; contains between 1.2 and 2.0 percent sugar. Here's where the terms grow deceptive, since *extra sec* literally translates as "extra dry."

Sec Medium sweet; contains 1.7 to 3.5 percent sugar. (But the term literally means "dry"!)

Demi-sec Sweet; contains 3.3 to 5.0 percent sugar. ("Half-dry" is the literal meaning. Jeesh.)

Doux	Very sweet; contains more than 5.0 percent sugar. Finally, terminology and meaning overlap—since *doux* (DOO) does mean "sweet."

Except for not using wines from different years, **vintage Champagne** is created in much the same way as nonvintage—though it's also aged longer, spending at least three, and often as many as five, years on its lees before riddling and disgorgement. Though vintage Champagnes are created from grapes from a single harvest—and it must be an extraordinary year for a house to declare a vintage—almost all vintage Champagnes are blends of different grapes and of wines from different vineyards. The great care taken to produce these wines is often evident when you drink them. I was fortunate enough, while researching this book, to sample a vintage 1995 blanc de blancs Champagne made by the house of Taittinger. Its delicate bubbles, its subtle **mousse** (the frothy "head" that forms on the surface of the wine when poured), its exquisitely fresh nose, its buttery mouthfeel (I felt as if my teeth were coated with cream!), and its prolonged finish made for one of the peak wine-drinking experiences of my life.

Besides vintage and NV Champagnes, many top houses also create extra-extraordinary wines called **prestige cuvées**. (The French word *cuvée* [koo-VAY] literally translates as "vat," but in Winespeak it usually means "batch," or "blend," and the term is often reserved for special wines.) Prestige cuvées, which are almost always vintage Champagnes, are usually blended only from wines from top-rated vineyards (the **grands crus**, or "great growths") and are treated to especially long ageing—up to seven years. Probably the best-known prestige cuvées are Dom Pérignon, made by Moët & Chandon, and Cristal, made by the house of Roederer. The latter was originally created in 1876, on the special request of Czar Alexander II, who wanted something nobody else had. (I supposed he was growing bored with all those Fabergé eggs.) The Bolsheviks didn't do anybody much good—but, hey, if it took the Russian Revolution to make Cristal available to the rest of us, let's raise a toast to the Reds.

A Bubble-Head and His Friends

I like Champagne—who doesn't?—but I'm a real bubble-head when it comes to choosing one over another. I'm lucky enough, however, to have three friends—Eric Mueller, his wife Ramona Ponce, and Ramona's sister Rachel—who have squandered a goodly portion of their adult existences in pursuit of the next Champagne fix. (There are, let's be honest, worse ways to spend your time.) Ramona's a costume designer, and though her champers fetish is perhaps a little less extreme than, say, Marilyn Monroe's (Monroe reportedly bathed in the stuff), she did once make herself an extraordinary hat topped with a gloved hand hoisting a Champagne glass. We should all advertise our passions so. Anyhow, rather than offering you my own Champagne recommendations, I thought I'd consult with these three roués, who were eager to share their hard-won knowledge with the public at large.

Ramona rhapsodizes about Roederer's prestige cuvée, Cristal: "Outstanding to breathtaking, depending on the vintage—but worth every penny, every time. Anticipation of it is like waiting for your first kiss. Memory of it—and longing for it—never fades. It's got a perfect balance of acid and fruit—crisp apple, apricot, and the merest hint of citrus. The mousse lasts and lasts. So does the finish. Everything's in perfect alignment. Who cares if it's the drug kingpin's bubbly of choice? If money were no object, this would be our house Champagne, too." On that last point,

Champagne's idiosyncrasies extend to its packaging: the toadstool-shaped cork imprisoned by a wire cage, the heavy glass bottle with an extra-deep indentation at the bottom. Also unusual is the fact that Champagne is sold in bottles ranging from the tiny (containing about one and a half flutes' worth of wine) to the preposterously enormous (one hundred–plus flutes). True, you'll also find other wines in a range of bottle sizes, but the greatest variety belongs to Champagne.

Champagne corks actually begin as straight-sided cylinders. Wider than ordinary corks, they have to be jammed into the bottles' necks—and they won't go all the way in. It's this tight pinch that causes the top part of the cork to swell, giving it its signature mushroom shape. The wire cage—it's called the **muzzle**, or, in French, the ***muselet*** (myoo-suh-LAY)—is there, of course, to make sure the cork stays put until the wine is opened. Many wine bottles have an indentation at the bottom; the term for this concave space is the **punt**, and it's an artifact from the days when bottles were hand-blown. The glassmaker's tool—the punty—would leave behind a small nipple, and pushing this protuberance up into a bottle's bottom ensured that the bottle would stand upright. But even today, when wine bottles are made of molded glass, Champagne bottles' extra-deep punts serve a practical purpose: they help equalize pressure throughout the bottle, making accidental explosion much less likely.

Some connoisseurs insist that Champagne from giant bottles tastes better than that dispensed from the ordinary, 750-ml variety. Others say that big bottles make for comparatively flat Champagne, since the wine is aged and riddled in smaller bottles and then transferred to the larger containers, resulting in some loss of pressure. I wouldn't know. My sole experience with Champagne from a truly huge bottle occurred on the New Year's Eve of

1999/2000. You remember Y2K, yes? Well so do I—sort of. The blowout I attended featured a Nebuchadnezzar of Veuve Clicquot. (That's the biggest bottle on the list on the next page; the drawing at right shows the relative sizes of a Nebuchadnezzar and a standard, 750-ml bottle.) The big bottle was opened at midnight; it took a surprising amount of effort to wrestle out the cork and three people to lift the bottle and pour—or, rather, slosh—the wine into the guests' eagerly proffered glasses. I drank some, of course (rather a good deal, I imagine), but though I clearly remember the great hilarity accompanying the event, I have absolutely no memory of how the Champagne tasted.

If you pull a bank heist and—while waiting for the Feds to catch up to you—decide to treat yourself to a Nebuchadnezzar of your favorite bubbly, you shouldn't have to worry about spilling it on the lovely oriental rugs in your robber's lair. Spend part of your ill-gotten proceeds on a specially designed cradle that makes pouring from a supersized bottle a snap. Proving that there's an Internet emporium for *everything*, a website called www.giantbottles.com sells these contraptions, which will set you back a couple of thou'. Since there won't be room for the cradle in your jail cell, though, you might want to lease rather than buy (some wine shops rent, or even lend, such cradles to their big-bottle-buying customers).

The bigger bottles are named after biblical personages—kings of Israel and Judah, Mesopotamian monarchs, one of the Three Wise Men, and an antediluvian codger whose sole claim to fame is that he lived 969 years. So far as I can tell, no one knows why these names, which have been used since the nineteenth century and which are used for both still- and sparkling-wine bottles, were chosen. Here, anyhow, is the list:

Split   The smallest bottle; holds 187.5 ml, or about 1½ flutes.

Half-bottle   Holds 375 ml, 2 to 3 flutes.

Bottle   Though heavier (because of the thick glass), holds the same amount as a standard wine bottle: 750 ml, or 5 to 6 flutes' worth.

Magnum   Equivalent to 2 standard bottles.

Jeroboam   Equivalent to 4 standard bottles. Jeroboam was a king of ancient Israel.

Rehoboam   Equivalent to 6 standard bottles. One of Solomon's sons, Rehoboam was a king of Judah.

Methuselah   Equivalent to 8 standard bottles. Methuselah was the old guy (see Genesis 5:27).

Salmanazar   Equivalent to 12 standard bottles. Salmanazar was an Assyrian king.

Balthazar   Equivalent to 16 standard bottles. Balthazar is the name traditionally given to one of the Three Wise Men. (In the Bible, they're anonymous.)

Nebuchadnezzar   Equivalent to 20 standard bottles! Nebuchadnezzar was a king of Chaldea.

Eric whispers a husbandly demurral: "If it be known, I'd trade away a bottle of Cristal for a Dom Pérignon [the Moët & Chandon prestige cuvée]."

Money, of course, is an object in most households. (You'll easily pony up $170-plus for a bottle of Cristal from even a recent vintage.) When it comes to more reasonably priced, NV Champagnes, marital harmony prevails between Mueller and Ponce. The pair are very partial to rosé Champagnes, especially those made by Billecart-Salmon and Nicolas Feuillatte. About the Billecart-Salmon, Eric says, "This is a very elegant, medium-body sparkler that goes *wonderfully* with food—especially pink-fleshed fish. 'Color coordinate' food with this wine and you've got it made." Ramona concurs, though she's more mix-and-match than Eric: "I think it goes with any fish or lighter meat, including veal, duck, and goose liver."

At about $60, though, the Billecart-Salmon still qualifies as a special-occasion bubbly. The Feuillatte rosé, at a little more than half the price, is, in Eric's assessment, "a real bargain for the superior tastes in this bottle, which has great balance between crisp dryness and lush pink and red fruit flavors." Ramona: "It also has some floral and herbal notes that make it extremely refreshing—and a great mixer with red-fruit liqueurs for spring and summer cocktails." (Rachel Ponce, however, dissents: "If you want a rosé, go with Gosset Grand Rosé, if you can find it. It's more expensive, but way worth it. I think it beats the hell out of the Nicolas Feuillatte.")

When it comes to non-rosé Champagnes—which represent 98 percent of the Champagne market—Eric and Ramona are again a model of marital concord: "Moët & Chandon Brut Imperial NV is a reliable standby—though it's somewhat of an underdog to the too-fashionable Veuve Clicquot." Ramona: "You really can't beat it for the price [about $25]. It's quite elegant: there's a taste of starched, beeswaxed Old World society in every sip."

Sister Rachel is a little more catholic in her advice: "I recommend buying the one on sale that you haven't tried yet. In the privacy of your own home, you can pop the cork of today's special, and nobody need know but you." Since Rachel—did I forget to mention?—is a sommelier, it makes good sense to take her experimental approach seriously. And it certainly makes a bubble-head like me feel a lot less dumb.

THE OTHER STUFF

Many wine books give non-Champagne sparkling wines short shrift. Unfortunately, this little book must do the same. What a shame, since the world's other bubblies—and sparkling wines are made virtually everywhere that still wines are made—offer such a panoply of pleasures.

Many are created using the traditional, or classic, method. (The French have gotten as proprietary about the term *méthode champenoise* as they are about the name Champagne itself, so makers elsewhere are less likely than in the past to identify their lees-aged, riddled sparklers as "Champagne method.") For a superb, dry, classic-method white sparkler whose finesse approaches that of Champagne (but which costs a fraction of the price), try Graham Beck Brut, from South Africa. (About $16, last time I looked.) California classic-method sparklers are legion. Though many are produced by companies owned or partly owned by well-known Champagne houses, the California wines tend to be fruitier (a result of the warmer climate) than their French cousins. The sparklers made by Piper-Sonoma (owned by the French house Piper-Heidsieck), by Roederer Estate (another name you should recognize by now), and by Iron Horse are extremely dependable, but with so many California sparklers to choose from (and so many selling for less than twenty bucks a pop), be adventurous.

The Spanish sparkling wine called **cava** is also made by the traditional method. (Pronounced KAH-vah, the name means "cellar" in Catalan, and most cava hails from Catalonia, in Spain's northeastern corner.) Though made in basically the same  way as Champagne, cava can taste quite different, because it's traditionally based on three indigenous Spanish grapes. (Macabeo, Parallado, and Xarel-lo are the names; Chardonnay, a legal ingredient in cava since 1986, is fast catching up, however.) Many cavas are serious wines—but their price tags make them very attractive to the Champagne-taste-on-a-beer-budget set. The giant Spanish winemakers Cordoníu and Freixenet are the most familiar cava brands, but you should feel very free to experiment with whatever your local wine shop offers.

The same goes for the Italian sparklers called **Prosecco**. (Prosecco is the name of the grape they're made from.) Hailing from the Veneto region of northeastern Italy, Proseccos are mostly created via the **tank method**, in which the wine is refermented in a pressurized tank and bottled afterward. (The tank method is sometimes called the **Charmat method** [shar-MAH], after its French inventor, Eugène Charmat.) Tending to be off-dry rather than dry, Proseccos don't have anything like the complexity of great Champagnes, but, hey, who's against indulging in simpler pleasures? The almost candylike fruitiness can be fun—and Prosecco makes a fantastic base for sparkling-wine cocktails that incorporate fruit or fruity liqueurs. (The famous Bellini cocktail, invented at Harry's Bar in Venice, couples Prosecco with puréed white peaches.) A recommendation? Well, Pisano Party Blu Prosecco Brut is, as its name implies, a terrific party wine, and its $11 price tag means you can invite *lots* of friends.

CHAMPOO?

The best way of chilling sparkling wine—of getting it cold enough to be pleasurable but not so cold that the character is dampened—is to do it in a Champagne bucket. Fill the bucket half-full with ice cubes, then add enough water to just cover the ice. Plunge the bottle deep into this ice-and-water soup, and twenty minutes to half an hour later you're good to go. (Perhaps needless to say, this method works well for any wine you want to chill.)

If this strikes you as too much trouble, you're awfully lazy. Or maybe you just don't own a Champagne bucket—in which case, do chill the wine in the fridge. (It takes three to four hours.) Experts seem to agree that it's a bad idea to let sparkling wine hang out in the refrigerator for too long a time—it gets so depressed in that morguelike environment—and that trying to quickly chill a bottle by sticking it in the freezer is a definite no-no. Store unopened sparkling wines as you would any others: on their sides, in a dark, reasonably cool, and vibration-free place. (For more on storing wines, see pages 344–347).

Nearly everybody agrees that sparkling wines should be served only in the narrow, stemmed glasses called flutes or the slightly more capacious tulip glasses (see page 84); by limiting the wine's surface area, these glasses restrict the rate at which the bubbles escape, prolonging the effervescence. And just about everybody disparages

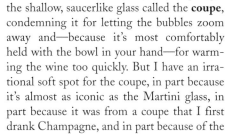

the shallow, saucerlike glass called the **coupe**, condemning it for letting the bubbles zoom away and—because it's most comfortably held with the bowl in your hand—for warming the wine too quickly. But I have an irrational soft spot for the coupe, in part because it's almost as iconic as the Martini glass, in part because it was from a coupe that I first drank Champagne, and in part because of the legend that the first coupe was modeled on the breast of that misunderstood, ill-fated French queen Marie-Antoinette. If the people have no flutes, let them quaff from coupes, I say.

Champagne and other sparkling wines are so closely associated with parties (and the launching of ships) that most people don't think of partnering them with meals. In fact, dry sparkling wines go terrifically well with a wide range of foods, including—my favorite—roast chicken. (Red-meat dishes aren't a great idea; neither are highly spiced foods.)

And what about leftover sparkling wine? The best strategy—and the only one *Drinkology WINE* can genuinely recommend—is to make sure there *isn't* any left over. Open a bottle, drink a bottle. (Or a half-bottle or split if you think a whole bottle won't get finished.) If you're drinking a sparkling wine slowly over the course of an evening, feel free, as the Old Wives do, to insert the handle of a spoon into the bottle's neck; I've no idea whether this time-honored technique actually helps keep a bubbly bubbly, but I always do it because it makes me feel virtuous.

Having advised you to drink up, I've got to testify that the effervescence of some well-made sparkling wines has some staying power even after the bottle is uncorked. Re-closing a bottle with a Champagne stopper (the stopper pictured is just one of many types available) and putting it in the fridge may keep  the wine vivacious for one or—at the outside—two days. But this is unpredictable, so don't get mad at the wine if it goes flat on you. If all the bubbles have fled, you might consider doing as famous fashionista Diana Vreeland advised her friends to do: wash your child's hair in the dead Champagne, to keep it blond. (If you're not the parent of a towheaded kid, there's still the option of using the wine for cooking.)

Believe it or not, more sparkling wine is made and consumed in Germany than anywhere else. It's called **Sekt** [ZEHKT], and the vast majority of it is awful: fruit-juicy, sudsy dreck made via the least noble sparkling wine–making process—**carbonation**. (That's right: the same method that puts the bubbles in Mountain Dew.) Little of this stuff makes it to our shores *(Gott sei Dank!)*, but you will occasionally find higher-quality, bottle-fermented Sekts from both Germany and Austria in better wine shops. If you run across the brut Sekt made by the Austrian producer Bründlmayer, buy it. It'll only set you back about $30—less than most Champagnes—and you'll be in for a very interesting experience. My tasting notes: "Yeasty! Hops-like! Almost like stout!" Of course, you don't always want a wine to remind you of beer (in fact, you seldom do), but I wish I could lay in a store of the Bründlmayer Sekt so that I could serve it whenever I fix a German- or Austrian-themed meal. I can't imagine a better accompaniment.

Finally, there are some lightly sparkling *(pétillant)* French wines that referment—or, rather, finish fermenting—in the bottle but that are never riddled or disgorged. This method is called, appropriately, the ***méthode ancestrale***—because it hearkens back to the way sparkling wines were made before the Widow Clicquot drilled holes in her kitchen table to make the first riddling board. There's an extremely unusual *méthode ancestrale* wine that I think you've just got to try. It's from the Savoie region of eastern France, and it's called Vin du Bugey Cerdon Demi-Sec Rosé. Sweet, raspberry-colored, and raspberry-flavored, it is—I admit—like soda pop. But what soda! Most of *Drinkology WINE*'s tasting crew thinks me insane, but I adore the stuff. Guess I'm still a wine baby, after all.

CHAPTER EIGHT

A Whirlwind Wine-World Tour

FROM YOUR LOCAL VINO STORE

WHEN IT COMES TO THE WORLD OF WINE, ALMOST EVERYBODY thinks globally but acts locally. Sure, some people regularly go on wine tours or at least arrange to visit a few wineries when on vacation in the U.S. or abroad. And sure, some people buy wine from far and wide over the Internet. But no matter who you are, I think it's safe to guess that you probably buy most of the wine you drink from wine shops, liquor stores, and/or supermarkets in your vicinity. The local wine shop is where most of us get acquainted with the wines of the world.

The world of wine is unknowably complex. There are some good, more or less comprehensive guides to the world's wines (see my recommendations on pages 356–358)—but none is exhaustive. That would be impossible. Knowing that this little book can't be anything like comprehensive, I decided on a different tack to introduce you, the less-than-well-traveled neo-oenophile, to the wine world. I visited a number of wine merchants in my general neighborhood, compiled and collated my

What can you tell about a wine from its bottle? Well, not all that much, but a bottle's shape and the color of the glass it's made from can provide a few clues as to the kind of wine it contains. The well-defined shoulders of the bottle at the left of the drawing opposite, for example, mark it as a **Bordeaux-type** bottle. It's the shape used for both red and white Bordeaux, and the pronounced shoulder serves a practical purpose when it comes to pouring older red Bordeaux, helping catch sediment before it reaches the bottle's neck. The Bordeaux shape has been widely adopted elsewhere, and it's often used for more "powerful," darkly pigmented red wines (California Cabernets, Australian Shirazes, various Italian and Spanish reds). In Bordeaux, red wine bottles are generally made from fairly dark green glass, which shades the wine inside from harmful ultraviolet light; in Spain, Italy, and elsewhere, dark brown glass is used at least as often as dark green.

Second from the left is a **Burgundy-type** bottle, traditionally used both for Burgundy's Pinot Noir–based reds and for its Chardonnay-based whites. The gently sloping shoulders are testimony to the fact that Pinot Noirs are generally less deeply pigmented—and therefore less likely to throw sediment or to need careful decanting—than some other reds. This shape has, if anything, been even more widely adopted internationally than the Bordeaux type; it's the kind of bottle used, for instance, for virtually all California Chardonnays.

The bottle in the center belongs to the **German type**; slender "flute" bottles like this one—often in a fairly vivid green glass—are typically used for Rieslings from the Mosel region. The profile is very similar to that of bottles used for the wines of Alsace and for other German white wines, though the glass of these bottles is likelier to be brown rather than green.

The shape of the **Champagne bottle** (second from the right) is similar to that used for many sparkling wines. Sometimes slightly bulbous, sparkling wine bottles have thick walls, making them wider and significantly heavier than bottles used for still wines. (The well-fortified walls provide insurance against explosion.) Green is the color of choice for many sparkling wine bottles, though bottles for Italian Proseccos are often cobalt blue.

The shape and dark color of the bottle at the far right are typical of many **Port bottles**. The **stopper cork** sealing this bottle can be replaced after opening. The glass is such a dark green that it appears to be black; again, the color's purpose is to protect the wine inside.

BORDEAUX   BURGUNDY   GERMANY   CHAMPAGNE   PORT

impressions, and organized this "whirlwind wine world tour" based mostly on my on guesses about what you're likely to find when you trip into your own local wine emporium.

The shop we'll visit doesn't exist in reality—it's an imaginative reconstruction. And I've edited down our made-up shop's holdings pretty significantly. Even moderate-size wine shops often carry two thousand or more different wines, but in what follows, I won't discuss more than a few score, altogether. The principle is to provide you with a passing introduction to some of the wines you're most likely to find— and to make some suggestions regarding things you might try, if you run across them in your own, real-world neighborhood shop. (And, as always, I'll keep your pocketbook in mind, only rarely venturing higher than $30 a bottle.)

UNITED STATES

Wish they all could be California wines? Well, entering an American wine shop, you may feel your wish has been granted—so long, that is, as you don't venture too far beyond the front of the store. In many U.S. shops, the first thing you see when you walk in are the California wines. They're grouped by varietal: the Chardonnays first, possibly, and the Cabernet Sauvignons second. There are dozens of California Chards and Cabs, ranging in price from $10 or so right on up the scale. (The Chardonnays top out at about $60; the sky's the limit with the Cabernets.)

The Chardonnays and Cabernets may each occupy a whole floor-to-ceiling shelving unit. They're likely to be followed by other California varietals: a large-ish group of Merlots, a slightly smaller selection of Sauvignon Blancs, and then some Pinot Noirs, some Zinfandels, and a smattering of other California wines, including a few more varietals (a couple of Viogniers and Syrahs; a Petite Sirah or two; a Chenin Blanc) as well as some blended, "branded" wines like those made by Bonny Doon.

All told, the California wines may account for as much as a sixth of the total stock. Maybe more, if you count in the generic "jug" wines and so-called **fighting varietals** from California that the shop also carries. ("Fighting varietals" is the name given to the inexpensive, mass-produced, but varietally labeled wines made by big California makers. Quality-wise, they're in between the generics and the fine table wines. In recent years, inexpensive fighting varietals have been battling for bargain-hunters' loyalty against even cheaper, **"extreme value"** wines, which also carry varietal labels. The most famous are the Charles Shaw label wines sold by the Trader Joe's chain—nicknamed "two-buck Chuck" because they've sometimes retailed for as little as $1.99 a bottle.)

In according California such prominence, our typical wine shop is bowing to economic reality. Not only does the state produce 90 percent of the wine made in the U.S., but three out of every four bottles of wine sold in this country come from California. However large it seems, though, the selection of California wines in a typical shop is actually quite limited (especially outside California). The state now has about a thousand wineries—ranging from the tiny to the immense—and more than a hundred different grape varieties are grown there. Virtually every style of wine is made in California: sparkling wines, sherry- and port-style fortified wines, and even some highly regarded dessert wines modeled on the sweet, late harvest wines of France and Germany. Yes, our imagined shop does stock a few California bubblies in the sparkling wines section, but otherwise the choice is mostly limited to dry red and white table wines. They're what people come in looking for—the Chards and Cabs, especially.

Forty years ago, things would've been different. It may surprise you to learn that California's current dominance in the American fine-wine market is a fairly recent phenomenon. Yes, wine's been made in California ever since Catholic missionaries carried *vinifera* vines there from Mexico in the 1770s, and commercial winemaking got started in California during the years following the Gold Rush of 1849. The **Sonoma** and **Napa** valleys, northeast of the then-burgeoning city of San Francisco, were on their way to becoming established winemaking centers by the early 1850s. By the late nineteenth century commercial winemaking had expanded to areas up and down California's coast, from Mendocino County in the north down to Santa Barbara County, about seventy miles above Los Angeles.

But then something happened: Prohibition. A few makers, including familiar names like Inglenook, Charles Krug Winery, and Beaulieu Vineyard—all established in the nineteenth century—survived America's "dry spell," but most went under or started growing table grapes (or grapes for raisins) instead. Though the revived industry grew during the decades following the Second World War, postwar California mostly produced cheap generics—the so-called "burgundies," "chiantis," and so on—that pandered to the new middle class's desire for sophistication without blemishing its near-total ignorance of Old World wine culture.

Even Malibu has vineyards now

If this were the 1950s or '60s, then, our shop's fine-wine offerings would mostly be French. The fine table wines from California would be very few. But then something else happened. Beginning around 1970, a flood of new people entered the California winemaking biz—many of them professionals from other fields who took early retirement (with or without pensions), bought up old vineyards or created new ones, and went for broke. Against all odds, they succeeded—not just in selling their wines, but in educating American drinkers about fine wines and, ultimately, in helping turn Napa and Sonoma counties into gustatory destinations rivaling those of Europe. The trend begun by these latter-day pioneers continues: each year, more and more world-weary film directors, dentists, and airline pilots decide that what they really want to do with the rest of their lives is grow grapes and make wine. For cripes sake, even Malibu has vineyards, now.

Enough history, already. What you want is a little guidance in choosing a California wine. So let's begin at that first shelving unit:

California Chards. If it's an oaked Chardonnay that interests you, I'll repeat the suggestion, made back in chapter 6, that you choose one made in the **Edna Valley**. (By the way, Edna Valley, like many of the other places you'll see on American wines' labels, is a federal government–designated **American Viticultural Area**, or AVA. See the sidebar on the next page.)

You'll remember, I'm sure, that *Drinkology WINE* is not particularly enamored of heavily oaked Chards, and so I want to direct your attention to a number of the new, **unoaked Chardonnays** that a growing number of California winemakers are creating. If your wallet's burning a hole in your pocket, there's the Arcadia Chardonnay by Napa Valley's famous Stag's Leap Wine Cellars. At $45, it's certainly a pricey white wine—but its crispness coupled with the great range of fruit flavors it conveys (everything from pear to tangerine) make it worth the money. At a lower price point, consider the Laurel Hill Chardonnay made by the Mayo Family Winery of Sonoma County (about $15) or the aptly named Metallico (because it's fermented in steel tanks, not oak barrels) by the Morgan Winery of Monterey County (about $20). Seems like all of the new crop of unwooded California Chards share a bright acidity, a mineral substructure, and a cornucopia of fruit. I like the trend.

California Cabs. Of all the grapes grown in California, Cabernet Sauvignon is the variety most fundamentally identified with the state's fine-wine industry. In fact, Cabernet's importance in Napa is so great that you could *almost* say that Napa = Cabernet and Cabernet = Napa. Back in chapter 5, I wrote that wine experts

You could almost say that Napa = Cabernet

have taken to disparaging moderately priced California Cabs—but are they right to do so? To rush to my own judgment, I selected three medium-price-range Napa Cabernets made by well-known makers, and, for good measure, threw in another commonly available California Cab, this one from Sonoma. All were 2001 vintage. Tasting them in tandem, here's what I found (I begin with the least satisfactory):

Wine #1 Sterling Vineyards Napa Valley Cabernet Sauvignon (about $24): A thin though somewhat floral nose. Watery and vegetal in the mouth. Weak tannins. A negligible finish. Indeed, not a very good wine, showing no ageing potential whatsoever.

Wine #2 Louis M. Martini Napa Valley Cabernet Sauvignon (about $20): Better. A more powerful, smoky nose. Mildly tannic. At first, shows a thinness of flavor similar to the Sterling's, but the flavor develops over the long finish, with strong, bright berry notes shining through at the end. Ageing potential: who knows?

Wine #3 Pine Ridge Rutherford–Napa Valley Cabernet Sauvignon (about $40): The leap in price appears to make a big difference. The nose possesses something of Cabernet's trademark "cigar box" scent. Though not terribly aggressive, the tannins are definitely present. And so's the fruit, which envelops the tongue. The nice, long finish reminds me of wood smoke—a sign of French oak? Very drinkable right now, but it has the structure to sustain it. (Note, by the way, that this wine specifies a particular Napa Valley AVA: Rutherford.)

Wine #4 Ravenswood Sonoma County Cabernet Sauvignon (about $21): The lone Sonoma representative—and the champ, hands-down. On the nose, shows the classic Cabernet combo of tobacco and black fruit, with a slight floral fragrance, as well. The tannins pack a punch, at first subduing the fruit—which does, however, come through clearly at the long finish. The acid is subtle, but there (and balanced with the other components). I'd guess this wine—very good now—will get even better with age. (I tasted it in the afternoon, then decanted it and served it with a meatloaf dinner that evening, by which time the fruit had grown delectably ripe.)

The lesson? Well, you sure can't generalize from such a small sample. The results were, however, interesting. The Sterling was a rip-off at $24. The Martini was an adequate if underwhelming wine. The Pine Ridge—a maker I admire—was certainly better than adequate, but the experience didn't seem to justify the forty-buck price tag. The Ravenswood, though, sustains one's faith that there are very good, reasonably priced California Cabs out there; maybe you'll get lucky and find some others.

Other California Varietals. Of all the fine-wine grapes grown in California, the leaders, besides Chardonnay and Cabernet Sauvignon, are Merlot, Pinot Noir, Sauvignon Blanc, and Zinfandel. Let's leave the Merlots aside—as you'll see in a moment, you're likely to get better quality at lower cost if you go with a Washington State Merlot. If it's a Sauvignon Blanc you're wanting, we'll suggest one from Monterey County or the Santa Ynez Valley (perhaps the Firestone Vineyard S.B., a tasty bargain at about $11 a bottle)—while reminding you that California S.B.'s are usually fruitier (less grassy and acidic) than their European counterparts. In fact, that's a claim that can be reasonably made about California's fine wines in general: more often than not, they're **fruit-driven**.

If you're curious about Zinfandel's earthy texture/flavor and alcohol wallop, I'll recommend that you try an **old vine** Zinfandel—but don't come crying to me if the experience proves a little too rugged for your delicate sensibilities. ("Old vine," by the way, is a vague term with no legal meaning. Some "old vines" are centenarians; some are just middle-aged.)

I'm much more enthusiastic about California Pinots: besides the BearBoat Pinot Noir recommended in chapter 5 (a true bargain at under $20), I especially like the Carneros Pinot Noir made by Étude Wines of Napa, though, at about $40 a bottle, it's a stiffer investment. By the way, **Carneros** (or Los Carneros) is an unusual AVA: it straddles Napa and Sonoma counties at their southern ends and because of its topography takes greater advantage of the cooling morning fogs that roll in from the Pacific. That's what makes it a suitable place to grow the cooler-temperature-loving Pinot Noir.

In Napa County, it actually gets hotter the farther *north* you go, and, in fact, it's true of California as a whole that climate doesn't necessarily correlate with latitude. That's why, for example, Pinot Noir also succeeds in Santa Barbara County, whose winegrowing areas, though hundreds of miles *south* of Napa and Sonoma, are much cooler because of their greater access to the influence of the ocean. If you're a fan of the 2004 movie

Californian climates don't correlate with latitude

Sideways, you'll recall that the film's Pinot-crazed protagonist, Miles, conducted his wine pilgrimage in Santa Barbara County's **Santa Ynez Valley**. Pinots featured in *Sideways* include, among others, those made by the Hitching Post (the restaurant where Miles and company took many of their meals) and by the Au Bon Climat winery. (Both wineries, like many others in California and elsewhere, create varietals of a number of different **tiers**. Though low-end Pinots from Santa Barbara County retail for about $20, a **single-vineyard** "cuvée" or a "reserve" wine can cost a lot more, without necessarily being a better wine.)

Nonalcoholic wines from California. Before we leave California for parts north and east (and just a little farther back in our imagined wine shop), let me mention one more thing. If you have family or friends who don't, for whatever reason, drink alcohol, that's not necessarily a reason for them to be totally excluded from the enjoyment of wine. There are lots of nonalcoholic wines on the market, but I bring this topic up in connection with California because the California winemaker J. Lohr creates some noteworthy **dealcoholized wines**, bottled under the Ariel label. Though the experience of drinking these wines—which include, among others, a Chardonnay, a Cabernet Sauvignon, a Merlot, a Zinfandel, and even a sparkler called Ariel Brut Cuvée—doesn't quite match that of drinking "real" wine (they're missing the weight and "heat" of alcohol), it comes amazingly close. That's because they're made in the same basic way—except that the finished wines are deprived of their alcohol through what's called a cold filtration, reverse-osmosis process. (This differs from the evaporation process used to make many other nonalcoholic wines, which, because it employs heat, can seriously damage a wine's flavor.) At about $8 a bottle, the Ariel dealcoholized wines are also terrific values. (Note: No nonalcoholic wine is completely alcohol-free; the Ariel wines contain less than 0.5 percent alcohol, however—a lower alcohol content than fresh orange juice.)

Washington State. No other state even approaches California in the amount of fine wine produced, but vintners all over the U.S. are rivaling California on the level of quality. Washington State and Oregon provide California's main domestic competition, and you're likelier to find their wines in an Anytown, U.S.A., wine shop than wines from Virginia, say, or Texas. After California, Washington is the largest producer of *vinifera* based wines, so let's start there.

Who'da thunk that you could make fine table wines in Washington? In fact, before a few decades ago, almost nobody *did* thunk it. In 1969, the state had two wineries; today, it boasts about 150. The vast majority of them are located in the southeastern corner of the state, in the **Columbia Valley**, Yakima Valley, Walla Walla, and Red Mountain AVAs. The climate here is *very* different from that of temperate, rain-soaked Seattle. Because the region is cut off from the ocean's moderating effects by the Cascade Mountains, which also act as a rain shield, its summers are hot and very dry (vineyards are irrigated), and its winters are *cold*. There's sometimes the risk of *vinifera* vines dying during extended freezes; on the other hand, the region's northerly latitude adds hours of sunlight to each day during the growing season. The white-wine varieties associated with northern Europe flourish here, but, interestingly, so do red-wine varieties like Merlot, Cabernet Sauvignon, and Syrah/Shiraz. (An interesting aspect of Washington viticulture is that eastern

Washington's range of varietals is incredible

Washington's sandy soils don't appeal to the *Phylloxera* aphid, so vines here are generally ungrafted.)

Unfortunately, relatively few Washington wineries have strong national distribution. But those that do are worth paying attention to. Don't turn up your nose at the big, well-known Washington State makers just because their names are familiar and their wines are relatively inexpensive. Wineries like Hogue Cellars, Covey Run, Columbia Crest, and Chateau Ste Michelle (all in the Columbia Valley) may produce hundreds of thousands of cases per year, but their wines regularly cull scores in the high 80s and 90s from the *Wine Advocate, Wine Spectator,* and other raters. Each of these wineries produces numerous varietals, and each offers several tiers of wines: the ones at the low end going for as little as seven or eight dollars a bottle and the highest-end reserves rarely exceeding $40. The range of varietals really is incredible. For example, Covey Run's Quail Label series (the maker's lowest tier, with wines averaging about $10 a bottle) includes a Cabernet Sauvignon, a Chardonnay, a Chenin Blanc, a Gewürztraminer, a Merlot, a Muscat, two Rieslings, a Sauvignon Blanc, and a Syrah, as well as a varietal made from a grape that in Washington State is called Lemberger. (This last is really worth trying: the grape's the same as an Austrian grape called Blaufränkisch; Washington's the only place in the U.S. that the variety—whose wines resemble the fresh 'n' fruity Gamay-based wines of Beaujolais—is grown.)

But we need to focus our attention, and here, in a spirit of experimentation, is what I suggest you do. Concentrate on Washington State's Merlots—commonly described as "succulent," "luscious," and "chocolatey." I'll give you two options:

• Taste "vertically" (so to speak), trying each of the Merlots made by a single maker. For example, stick with Hogue Cellars, and sample the low-end Hogue Label Merlot (about $10), the mid-tier Hogue Genesis Merlot (between $15 and $20), and the high-end Hogue Reserve Merlot ($30+). These wines differ according to the quality of the grapes used, the amount of oak ageing each receives, and so on. Can you detect the differences? Which do you like better, and why? (You might want to taste them blind to ensure you don't automatically choose the most expensive as your favorite.)

• Alternately, conduct a "horizontal" sort of tasting, trying one Merlot from each of three or four different makers—but make sure they're from equivalent tiers and the same vintage. If you want to take the low road, fine: taste a Hogue Label Merlot against a Covey Run Quail Label Merlot, against Columbia Crest Two Vines Merlot, against a Chateau Ste Michelle Columbia Valley Merlot. The whole exercise may set you back a total of $40, and—who knows?—you might discover your own "house Merlot" in the process.

Oregon. Wine-wise, Oregon could be described as "the Land of the Two Pinots": Pinot Noir and Pinot Gris. Though lots of other varieties are grown here—including, increasingly, Chardonnay—Oregon's fine-wine reputation hinges on the outstanding results that the state's winemakers have achieved with these two varieties.

Oregon, like Washington State, is a late (but winning) entry in the winemaking race. Wine grapes weren't grown here until forty or so years ago, and back then few bettors would've given the state very good odds of viticultural success. That's because the **Willamette Valley** of western Oregon—where a few brave souls established vineyards in the 1960s and where most of Oregon's wine indus-

Oregon is the Land of the Two Pinots

try is now concentrated—doesn't, on the face of it, seem to lend itself to the growing of grapes. It's cold and it's damp. Turns out, though, that the Willamette Valley's climate is very akin to that of Burgundy, which means that Pinot Noir relishes it. (In what seem replays of the notorious Paris Tasting—see pages 128–131—Oregon Pinot Noirs have several times outscored famous red burgundies at competitions pitting American against French wines.) Pinot Gris—which, remember, originally appeared in the vineyards of Burgundy as a mutation of Pinot Noir—is equally at home here.

So it's with Willamette Valley Pinot Noir and Pinot Gris varietals that you should kick off your friendship with Oregon's wines. Among the labels you're likely to find in wine shops nationally are King Estate (Oregon's largest winemaker) and Eyrie Vineyards (which pioneered Pinot Noir and Pinot Gris cultivation in Oregon). Like many others in Oregon and elsewhere, these winemakers produce several categories, or tiers, of wines: the ordinary "estate" wines are usually priced in the $15 to $25 range; single-vineyard and reserve wines can be substantially higher. King Estate's vineyards, by the way, are certified organic.

New York State. I'm not a native New Yorker, but having logged twenty-seven years of residence in the state, I hope you'll forgive me for just a touch of boosterism when it comes to New York wines. I have space here for only a few suggestions, but I hope that the next time you're in Manhattan, you'll make it a point to drop in at either of the two Vintage New York shops, which carry an impressive array of wines by New York State vintners, large and small. The shops, which are at the corner of Broome and Wooster Streets in SoHo and at Broadway and 93rd Street on the Upper West Side, feature tasting bars where you can quickly get acquainted with the surprising range of New York wines. (You can visit Vintage New York on the Web at www.vintagenewyork.com.)

Of course, you won't find anything like that variety in a typical wine shop—not even in New York! If your local wine merchant does carry New York wines, I suggest you look first for Rieslings from the **Finger Lakes** region—not just the pellucid Riesling, mentioned in chapter 6, made by Hermann J. Wiemer, but also the luscious dry and off-dry Johannisberg Riesling varietals produced by Dr. Konstantin Frank Vinifera Wine Cellars (about $16). Back in the 1950s, the eponymous

Dr. Frank, a Russian immigrant, drew nay-sayers' jeers when he insisted that European *vinifera* varieties, if carefully cultivated, could survive the frostbitten winters of the Finger Lakes, in the west-central part of the state. But the good doctor's prognosis was correct, and his efforts forever changed New York winemaking, which formerly had mostly depended on cold-hardy native American and French hybrid varieties.

As you learned in chapter 2, the best known of New York's other winegrowing regions, the **North Fork** of Long Island, has an altogether balmier climate than the Finger Lakes. *Vinifera* vines have an easier time of it here, and the resulting wines are generally more lushly fruity and fuller-flavored than their inland counterparts, which tend toward the elegant/acidic side of the spectrum. Of North Fork wines, I'd recommend anything by the Lenz Winery, with the proviso that Lenz's wines tend to be a little pricier than may be justified.

One final note: the French hybrids that once played a larger role in New York's wine industry are still grown here. One of these grapes, Vidal Blanc, is especially worth mentioning. This is the variety used in many Canadian icewines (see page 174), and Finger Lakes makers also employ it and other hybrids for similar frozen-grape-based confections. But dry and off-dry Vidal Blanc varietals are also made by some New York State producers; if you see one, snatch it up—but try to make sure it hasn't been oaked, since barrel fermentation and/or ageing depresses this otherwise breezy, cheerful wine.

AUSTRALIA

The next stop on this whirlwind tour is on the other side of the globe—but just a few steps farther into our imagined wine shop. It's the "Down Under" continent: Australia. These days, however, Australia is anything but down under when it comes to its wines' presence on American wine shops' shelves. Australia is currently vying with Italy for second place in the amount of wine exported to the U.S., and even a medium-size shop is likely to stock dozens of Australian wines. Though at least seventy different varieties are grown in Australia, a few dominate the export market, including Chardonnay, Cabernet Sauvignon, and the grape that comes immediately to most people's minds when they hear the phrase "Australian wine": Shiraz.

Shiraz, as we learned back in chapter 5, is the same grape as Syrah—so important an ingredient in the blended red wines of the southern Rhône Valley and also an important varietal in California. At their best, Aussie Shirazes are saturated with fruit—black raspberry, black cherry, and blackberry are common descriptors—while almost always carrying at least a hint of that black-pepper spiciness that's Syrah's/Shiraz's calling card. (At their worst, they can have an "overcooked" taste or a pepperiness that obscures other flavors.) Despite their power, Shirazes from Australia are usually extremely user-friendly: not overly tannic, versatile with meat-based meals, ready to drink when released. You don't need a wine education to like them, and that—coupled with the fact that so many are so reasonably priced—is reason enough for their popularity.

Aussie Shirazes are very user-friendly

On the down side (at least for me) is the predictability of Aussie Shirazes, at least in *Drinkology Wine*'s preferred price range of $10 to $20. I grabbed half a dozen off the shelf—some by very well-known makers like Penfolds and Jacob's Creek, others (like Alliance) whose labels were less familiar to me. The wines weren't indistinguishable, certainly, but they were closer in fragrance and taste than you'd expect six randomly chosen wines, even of the same type, to be. All were high-alcohol (13.5 to 14.5 percent), and the alcohol sensation was always definitely discernible on the nose. Each was vaguely, inconsequentially tannic. Several had a chocolate-covered cherry flavor; only one was noticeably woody (a mildly unpleasant effect). None strove for complexity. Though I wouldn't mind having any of these wines with a lamb burger or a spaghetti bolognese, none told me anything I didn't know before—which, depending on your point of view, might be a good thing. (To escape this homogeneity, you might have to spend more. Just a few nights before, I'd had an Australian Shiraz—a Hugo McLaren Vale 2001 Reserve; about $32—whose stewed fruit and dark chocolate flavors bordered on the awesome.)

Though our whirlwind wine-world tour demands that we barrel on, I don't want to leave Australia behind before mentioning that the continent's growers and winemakers have, over the past couple of decades, fomented a vinous revolution. Though fine-wine making in Australia is barely fifty years old, the techniques developed there over the past half-century have influenced grape growing and winemaking nearly everywhere. Australia's limited labor pool necessitated the mechanization of virtually every **Australian winemakers led a vinous revolution** aspect of vine cultivation and vinification, and technologies born in Australia have made their way around the globe. Moreover, Australians have never been particularly entranced by the idea of *terroir*—at least not in the European sense of adulating the uniqueness of sometimes tiny plots of land and the specificity of their wines. The great majority of Australian wines, varietals included, are made from grapes from different vineyards (sometimes separated by hundreds of miles), and

Australian makers have focused their attention on *blending* to achieve complexity of flavor and consistency of product. (This doesn't mean that location is utterly unimportant: the **Coonawarra** region of South Australia is, for example, celebrated for its Cabernet Sauvignons, and the **Barossa Valley**—also in South Australia—for its Shirazes.)

Australian winemakers' skill in the cellar has also led to a great demand elsewhere for their services: Aussies are now installed as chief winemakers at wineries from Long Island to Sicily, and an itinerant class of Australian enological consultants jets hither and yon, dispensing advice to anyone who can afford their services. From the early 1990s on, these **flying winemakers** have had an enormous impact on the world's wines, and in recent years others besides Australians have gotten into the "flying winemaker" game. (In fact, the most famous is probably Frenchman Michel Rolland.) Whether the flying winemakers' impact has been good (improving overall quality) or bad (remaking wines everywhere in a homogenized, "international" image) is a matter of enormous controversy.

NEW ZEALAND

Next, we bound over the Tasmanian Sea to the South Pacific country of New Zealand. Because of their geographical proximity (though, actually, they're separated by a thousand miles of water) and their shared cultural traditions (both were colonized by Britain), Australia and New Zealand tend to get lumped together in our minds—and their wines shelved together in our wine shops. This makes sense in another way, too: New Zealand's contemporary fine-wine industry was given a shot in the arm by one famous Australian winemaker (more about that in a moment). But in some ways it makes no sense at all: Australia's winegrowing regions are generally hot and arid; New Zealand's—among the southernmost vineyards in the world—are generally cool and rainy. Many of Australia's wines are fruit-laden powerhouses; New Zealand's are often marked by what Winespeakers call elegance and finesse. Australia's most famous varietal, Shiraz, is a red wine; New Zealand's is a white—Sauvignon Blanc.

New Zealand's fine wine industry is among the world's youngest. Historically, the country's strong Prohibitionist tendencies and restrictive wine and liquor laws (now mostly repealed) interfered with its growth. Moreover, a nasty (and to some extent ongoing) struggle with *Phylloxera* infestations long led New Zealand growers to focus on pest-resistant American hybrids rather than *vinifera* varieties—and the poor-quality wines that resulted merited no international notice. This didn't begin to change until the late 1970s/early 1980s, and the world at large didn't become aware of how good the new generation of New Zealand wines could be until 1986.

We can assign such a specific date to the event because that was the year that a wine called Cloudy Bay Sauvignon Blanc first appeared in Britain and America. (The wine had debuted in New Zealand just one year before.) The Cloudy Bay winery was the brainchild of Australian winemaker David **Wine writers went crazy for Cloudy Bay** Hohnen, who had first tasted N.Z. Sauvignon Blancs in 1983 and shortly afterward decided to set up his own operation in the **Marlborough** region of New Zealand's South Island. Wine writers—and wine drinkers generally—went crazy for this new wine's sensational combination of herbal and fruit flavors complemented by citrusy acidity, and the fanaticism has hardly diminished two decades later. Cloudy

Bay, now owned by the Champagne house Veuve Clicquot, produces sixty thousand cases of the stuff each year, and a goodly number are shipped to the U.S.—but just try to find a bottle! (If you do, buy it. It's not terribly expensive, just hard to lay your hands on.)

But if Cloudy Bay Sauvignon Blanc's extraordinary popularity renders it elusive, there's no reason to despair: there are plenty of other New Zealand makers creating outstanding Sauvignon Blancs. In fact, it's difficult to find a bad one. *Drinkology WINE* randomly plucked four bottles of 2004 vintage N.Z. Sauvignon Blancs off a neighborhood wine shop's shelves. All were from the Marlborough region; all were in the $12 to $20 price range; and three of the four were excellent, showing Sauvignon Blanc's knockout combo of grassy/herbal pungency and crisp, citrusy fruit. The fourth—interestingly, the highest-priced of the quartet—was marred by a slight wateriness, but it was a very drinkable wine all the same. (It should be noted that 2004 is considered a very good year for Marlborough Sauvignon Blancs.)

Though you should probably get acquainted with New Zealand's wines by sampling some of its Sauvignon Blancs, you shouldn't stop there. New Zealand Pinot Noirs are up-and-coming contenders against those of California, Oregon, and Burgundy. (By now, it shouldn't surprise you that Pinot Noir can make a go of it in New Zealand's relatively cool climate.)

SOUTH AMERICA—ARGENTINA AND CHILE

The first thing you need to know about the wines of Argentina and Chile—the next stops on our world tour—is that they are probably the *best wine values* on the planet (and, by extension, in your local wine shop). Whether they'll remain so for long is hard to say, since price does have a way of catching up with quality, but for now it remains possible to buy superb Argentine and Chilean wines for well under $20 a bottle. What's more, your choices keep expanding, as more and more South American wine makes its way to the United States each year.

Wine has been made in Argentina and Chile since the mid-sixteenth century, shortly after the Spanish conquest. But South American wines' rise to international prominence is a very, very recent phenomenon. A number of factors— the fall of oppressive military dictatorships, an influx of foreign investment, the widespread

Malbec just loves its adopted home

adoption of modern winemaking techniques—coalesced to invigorate the wine industries in both Chile and Argentina in the 1990s. We're the beneficiaries. (American wine drinkers are also inadvertently the beneficiaries of Argentina's monetary troubles during the early 2000s, which have kept its wines' prices absurdly low.)

I asked my friend Elizabeth Aldrich, an American who's lucky enough to have a second home in Chile, to explain for us the wines she knows and loves so well. (See the sidebar on pages 247–250.) I've assigned myself the easier job of talking about Argentina's wines —easier because what you, as a wine newbie, need to know about Argentine wine can be summarized in one word: *Malbec*.

Malbec, you'll recall from chapter 5, is the red-wine grape, originally from Bordeaux, whose star has risen in Argentina even as it's sunk in its native land. For reasons unknown, Malbec does extraordinarily well in its adopted home—especially in the foothills of the Andes Mountains in the region of **Mendoza** in west-central Argentina. (Mendoza, which includes the subregions of Luján de Cuyo and Maipú, produces about two-thirds of Argentina's wine.) The Mendoza region is sunny (averaging something like 320 cloudless days per year), is almost desert-dry (necessitating irrigation), and has an exceedingly wide **thermal amplitude**, which simply means that it enjoys warm days and cool nights—a variation that grapevines love.

No less an authority than wine guru Robert Parker has declared Argentine Malbec the wine of the future: "By the year 2015," he writes, "the greatness of Argentinean wines made from the Malbec grape will be understood as a given." Here's one place, then, that newcomers to the world of wine can jump ahead of the curve. Some of your oenophile friends may never have tasted an Argentine Malbec; introduce them to the wine and you'll retain bragging rights forever.

The Mendoza region Malbecs and Malbec-based blends I sampled—and which ranged from just $9 up to about $40 a bottle (an unusually high price for a Malbec)—were without exception very good. Here are some notes. Trumpeter Malbec/Syrah 2003 ($9): "This very fruity, chewy wine is almost too delicious for me." Felipe Rutini Malbec 2002 ($15): "A thin nose, but it really makes up for it on the finish—the wine's flavor *expands* in the mouth." Alamos Malbec 2003 ($12): "Tobacco on the nose; a beautifully dry finish. The tannins, though definitely present, aren't at all bothersome. I even like the untamed oak in this wine." Cateña Malbec 2001 ($20): "Layers and layers of flavor: chocolate, earth, fruit." Cateña Alta Malbec 2001 ($40): "An extremely dramatic wine; the flavor is *explosive* in the mouth."

Not a bad showing for five randomly selected wines, huh? Advisory: Do beware of going too low on price. You can find Argentine Malbecs for six or seven dollars a bottle, but these are likely to be thin on flavor because their makers permit very high yields. (Hence the rock-bottom prices.)

CHILE? COOL.
BY ELIZABETH ALDRICH

Before my first trip to Chile in the late 1970s, my wine-tasting experience had been limited to whatever I could afford on my meager dancer's salary and whatever my friends brought to our potluck dinners. (Looking back, I remember everything seeming sugary-sweet, and I strongly suspect that few of the bottles had corks.) The gusto with which my new Chilean friends drank and talked about wine therefore came as a colossal revelation—and an education. At the end of that first visit, I lugged home twelve bottles of Chilean wine, all purchased at a Santiago supermarket for under three dollars a bottle.

On returning to New York, I discovered that my local liquor store did indeed stock some decent and inexpensive Chilean wines. In those days, it was possible to buy a good Chilean wine for $5. Regrettably, that price-point is today reserved for Gato Blanco and Gato Negro, which despite their jazzy labels are musts to avoid. But for just a few dollars more, you can sample Chilean wines of an entirely different caliber.

In 1548—more than seventy years before the *Mayflower* brought the Pilgrims to the shores of Massachusetts—Francisco de Carabantes, a Spanish priest, planted the first grapevines in Chile's Maipo Valley. It was France, however, that provided the chief inspiration for Chile's first three hundred years of winemaking; by the mid-nineteenth century, French-inspired châteaux dotted Chile's landscape, and wealthy Chileans engaged French winemakers and imported French vines for their estates.

Wine production worldwide changed forever when *Phylloxera* appeared in the 1860s. Within a generation, nearly two-thirds of Europe's vineyards had been destroyed. With no effective chemical or biological controls, grafting vines onto resistant rootstocks (from North America) is the only effective means of dealing with this pest, which continues to afflict nearly all major winegrowing regions of the world. But miraculously—perhaps owing to Chile's geographical isolation—*Phylloxera* has never affected Chilean grapevines. (It's never been a problem in Argentina, either.) Abandoning their devastated vineyards, many Basque, Spanish, and French winemakers fled to Chile, eager to begin anew, and for the next hundred years they produced solid, if not always distinguished, wines. Then, in the 1980s, Chile's economic and political fortunes changed. A number of important European winemakers—notably the Rothschilds (of Château Lafite-Rothschild fame) and Spain's Miguel Torres—bought out established Chilean vineyards. Wineries invested enormous sums in their operations, and by the early 1990s, with improved export markets, Chile had become the "Bordeaux of South America."

With about 265,000 acres of vineyards, Chile ranks tenth in the world in wine production. The country's twelve principal winegrowing regions occupy a series of valleys in the central part of the country. These valleys are protected on the east by the Andes and on the west by low hills (called the *cordillera*) that hug the coastline. The sun shines nearly every day, but the vineyards also benefit from the fogs that roll in off the ocean as the cold waters of the Humboldt Current mingle with the warm coastal air. The climate is semi-arid, and the vineyards are flood-irrigated (except in the Casablanca Valley, where drip irrigation is used). While summer days—in Chile, that means December, January, and February—may reach the upper 80s, nights are cool. These natural conditions are perfect for growing grapes.

Each of the twelve valleys, however, produces wines that are unlike those of the other valleys, and when purchasing a Chilean wine it is important to look at the label to identify the wine's place of origin. A Sauvignon Blanc from the Curicó Valley will taste very different than one from the

Casablanca Valley, and a Cabernet Sauvignon from the Maipo Valley is distinct from one produced in the Rapel Valley. Because of these differences, most of Chile's largest wine producers maintain vineyards in several valleys.

Although nearly twenty varieties are grown in Chile, most of the country's fine wines are made from Cabernet Sauvignon, Merlot, Chardonnay, and Sauvignon Blanc. In the Casablanca Valley, Chile's newest and potentially greatest winegrowing region, vintners have also had early success with Pinot Noir as well as with a grape called Carmenère. (Carmenère was an important vine in Europe until it was virtually wiped out by the *Phylloxera* epidemic.)

The Maipo Valley, located near the capital, Santiago, is the oldest and most prestigious winegrowing area in Chile. All of Chile's best-known vineyards have a major presence in the Maipo Valley, which is primarily known for its Cabernet Sauvignons. Among Maipo Valley reds, both Viña Santa Rita's Medalla Real Special Reserve Cabernet Sauvignon (about $18) and its Cabernet Sauvignon Reserva (about $12) have very intense color and flavors of raspberries and blackberries, with just a hint of vanilla. Santa Rita also makes a nice Reserva Merlot, which retails for about $12. One of the best Maipo wines for the money is Viña Santa Ema's Cabernet Sauvignon–Merlot blend (about $11). Santa Ema also makes my all-time favorite Chilean red: the Merlot Reserva, which can be had for about $12. If you're in the mood to treat yourself, try the Puente Alto don Melchor Cabernet Sauvignon made by the Maipo Valley's most famous winery, Concha y Toro. It may set you back about $45, but it's a wine you won't soon forget.

The Curicó Valley's Viña Echeverría (still run by a Basque family that emigrated to Chile in 1740) produces very fine reds: the Reserva Molina Cabernet Sauvignon (about $18) is highly recommended. Two great bargains

CHILE? COOL.

come from the Rapel Valley: Casa Lapostolle's highly satisfying Cabernet Sauvignon and Concha y Toro's delightful, medium-bodied Carmenère. (No matter what the valley of origin, you can hardly go wrong with a wine from Casa Lapostolle.) The Aconcagua Valley's Viña Errazuriz Cabernet Sauvignon is likewise an excellent buy. All three of these wines sell for about $10 a bottle.

The best Chilean whites come from the Casablanca Valley, located about fifty miles northwest of Santiago. Casablanca is a newcomer to the Chilean scene; most of its vineyards have only been producing since the late 1990s. Veramonte, the largest winemaker in the valley, produces a Chardonnay that is full of citrus and apple flavors, with just a hint of honey. Veramonte's Sauvignon Blanc, rich in tropical fruit and herbs, is just perfect for a hot summer's day. Both cost about $10. As of this writing, two of the Casablanca Valley's best Sauvignon Blancs—those made by Viña Mar and Casas del Bosque—are not yet available in the United States. As soon as they are, run—don't walk—to your local wine merchant and demand that they be stocked.

Though the Casablanca Valley is celebrated primarily for its extraordinary whites, its reds are also showing great promise. Veramonte's Primus (about $16), a blend of Carmenère, Merlot, and Cabernet Sauvignon that's aged for twelve months in oak barrels, is rich and full bodied, with tolerable tannins. Its Casablanca Valley Winemaker's Selection Pinot Noir is a steal at about $10.

Although the days of good $5 Chilean wines are long gone, it's still possible to experience a classy, complex wine from the world's longest, skinniest country for $12 or less a bottle.

SOUTH AFRICA

Question: What was Napoleon's favorite wine? I know you're thinking the answer has to be something grand from Bordeaux or Burgundy, right? Or maybe a rustic wine from his native Corsica? Or—at the outside—maybe one of those sweet Hungarian Tokays so popular with nineteenth-century monarchs?

Answer: None of the above. The wine most beloved by the Little Corporal was a sweet wine, yes, but it came from, of all places, *South Africa*. Called Constantia and made from Muscat Blanc à Petits Grains (see page 193), it was one of the most sought-after wines in Europe from the late eighteenth century through the mid-1800s. Unfortunately—no matter how strong your Napoleon complex—you can't try it for yourself. The firm that made it long ago went bust, though a relatively new winery, Klein Constantia ("Little Constantia"), bought up part of the original estate's land in the 1980s and now markets a wine called Vin de Constance, promoted as a re-creation of the original.

Given the extremely limited U.S. market for sweet, dessert-type wines, however, the South Africa section of your local wine shop is *much* likelier to stock a range of South African dry wines: probably a Shiraz or two, maybe a well-made Chenin Blanc (or Steen, as the South Africans call it; see page 187), and in all probability a number of Sauvignon Blancs. The overall selection will doubtless be small. That's partly an aftereffect of apartheid; an embargo prohibiting the importation of South African wine—and other products—into the U.S. wasn't lifted until the fall of the white-minority government in the early 1990s, so South African vintners are still establishing a reputation with American consumers.

Most of South Africa's vineyards—the South Africans charmingly call them **wine farms**—are in the country's **Western Cape Province**, and most, in fact, lie within 250 miles of the Cape of Good Hope. The South African wine regions you're most likely to find represented among the offerings at American wine shops are those clustered close to the provincial capital of Cape Town, especially the **Stellenbosch** and **Paarl** regions. Most of the international varieties are grown in South Africa, but the country also possesses a few varieties—crosses of European grapes, actually—that are found nowhere else. The best-known of these is Pinotage, a cross between Pinot Noir and another French red-wine grape, Cinsault. Pinotage varietals can be densely, exuberantly fruity. (The well-known South African maker Goats Do Roam produces a Pinotage–dominated red blend that costs less than $10.)

White wines, however, constitute something like 85 percent of the country's overall production, and it's South Africa's Chardonnays, Chenin Blancs, and, especially, Sauvignon Blancs that are gathering a devoted following abroad. As you've already heard me testify, I like New Zealand Sauvignon Blancs very much. By comparison, I think it would be fair to say that I've *loved* virtually every South African Sauvignon Blanc I've had. What distinguishes them for me is a creaminess that's missing from their New Zealand counterparts. A recent, spectacularly good (and affordable) find: Fairview Sauvignon Blanc, from the Paarl region (about $10 a bottle).

We're about to cross the great divide between the New World and the Old. From South Africa, we fly six thousand miles almost due north to what remains—and probably always shall remain—the greatest wine-making country on earth: France. The journey inside our imagined wine shop is a lot quicker: we simply walk to the opposite side of the store, where the Old World wines face off against their New World competitors. The largest Old World section belongs, of course, to France, which still exports more wine to the U.S. than any other country.

FRANCE

Thinking of conquering Gaul? Well, when setting out to learn about the wines of France, the only reasonable way to proceed is to admit defeat in advance. The numbers alone are mind-numbing: at the turn of the millennium, France was producing about *550 million* liters of wine annually. In the region of Bordeaux alone, there are roughly ten thousand *châteaux*. No, that doesn't mean that Bordeaux has a whole heck of a lot of *castles*: in Winespeak, the word ***château*** (pl., ***châteaux***; both pronounced shah-TOH) means a wine-growing, winemaking estate that bottles its own wines. There may be a castle on the property, or not. In any event, Bordeaux has *ten thousand* such estates—plus thousands of other growers who don't bottle their own wines but sell their grapes or their wine to other, larger operations. (By the way, in Burgundy and some other places in France, the word ***domaine*** [duh-MEN], rather than *château*, is used for "estate.")

Now, granted, much of the wine produced in Bordeaux (and in the other wine-growing regions of France, as well) never leaves France; some of it is of poor quality, and nobody pays it very much mind. Only a relatively small fraction of the estates of Bordeaux merit international attention. The trouble is, a "relatively small fraction" of ten thousand is still quite a daunting number: the fourth edition (2003) of Robert M. Parker, Jr.'s authoritative *Bordeaux: A Consumer's Guide to the World's Finest Wines* discusses the wines produced by nearly *seven hundred* different estates. (I counted.) But the true complexity of this situation doesn't really emerge until you add in the fact that each producer's wine differs—sometimes subtly, sometimes markedly—from vintage to vintage, and that many good Bordeaux wines (the reds and also some of the whites) get better as they age in the bottle, meaning that knowing *when* to drink a Bordeaux wine can be as important as knowing which to drink.

In short, it takes years of effort, including a lot of elbow-bending, even to begin to knowledgeably appreciate the wines of just *one* of France's many winegrowing regions. And the wines of France as a whole constitute a subject that's incomprehensibly vast and unfathomably intricate: the Burgundy region is even more complicated than Bordeaux—and differently so.

So do yourself a favor and *give up*. Relax, do some stretches, breathe deeply, pour yourself a nice, hefty glass of *quelque chose*, and come to terms with the fact that you'll probably never be an expert in *les vins de la France*. It's only then that you'll be able to begin your exploration with a non-self-defeating (in fact, a salutary) attitude. It's to be hoped that that journey of discovery will ultimately take you far and wide, though this little book can't do more than provide you with some basic wayfinding apparatus.

The AC System and Other Classifications. It was way back in chapter 1 that we first encountered the Appellation d'Origine Contrôlée (ah-pel-lah-SYAWn dor-oh-ZHEEN cawn-troh-LAY) system, or AOC (or AC) for short. You'll recall, I hope, that the AC system—which began being instituted in the 1930s and whose original purpose was to combat an epidemic of fraudulent mislabeling that was then doing serious damage to the French wine industry's reputation—assigns place-of-origin names to many of France's wines and that it strictly regulates numerous aspects of viticulture and winemaking in each designated appellation.

Most of the French wines you'll find in American wine shops carry AC designations, though such "appellation wines" represent something less than 50 percent of total French wine production. Wines that don't meet rigid AC standards—which specify the types of grapes that may be grown in each appellation, maximum yields, allowable winemaking practices, alcohol content of the finished wine, and so on—fall into one of three other categories: (1) **VDQS wines** (the acronym stands for *Vin Délimité de Qualité Supérieure*, desig-nating wines from areas that haven't

Some serious winemakers opt out of the AC system

yet qualified for full AC status), (2) ***vins de pays*** (vaan duh pay-YEE; lit-erally, "country wines," but better thought of as regional wines expressive of the areas in which they're made),   and (3) ***vins de table*** (vaan duh TAH-bl; usually simple but sometimes characterless wines made from grapes grown without any concern for limiting yield). Though *vins de pays* and *vins de table* are usually of lesser quality than appellation wines, it's important to recognize that this isn't *always* the case. Some quite seri-ous French winemakers choose to opt out of the AC system because they view its rules as oppressive and discouraging to experimentation. Though their "unorthodox" wines receive *vin de pays*—or sometimes even *vin de table*—designations by default, they may, in fact, be excellent.

As was briefly mentioned in chapter 1, rookie oenophiles are some-times confused by the *concentric* nature of French appellations—that is, that large appellations are often subdivided into smaller appellations whose boundaries may, in turn, contain even smaller appellations. The general rule, again, is that the more specific the territory (or *terroir*) denominated by an appellation, the better the wine. That rule, though, comes with several provisos: The first is that in poor vintages, the "best" appellations may produce wines of lesser quality than those that the surrounding, second- or third-rate appellations produce in good years. The second is that for wine newbies (and even for some people whose experience of French wine is rather substantial), it may be sometimes difficult to detect much of a difference between a top-rated appellation's wines and those of its less well regarded neighbors. And the third proviso is that even with these qualifying statements thrown in, I'm greatly oversimplifying the situation!

Adding to the complexity is that several of France's great wine-producing regions—Bordeaux, Burgundy, Champagne, and others—have classification schemes that overlay the AC system. These other classifications sometimes predate the *appellations contrôlées*, and they are region-specific—the precise classificatory terms and their meanings differ from one region to another. Bordeaux has four such schemes (yes, four), but, to illustrate how these classifications work, let's turn to Champagne, which presents a comparatively easy-to-understand case:

Though the Champagne appellation has thousands of vineyards, these are grouped into about three hundred *crus*. Now, the French word *cru* (KROO) literally means "growth," but it's better to think of a *cru* as a demarcated area—sometimes a single vineyard, sometimes (as in Champagne) a group of vineyards belonging to a certain commune, or village—that is ranked against other areas within a given classification scheme. (Make sense? I thought not. But stay with me.) In Champagne, each *cru* is accorded a quality ranking somewhere between 80 and 100 percent. (Don't ask why the scale begins at 80; there are certain things that one just doesn't need to know.) Anyway, of the three hundred or so Champagne *crus*, only seventeen are rated 100 percent; these are the **grands crus** (GRAW^n KROO, or "great growths")—the pinnacle within Champagne's classificatory system. Another thirty-eight possess ratings between 90 and 99 percent; these are the **premiers crus** (preh-MYAY KROO), which literally means "first growths"—even though these are the *second*-highest-rated areas. (All the other Champagne *crus*, rated 80 to 89 percent, are just plain *crus*.)

Now, if you're considering pouring yourself a Champagne bath, settling into it, and slitting your wrists, don't. Familiarity and comfort with this and the other classification systems will come over time. Or it won't—but there's still no need to contemplate suicide. Nobody will be quizzing you on this—unless, of course, you're intending to become a sommelier or have an annoying wine-snob spouse. (In the latter case, divorce is the more sensible option.)

Wine-wise, all Gaul is divided into innumerable parts, but it's likely that your local wine shop's French offerings will mostly be composed of wines from only six major regions, including Champagne (but Champagnes will be shelved with the other sparklers). The others are Bordeaux, Burgundy, the Loire Valley, Alsace, and the Rhône Valley.

A (Very Brief) Introduction to Bordeaux. If you've been dutifully following along, you'll have picked up bits and pieces about Bordeaux throughout this book. The many references have been inevitable, since Bordeaux is the source of so much of the world's wine culture and, not incidentally, the homeland of several of the "international" grape varieties, including Cabernet Sauvignon, Merlot, and Sauvignon Blanc.

You've learned that Bordeaux is renowned for its dry red, dry white, and sweet white wines; that red Bordeaux are usually blends of some combination of Cabernet Sauvignon, Merlot, and Cabernet Franc (with Petit Verdot and, very occasionally, Malbec playing minor parts); and that white Bordeaux, both dry and sweet, are usually blends of Sauvignon Blanc and the grape called Sémillon. (Sémillon often plays the dominant role.) And you've learned that the best red Bordeaux, dry white Bordeaux, and sweet, botrytized white Bordeaux are all noted for their ability to evolve in the bottle, ultimately becoming wines of great depth and complexity. If you've been paying especially close attention, you'll also have inferred that many of the world's red wines (especially those based on Cabernet Sauvignon) represent attempts by winemakers elsewhere to emulate the greatness of Bordeaux.

It's time to amplify that knowledge with a little bit of geography and just a *soupçon* of Bordeaux history. *Bordeaux* (which is also the name of the region's largest city) roughly translates as "the edge of the waters"— an extremely apt name, given how important nearness to the sea has been in determining the character of Bordeaux' wines and aiding their rise to international prominence.

Situated in the southwestern corner of France, the Bordeaux region surrounds the Gironde estuary and its two main tributaries, the Dordogne and Garonne rivers. The Gironde penetrates far inland, carrying the Atlantic Ocean's moderating influences with it, creating a climate that, when the weather behaves itself, couples the best aspects of Mediterranean and cooler winegrowing regions. (Spring frosts can, however, sometimes wreak havoc on a vintage, as can autumn rains.) In the years before the development of efficient overland transport, the sea's proximity also made it easy for Bordeaux to ship its wines abroad. For centuries, Bordeaux' chief foreign market was Great Britain, and the Brits' passion for claret (their word for red Bordeaux) secured Bordeaux' fame.

You may recall, too, that the Bordeaux appellation, which encompasses a huge chunk of territory (almost 250,000 acres of vineyards— almost as much as in *all* of Chile), contains more than fifty smaller appellations.

The Brits' passion for claret secured Bordeaux' fame

Only a handful, however—well, maybe two handfuls— deserve being committed to memory (if, that is, you have the inclination).

The *extremely simplified* map of Bordeaux on the following page shows the best-known appellations. On the **left bank** of the Gironde is the **Médoc** (may-DAWK), divided into the Bas-Médoc (BAH may-DAWK; meaning "lower Médoc"—that is, downriver; nearer the sea) and the **Haut-Médoc** (OH may-DAWK; "upper Médoc"). Note: If a wine's label simply carries the Médoc appellation, it's from the Bas-Médoc—a peculiarity of the AC system.

It's the Haut-Médoc that merits your chief attention, since it contains four communal appellations whose red wines are known the world over: **St.-Estèphe** (saant eh-STEFF), **Pauillac** (poh-YAK), **St.-Julien** (saan zhoo-LYAA[n]), and **Margaux** (mahr-GOH). If you're already feeling overwhelmed by the hard-to-say place names, just remember this: the Médoc as a whole is Cabernet Sauvignon country; most of its red wines have Cabernet as their primary constituent—and the best are therefore superbly structured wines capable of extended evolution in bottle.

South of the Médoc and arrayed along the left bank of the Gironde's southerly tributary, the Garonne, are the appellations of **Graves**

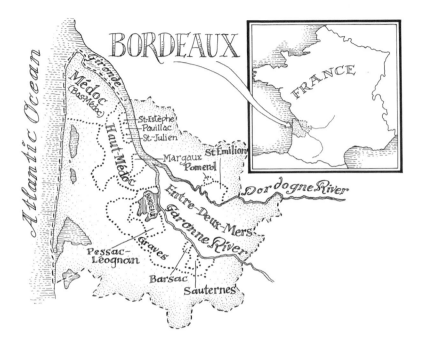

(GRAHV), **Pessac-Léognan** (peh-SAK lay-oh-NYAAⁿ), **Sauternes** (soh-TAIRN), and **Barsac** (BAR-sak). Though Graves and Pessac-Léognan produce both red and white wines (and, in fact, Pessac-Léognan is home to one of the top Bordeaux reds, Château Haut-Brion), this whole area is mostly white wine territory. Pessac-Léognan—which was carved out of the larger Graves district in 1987—is the source of Bordeaux' most highly regarded dry whites; Sauternes and Barsac are the most important of the appellations producing sweet, botrytized whites.

Between the Garonne and the Dordogne rivers lies a large, wedge-shaped swathe of land called **Entre-Deux-Mers** (awntr duhr MAIR; somewhat hyperbolically, the name means "between two seas"). Both white and red wines are made here, but only whites may carry the Entre-Deux-Mers appellation. (The reds are labeled simply *Appellation Bordeaux Contrôlée*.)

Traveling north from Entre-Deux-Mers and heading across the Dordogne River to its **right bank**, we again enter red wine territory. The most important of the right-bank appellations are **St.-Émilion** (saan tay-mee-LYAW[n]) and **Pomerol** (paw-meh-RAWL). Here, Merlot reigns supreme, though, once again, it's usually blended with other varieties.

Now that you've got the lay of the land down pat (yeah, right), let's turn to the Bordeaux classifications. If you have any wine knowledge at all, you've probably heard the term **classified growths** used in connection with Bordeaux wines. (I know: "classified growths" sounds as if it means medically categorized tumors; the French *crus classés* just doesn't translate felicitously into English.) There are, as I've said, four classifications in Bordeaux. The earliest and most famous is the **1855 Classification**, which was performed at the behest of French emperor Napoleon III and which, with extremely little revision, has remained in effect ever since. It places the top sixty red wine–producing *châteaux* of the Haut-Médoc and one Pessac-Léognan (formerly Graves) *château* (the aforementioned Haut-Brion) into five categories, ranging from the *premiers crus* ("first growths") through the *deuxièmes* ("second"), *troisièmes* ("third"), *quatrièmes* ("fourth") and *cinquièmes* ("fifth") *crus*. (Respectable Médoc wines that don't rate a spot in the 1855 Classification may be

> **It's a mark of distinction for a wine to be classified at all**

labeled *cru bourgeois*.) Don't make the mistake of thinking that a fifth-growth Médoc is a poor quality wine: it's a mark of distinction for a wine to be classified at all.

You can find the full 1855 Classification, as well as background information on each of the Médoc *châteaux*, at several sites on the Web (www.cellarnotes.net/medoc_classification.htm provides an especially thorough overview). You're probably at least vaguely familiar, however, with the names of the five first-growth *châteaux*, which, besides Haut-Brion, include Château Lafite-Rothschild, Château Margaux, Château Latour, and Château Mouton-Rothschild (the last being a late addition, joining the first rank only in 1973). And unless you're independently wealthy or regularly rub elbows with those who are, your acquaintance with these wines is likely to *remain* vague, since they are inordinately expensive. Price depends partly on the quality of a vintage and partly on the vagaries of the luxury-goods market: 2000 vintage first growths averaged a whopping $463 per bottle on release; the average price, on release, of a 2001 vintage first growth was "only" $173.

The year 1855 also saw the establishment of a classification of the sweet white wines of Sauternes and Barsac. (Only one wine inhabits its topmost rank: Château d'Yquem [see page 170], designated a *grand premier cru*, or "great first growth.") The top red wines of St.-Émilion were classified a century later, in 1955, and the top wines of Graves in 1959. Now, mind you, the classifications provide only a generally accepted consensus about which *châteaux* have historically produced the finest wines in these few Bordeaux appellations. There are thousands of wines from these and the other Bordeaux appellations that are excluded from the "who's who"–type lists. For example, the *châteaux* of Pomerol—a number of which produce reds regarded as among Bordeaux' best—remain unclassified. Go figure.

So here's the question: What do you *do* with all this information? One thing's for certain: The little I've given you so far won't be much help when you're standing in a wine shop scratching your *tête* and trying to select a Bordeaux. What you need is *informed, detailed advice*—advice about vintages, about makers, about whether a wine is drinkable now or needs to be held for a few (or even many) years, and—here's the most important thing—about whether a particular Bordeaux is even any good at all. It's to be hoped that your wine shop's staff will be able to help you choose—but take it from me, that's a bit of a crap shoot.

So what *do* you do? Well, if you're planning on having more than just the occasional bottle of Bordeaux, you've got to turn your interest into an avocation. You've got to study: Robert Parker's *Bordeaux: A Consumer's Guide* is, as mentioned above, the essential reference. (It's updated every

---

BORDEAUX CHEAT-SHEET

Here are the top Bordeaux appellations, listed by the kind of wine(s) they're best known for. The dominant grape variety or varieties appear after the appellation's name.

Reds
Margaux (Cabernet Sauvignon)
Pauillac (Cabernet Sauvignon)
Pomerol (Merlot)
St.-Émilion (Merlot)
St.-Estèphe (Cabernet Sauvignon)
St.-Julien (Cabernet Sauvignon)

Reds and Dry Whites
Graves/Pessac-Léognan (Cabernet Sauvignon/Sémillon and Sauvignon Blanc)

Sweet Whites
Barsac (Sémillon and Sauvignon Blanc)
Sauternes (Sémillon and Sauvignon Blanc)

few years.) *Wine Spectator* and the other wine rags regularly rate Bordeaux and run special features whenever the latest vintage to hit the market appears. (And, in fact, earlier, when many Bordeaux wines—still in barrel—are given their first public tasting in the March following the harvest.) There are, in fact, endless resources available. So get crackin'.

If, however, you don't want to turn the wines of Bordeaux into a lifetime's passion, I can offer just a few tentative suggestions. First, if you're just beginning your exploration of red Bordeaux, it may make sense to start with a reasonably priced wine from St.-Émilion or Pomerol—something in the $25 to $35 range. Because St.-Émilion and Pomerol wines, all of which are reds, are mostly dominated by Merlot, they are generally rounder and softer—and drinkable earlier in their lives—than the Cabernet Sauvignon–dominated reds of the Médoc.

If it's a dry white wine you're interested in, the going's a little easier: assuming you like the "serious" style—these are wines to drink attentively, not unconsciously quaff—you'll probably be pleased with virtually any Pessac-Léognan AC white you pull off the shelf. With a little advice from a wine shop salesman, *Drinkology WINE*'s tasting crew sampled five recent-vintage Pessac-Léognan whites ranging from about $30 to about $40 a bottle, and we liked them all. (Our collective favorite, in case you're interested, was a Les Planticrs du Haut-Brion 2000, whose nose reminded our tasters of burlap, banana, and egg cream, and whose flavor was a wowie-zowie combo of clove, cinnamon, and orange rind.)

If you've never tried a Bordeaux dessert wine and would like to, I'll make a suggestion some will consider lowbrow: try the Sauternes made by Barton & Guestier, a long-established, respected Bordeaux ***négociant*** (nay-goh-SYAWn)—that is, a wine merchant. (Many *négociants* blend and bottle wines under their own labels; some also own vineyards.) The

Do I Detect a Note of Motor Oil?

Garage bands occasionally knock the rock 'n' roll world on its ear. So-called **garage wines** have done something similar in the rarefied precincts of Bordeaux. The trend began twenty-plus years ago, when several members of the Thienpont family (Belgians who've been making wine in Bordeaux for seventy years) bought a couple of acres of vineyard in Pomerol and started making tiny quantities of finely crafted wine in, yes, a revamped garage. They christened their product Château Le Pin, and the wine wasn't just a hit—it was a blockbuster, drawing critical raves and commanding prices rivaling, then exceeding, those of some top Bordeaux *châteaux*. The Thienponts' success inspired others, often people with full-time jobs in other trades, who were determined to create their own, superior Bordeaux wines on a very small scale. Though not all these do-it-yourself *vignerons* ("winemakers") ply their second profession in garages, the French press dubbed them *les garagistes*—and the name stuck. (A politer term for these diminutive winemaking operations is **microchâteaux**.) Nowadays, the "garage wine" phenomenon isn't limited to Bordeaux, nor even to France: in Australia, California, South Africa, and elsewhere there are legions of small-time makers convinced that by lavishing attention on their little plots of vines, harvesting at the moment of perfect ripeness, and lovingly fashioning their wines, they can outperform the big, well-known producers—in quality, in critical kudos, and in the prices they can charge. Price, of course, is often a function of rarity—something that wineries (if you can call them that) releasing only a couple of hundred cases a year have no trouble achieving. In California, these limited-quantity artisanal wines are usually called **cult wines**—for the fervent, cultlike following they kindle.

B&G Sauternes isn't extraordinary, but it's a good-enough introduction to this unusual genre of wine; plus, it's widely available and retails for what, for a Sauternes, is an exceedingly reasonable price: about $30. (That's for a full bottle; many Sauternes and Barsacs are more commonly sold in half-bottles.)

Or, you know, you could just pick your Bordeaux—red and white, dry and sweet—at random, and see what you come up with. If you don't like what you get (assuming you don't spend too much), just chalk it up to experience; if you do, buy a case. I find it instructive that the most satisfying red Bordeaux I sampled during the writing of this book was a stray gift from a business client. From an unprepossessing appellation, Lalande de Pomerol (which is sort of Pomerol's "backyard," if you will), this Château Jean de Gué Cuvée Prestige 2000 was incredibly velvety—pure tongue-cloaking Merlot lushness. I looked the gift horse in the mouth and priced it on the Web; it retails for about thirty bucks. *Incroyable.*

An (Equally Brief) Introduction to Burgundy. Bordeaux is complex; Burgundy is *murder.* The mind-boggling intricacy of this celebrated wine region—Bourgogne (bohr-GUNyuh), in French—is partly a result of history. Up until the French Revolution, winemaking in this sliver of territory in east-central France was mostly the province of monasteries and landholding aristocrats. In 1791, the Revolutionary government broke up these holdings, selling them off in smallish parcels. The Napoleonic Code—the legal system introduced in France during the early nineteenth century—led to the vineyards' further subdivision, since its inheritance laws mandated that on the death of a landowner his property be divvied up equally

Bordeaux is complex; Burgundy is *murder*

among his sons. The heirs' portions were, of course, divided again on *their* deaths—and so on and on down through the generations.

If you add in the transfer of property through marriage and the buying and selling of land that always goes on, you can begin to imagine the sort of situation that exists today in Burgundy. A single vineyard may have scores of owners, some with only a few rows of vines to their names, and, conversely, a given producer may own plots in a number of different vineyards. Granted, many of Burgundy's smaller growers sell their grapes or juice to *négociants* (merchants), who vinify, age, bottle, and sell the wine. (Many *négociants*, who together control nearly two-thirds of the Burgundy wine trade, also have their own vineyards and/or plots within a number of different multi-owner vineyards.) But numerous relatively small growers make and bottle their wines themselves. If a Burgundy producer bottles his—or, nowadays, her—own wine, the label will carry the phrase *mis en bouteille au domaine,* "put in the bottle at the estate." (But note that in Burgundy the word *domaine,* unlike *château* in Bordeaux, doesn't necessarily denote a single, contiguous chunk of property.)

Burgundy's complexity, however, doesn't only have to do with how ownership of the vineyards is apportioned; it also has to do with the character of the land itself. So infinitely variable are Burgundy's *terroirs* that distinctions are drawn not just between wines from different vineyards but between wines from separate, miniscule—even adjacent—plots within the same (small) vineyard. Nowhere in the world is *terroir* paid so great homage as in Burgundy, and it's fair to say that no winegrowing region on earth is as intimidating to the uninitiated. By the same token, it's this dazzling diversity that appeals to Burgundy lovers.

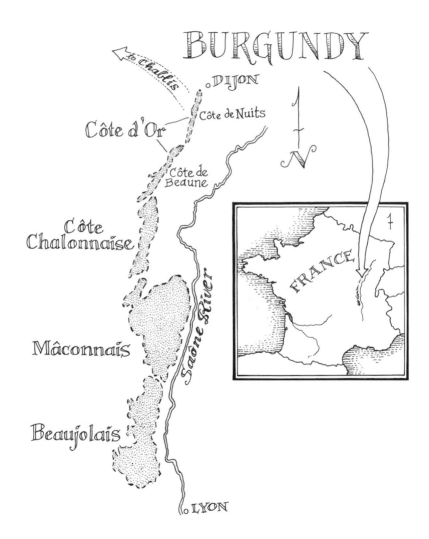

The main part of Burgundy—see the map at left—stretches south from just below the city of Dijon, roughly paralleling a little river called the Saône. The region's heartland, the **Côte d'Or** (koht-DOR; "slope of gold"), is at the upper end of this strip, and consists of a band of vineyards on the east- and southeast-facing slopes of a series of limestone hills. The Côte d'Or is divided into northern and southern sections: the **Côte de Nuits** (koht duh NWEE), which produces many of Burgundy's most renowned red wines, and the **Côte de Beaune** (koht duh BOHN), the source of Burgundy's most celebrated white wines and a number of notable reds.

As the hills extend south of the Côte d'Or into the **Côte Chalonnaise** (koht shah-luh-NEHZ) and then into the **Mâconnais** (mah-kuh-NAY) districts, the geology gradually changes, with the limestone being replaced by granite. In Burgundy's southernmost district, **Beaujolais** (boh-zhuh-LAY), the hills begin to peter out, and the land grows flatter. Though part of Greater Burgundy, Beaujolais is often treated separately because its wines are so different from the others produced in the region. Technically, **Chablis**, which lies sixty miles northwest of the Côte d'Or, is also part of Greater Burgundy, though discussions of French wine likewise often treat Chablis separately because the "austere," often unoaked Chardonnay-based whites that are its claim to fame are unlike the whites of the Côte de Beaune, Chalonnaise, and Mâconnais.

Though the appellation systems differ from district to district in Burgundy, a somewhat consistent pattern prevails, which might be graphically summarized like so:

Burgundy → (Specific) Region → Village → Vineyard

Understanding this pattern is essential to understanding how Burgundy's wines are named and—by extension—ranked.

First, there's **Burgundy *as a whole***: a wine labeled *Appellation Bourgogne Contrôlée* might come from many places within the region—usually from vineyards on the plain below the slopes—and such wines are often poor in quality. Then there are other, **more precise regional appellations**: for example, a wine labeled *Appellation Bourgogne Hauts-Côtes de Nuits Contrôlée* comes from vineyards in the hills (*Hauts-Côtes* = "Upper Slopes") above the Côte de Nuits proper.

Then there are the **villages, or communes**: the Côte de Nuits, for example, has eight villages that are allowed to have their own appellations. One of these is Nuits-St.-Georges; an *Appellation Nuits-St.-Georges Contrôlée* is not just from that specific village but is in all probability of a higher quality than a Burgundy with a regional appellation.

And then—here's where the plot really thickens!—there are the **vineyards**. Some village-appellation wines are identified with a particular vineyard. For example, sitting on my desk is a bottle of Nuits-St.-Georges AC wine by a maker called Domaine Jean Grivot. (A very trustworthy maker, by the way.) The most prominent name on this wine's label is that of the appellation: Nuits-St.-Georges. But below this, in smaller type, is the designation "Les Charmois," which means that this wine—a red—is made from grapes grown in the Les Charmois vineyard.

But the discrimination among wines doesn't stop there. Many of the vineyards of the Côte d'Or are **classified vineyards**: the topmost tier are the ***grands crus*** (only thirty-three rate this distinction); below them on the scale are the ***premiers crus*** (of which there are—oh, dear—more than 560). Burgundies from *grand crus* and *premiers crus* are identified as such on their labels (the abbreviation *1er cru* is often used for "*premier cru*"). The *grands crus* are, in fact, appellations unto themselves;

they're also the rarest Burgundies, together accounting for only 1 percent of the region's production.

So this must mean that a *grand cru* Burgundy—at the pinnacle of the appellation heap—is a magnificent wine, right?

Well, not so fast. An often-cited example of just how complicated things can become in Burgundy is provided by a very famous vineyard called the Clos de Vougeot. (It's in the village of Vougeot in the Côte de Nuits district.) This stone wall–enclosed vineyard (that's what *clos* means) has 120 or so acres—making it the largest *grand cru* vineyard. Not only is this property divided up among about *eighty* different owners— many of whom bottle

Burgundy's *grand cru* vineyards are themselves appellations

their own wines—but the vineyard also embraces several distinct *terroirs*, with the uppermost portion of the vineyard considered superior to those farther down the slope. As if all this weren't enough to contend with, there's the matter of the weather. Burgundy's is unreliable. Remember, this is a northerly winegrowing region, and one that's far inland, robbing it of the tempering influence that a large body of water could provide. By now, you're well aware of what this means: that vintages can differ markedly in quality. Making an educated selection of a Clos de Vougeot wine therefore involves knowing (1) something about the reputation of the grower/maker, (2) something about where that maker's plot or plots are located in the vineyard, *and* (3) something about the relative quality of the vintage. A randomly selected Clos de Vougeot Grand Cru AC wine is guaranteed to be expensive (prices begin at $65–$70 a bottle for a recent-vintage wine and skyrocket from there); whether its price will be justified is very hard to say.

Burgundy Labels

Of all French wine labels, those on Burgundies can be among the most difficult to interpret. This (made up) example shows the meanings of various elements that often appear on Burgundy labels.

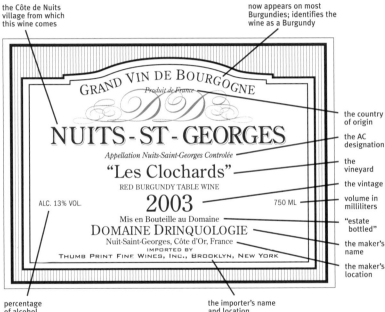

the Côte de Nuits village from which this wine comes

now appears on most Burgundies; identifies the wine as a Burgundy

GRAND VIN DE BOURGOGNE
Produit de France

NUITS - ST - GEORGES
Appellation Nuits-Saint-Georges Controlée
"Les Clochards"
RED BURGUNDY TABLE WINE
2003

ALC. 13% VOL.

750 ML

Mis en Bouteille au Domaine
DOMAINE DRINQUOLOGIE
Nuit-Saint-Georges, Côte d'Or, France
IMPORTED BY
THUMB PRINT FINE WINES, INC., BROOKLYN, NEW YORK

the country of origin

the AC designation

the vineyard

the vintage

volume in milliliters

"estate bottled"

the maker's name

the maker's location

percentage of alcohol by volume

the importer's name and location

Mercifully, only Pinot Noir is grown within the confines of the Clos de Vougeot! And that points to the *only* thing about Burgundy that's relatively simple. In much of the region, only two grape varieties are now grown: Pinot Noir (for reds) and Chardonnay (for whites). But given that both of these grapes are renowned for their ability to convey differences in *terroir*, knowing this hardly gives you a leg up. (Beaujolais is, by the way, the major exception to the Pinot Noir/Chardonnay rule: its red wines—only a tiny amount of Beaujolais wine is white—are all made from the Gamay grape. A white grape called Aligoté figures in a very few white Burgundies.)

If you're contemplating a love affair with Burgundies—red, white, or both—make sure: (1) that you're of a fearless and adventurous temperament; (2) that you have an aptitude for memorizing (sometimes very odd) French names; (3) that you have time to kill and money to burn; and (4) that you're able to endure disappointment with relative *sang froid*—since Burgundies, even the priciest ones from the classified vineyards, can let you down almost as often as they can lift you to the heights of ecstasy that Burgundy lovers describe in almost religious terms.

In the unlikely case that you're not catching my drift, I'm implying that mastering Burgundy requires a lifetime of work and study—oh, and yes, pleasure, as well. Hugh Johnson and Jancis Robinson's magnificent *World Atlas of Wine* can help you grasp Burgundy's jigsaw-puzzle geography. Other valuable references include Nicholas Faith's *Burgundy and Its Wines* (a superb introduction to the region, with great photos), Anthony Hanson's *Burgundy,* and Matt Kramer's encyclopedic *Making Sense of Burgundy* (the last unfortunately out of print but available—for a hefty sum—from online used-book sellers).

But does this mean that you, a study-averse wine newbie, should simply *forget* Burgundy and seek your vinous pleasures elsewhere?

Well, I fear the answer has to be yes and no. If you're just in the mood for a nice Pinot Noir and have twenty to forty dollars to plunk down for it, do yourself a favor and choose a higher-end Oregon or New Zealand Pinot rather than a red Burgundy. If you're just in the mood for a good Chardonnay made in the Burgundian manner, choose a higher-end oaked Chard from California. No, these New World imitators may not waft you to the beatific heights of the greatest Burgundies, but the plain truth is that *unless you know what you're buying,* you're much less likely to be disappointed—especially at this price-point.

CÔTE D'OR CHEAT-SHEET

Granted, Burgundies from the Côte d'Or are expensive, but you'll find lots of village-appellation wines in the $25 to $50 price range. Here are some frequently encountered Côte d'Or village (or commune) appellations, listed by the kind of wine (red, white, or both) that each is best known for and noting whether the commune is in the Côte de Nuits (CN) or Côte de Beaune (CB). Remember, all the reds are made from Pinot Noir; all the whites from Chardonnay.

Reds
Beaune (CB)
Chambolle-Musigny (CN)
Gevrey-Chambertin (CN)
Morey-St.-Denis (CN)
Nuits-St.-Georges (CN)
Pommard (CB)
Santenay (CB)
Volnay (CB)
Vosne-Romanée (CN)

Reds and Whites
Aloxe-Corton (CB)
Chassagne-Montrachet (CB)

Whites
Meursault (CB)
Puligny-Montrachet (CB)

On the other hand, if it really is a *Burgundy*—red *or* white—that you're hankering to sample, do recall that the majority of Burgundies are bottled and sold by *négociants*. In fact, at typical, medium-sized American wine shops catering to ordinary, middle-class folk, it's likely that most of the Burgundies on sale will be village-appellation wines produced by better-known *négociants* such as Bouchard Père & Fils, Joseph Drouhin, Faiveley, Louis Jadot, Labouré-Roi, and Louis Latour. (The *négociant*'s name appears prominently on the label.) Now, these *négociants* naturally have a big financial stake in their wines' reliability. That doesn't mean that by choosing, say, a Louis Jadot Chassagne-Montrachet, you'll be getting the best that Chassagne-Montrachet (a village in the Côte de Beaune that's especially famous for its white wines) has to offer. It means (1) that it probably won't be dreadful and (2) that it may, in fact, be quite interesting.

And there are yet other—and less expensive—options. For example, you might want to begin your exploration of the wines of Burgundy by working "from the bottom up," so to speak: that is, by sampling some of the less highly regarded but often very interesting wines from Burgundy's more southerly districts: the Chalonnaise, the Mâconnais, and Beaujolais.

The Chalonnaise embraces a small number of appellations that produce reliably good, if not sublime, reds. The best-known of these is **Mercurey**, and the widely available Mercurey AC wine made by Domaine Louis Max—its crown- and swag-bedecked red label is instantly recognizable—offers a presentable introduction to Burgundy-style Pinot Noir for about $30 a bottle.

The Mâconnais is (mostly) white-wine territory; its oaked Chardonnays may not equal those of the Côte de Beaune in subtlety and depth, but, once again, they provide a perfectly acceptable introduction to the region's white wine style. You might try any of the nearly countless **Mâcon-Villages** wines on the market; many are simply called Mâcon-Villages, but many have the name of a specific village attached: Mâcon-Lugny, for example, or Mâcon-Viré. The latter can get a bit pricey (upwards of $30), but—who knows?—you may happen onto a swell Mâcon-Villages for as little as $10 a bottle.

Or you might be totally outlandish and strike up your acquaintance with the region with the "Un-Burgundy Burgundy"—Beaujolais. Beaujolais' red wines (reds account for 98 percent of production) are

Beaujolais is the "Un-Burgundy" unlike other red Burgundies for two reasons: they're made from Gamay instead of Pinot Noir, and they're vinified in an unusual way that has a definite effect on their smell and taste. The process, called **carbonic maceration**, involves filling large fermentation vessels with *whole* bunches of grapes. The grapes nearer the bottom are crushed by the weight of those above, and, as they ferment, the carbon dioxide that's released drifts upward through the tank, causing the upper layers of grapes to undergo what's called *intracellular fermentation*. There's no need for you to understand the biochemistry—just that this vinification method gives Beaujolais its distinctive banana- and pearlike aromas and flavors.

If you're familiar with Beaujolais at all, it's probably through the Beaujolais Nouveau that arrives in wine shops, accompanied by a great deal of fanfare, at Thanksgiving time each year. But this extremely young wine—which, granted, can be vivacious and refreshing—only hints at the pleasures delivered by more serious Beaujolais. A couple of rungs up the quality ladder are the wines called Beaujolais-Villages, produced in the hillier, northern part of the Beaujolais district. Though these are also meant to be drunk young (i.e., within a couple of years of the vintage), Beaujolais-Villages' flavor is deeper and more subdued than that of Beaujolais Nouveau.

Best of all, though, are the barrel-aged wines from the so-called **Beaujolais Crus**—ten communes in northern Beaujolais that are permitted to have their own appellations. The names are Brouilly, Chénas, Chiroubles, Côte de Brouilly, Fleurie, Juliénas, Morgon, Moulin-à-Vent, Regnié, and St.-Amour. (Their labels may or may not identify them as Beaujolais.) You're likely to find a number of Beaujolais Cru wines in many U.S. wine shops, and many of these will have been produced by Georges Duboeuf—a famous Burgundy *négociant* who, besides being a relentless promoter of the Beaujolais Nouveau phenomenon, has worked tirelessly to improve the wines of the district as a whole. (Duboeuf's Beaujolais Cru wines retail in the neighborhood of $15.) I really like Beaujolais with Middle Eastern food; its tireless fruitiness (present even in the Beaujolais Crus, which may, however, be missing the banana/pear notes mentioned earlier) nicely complements the spice-herb mix of Turkish and other, related cuisines.

The Loire: A Quick Trip Upstream. On the one hand, it's idiotic to try to characterize all the diverse wines of a given French winegrowing area with just a few hastily chosen words. On the other, a slapdash description might be helpful to the wine newbie eager to get her bearings in the confusing precincts of a wine shop. So, with appropriate trepidation, I offer the following flashcard-quick synopsis of the Loire Valley wines you're likeliest to find at your local wine merchant: they're *clean, light, bright, personable, and undemanding.* And unlike Bordeaux and Burgundies, the Loire Valley wines carried by your local shop probably won't stray very far beyond *Drinkology WINE*'s preferred price range of $10 to $30. In fact, few will exceed $20 a bottle. The appeal is well put by poet Wayne Koestenbaum, who in his book *Model Homes* compares one of the vaunted white wines of Burgundy to its humbler Loire counterparts:

> I can't afford Meursault,
> But Muscadet and Touraine from the Loire
> Taste pure, and stretch the vinous dollar far.

The first thing a neo-oenophile needs to know about the wines of the Loire is that the word "Loire" (LWAH^r) almost never appears on these wines' labels. Far from being a single, contiguous winegrowing region, the Loire is a *series* of regions strung along hundreds of miles of the Loire River from where it empties into the Atlantic near the city of Nantes eastward to Sancerre (much closer to Burgundy than to the ocean) and then southward to the Auvergne. (Auvergne wines make only rare appearances in U.S. wine shops, so I skip them here.) Despite this sizable geographic stretch, however, many of the dry and off-dry Loire wines you're likeliest to encounter share a number of commonalities: they're generally simple and crisp, relatively low in alcohol, and usually marked more by acidity (in the good, refreshing sense) than by fruit. The most famous of the Loire's wines are its whites, but there are a few reds and rosés that you should pay attention to, as well. So let's begin our quick trip upriver from river's mouth to its eastern reaches:

The white wine known as Muscadet dominates the **Nantais** (nahn-TAY), the westernmost part of the Loire. Now, I've already sung Muscadet's praises in chapter 6, but let me briefly refresh your memory: light and creamy (because they're allowed to rest *sur lie*—"on the lees"—after fermentation), the best Muscadets partner extremely well with seafood. (They're also ever so slightly fizzy, underscoring their refreshment.)

Traveling eastward, we next come to the region known as **Anjou and Saumur** (ahⁿ-ZHOO; soh-MYOOR). This is the beginning of the territory vaguely defined as the "middle Loire," where two grape varieties dominate: Chenin Blanc (for whites) and Cabernet Franc (for reds). Well-regarded Angevin whites include the *moelleux* ("sweet") Chenin Blanc–based wines of the **Côteaux du Layon** appellation and the dry wines of **Savennières** (also based on Chenin Blanc and easier to find in U.S. wine shops, though rarely under $20). Anjou and Saumur's Cab Franc–based reds are renowned—if that's the right word—for how very *easy* they are to drink. The best known is **Champigny-Saumur**, but **Anjou-Villages** reds provide an all-but-identical experience for a lower price. These red wines perform well as aperitifs.

For reds that are a bit more substantial, and for whites that some consider the *sine qua non* of Chenin Blanc–based wines, we move just a little farther upstream, to the **Touraine** (too-REHN) region, which surrounds—and whose name derives from—the city of Tours. Commonly dubbed the "garden of France," Touraine is a picture-postcard land of fairytale Renaissance châteaux. The Touraine region's best known reds come from two appellations near its western boundary: **Chinon** and **Bourgueil**. These aromatic Cabernet Franc–based wines taste—to my palate, anyway—remarkably like cherries. The differences between Chinon and Bourgueil are subtle, though Chinons are usually silkier, Bourgueils brusquer.

Touraine's stellar Chenin Blanc–based whites come from the **Vouvray** appellation on the Loire's right (north) bank just east of the town of Tours and from the less well known **Montlouis** appellation directly across the river. Now, the experts will tell you—and I trust them on this—that there are great Vouvrays and then there are mediocre Vouvrays. By "great Vouvrays," they usually mean the sweet *(moelleux)* or very sweet *(liquoreux)* Vouvrays made from noble rot–infected grapes. But these wines are expensive, hard to find in typical American wine shops, and often require significant in-bottle maturation to "achieve their potential," as the Winespeakers say. But I'm here to tell you that I like just fine many of the dry *(sec)* or, more commonly, off-dry *(demi-sec)* Vouvrays that you'll find in your local shop for $10 to $15 a bottle. I've hardly met a Vouvray I didn't cotton to. The green-apple flavor is scrumptious; the zingy acid gives my palate a lift; and (in an off-dry Vouvray) the hint of sweetness is a perfect foil for spicy dishes. If you have the money and want to go a step up, try one of the *sec* or *demi-sec* Vouvrays made by Domaine Huet (in the $25–$30 range); this respected maker is also notable because it follows *biodynamic* viticultural principles in all its vineyards (see the sidebar on page 282).

Besides Chinons, Bourgeuils, Vouvrays, and (possibly) wines from Montlouis, you're also likely to encounter both red and white whites labeled simply *Appellation Touraine Contrôlée.* The regulations for Touraine AC wines are unusually loose, meaning that these wines, which are often blends, might be made from any number of different grapes. The labels—oh, France, why do you *do* this to us?—generally give no indication of the constituent varieties, which means you can really be surprised by a Touraine AC wine. For instance, many Touraine AC whites, in contrast with the Chenin Blanc whites for which the middle Loire is better known, are based mostly on Sauvignon Blanc. Not that you'd necessarily

Touraine AC regulations are unusually loose

recognize the grape from these sometimes off-dry wines' flavor, which can be almost lushly fruity. (Try, for example, the unusual and delicious Touraine AC white made by Les Trois Chênes—about $15.)

That style certainly stands in contrast with that of the white wines of the last Loire region we'll visit: the **Sancerrois** (sahn-seh-RWAH), whose best-known appellations are **Sancerre** and **Pouilly-Fumé**. Here, in the eastern reaches of the Loire Valley, Sauvignon Blanc and Pinot Noir dominate, but it's the white, S.B.–based wines that you should pay most attention to. The whites of Sancerre, especially, stand as a global benchmark for unoaked, cool-climate Sauvignon Blancs—their "grassiness" often accompanied by grapefruit and/or asparagus flavors and by a distinct, and weirdly agreeable, whiff of cat pee on the nose. (If describing this ammonia-like scent as "cat pee"–like bothers you, use the less noxious-sounding French term: *pipi du chat*.) For sheer refreshment, Sancerres are among *Drinkology WINE*'s favorite whites, and their affordability— many sell for around $15 a bottle—seals the deal. (Equally affordable Pinot-based Sancerre rosés can be pleasant accompaniments to summertime suppers.)

Directly across the river from the Sancerre appellation is that of Pouilly-Fumé, whose white wines have a weightier character than those of Sancerre. Some describe them as "smoky" (*fumé* means "smoked"); some as more "Burgundian" than other Loire whites. Whether you'll really be able to distinguish them from Sancerres depends on how prodigious your palate is—but your wallet will know the difference, since they're generally more expensive.

Though we've barely skimmed the surface of the Loire, it's time to move on to parts north and south, for—*very* brief—reconnaissance of the two other French regions you're likely to find represented in your local wine shop. If you'd like to continue your exploration, get hold of a

When the Moon Is in the Seventh House . . .

. . . does it mean it's time to pick the grapes? It may astonish you to learn that a number of serious winemakers—more and more all the time, in fact—are consulting astrological tables in managing their vineyards.

On the one hand, **biodynamic viticulture** is simply an extension of organic viticulture. Chemical fertilizers and pesticides are eschewed. But adherents of the biodynamic philosophy go a step further by scrupulously focusing on the ecological character of their vineyards in all its biologically interactive complexity. The purpose isn't just to avoid toxins but to bring the vineyard "into harmony" with itself. The uniqueness of each particular locale is emphasized; thus, though manure may be used as a fertilizer, it's much better, from the biodynamic point of view, if that manure comes from farm animals living on the same estate.

But these winemakers don't just pay attention to their vineyards' terrestrial specificity; they also cast their gaze toward the heavens. Following principles outlined in the early twentieth century by Austrian philosopher (or kook?) Rudolph Steiner, biodynamic winemakers set themselves the task of bringing the dynamics of the vineyard into harmony with the rhythms of the cosmos—as astrologically defined. The signs of the zodiac and the positions of the planets and the moon help determine when to prune, when to weed, when to harvest, and so on.

The really strange thing, though, is that biodynamic viticulture hasn't been embraced only by people who are mystically inclined. A sizable cadre of perfectly level-headed folk—including some established winemakers not temperamentally given to New Age pursuits—have signed on, because (they say) the biodynamic approach *works*. Of course, critics and consumers actually have the final say in whether it results in better wines—and the jury's still out. Some wine shops now have special sections devoted to biodynamic (and organic) wines from places around the world.

copy of Jacqueline Friedrich's encyclopedically comprehensive *Wine and Food Guide to the Loire.*

Alsace. Chances are that somewhere in your local wine shop there's a corner—maybe no more than a shelf, maybe just half a shelf—devoted to wines from Alsace. Sometimes the Alsatian wines will occupy a spot in the larger French wines section; sometimes they'll be shelved next to, or even among, the German wines. This makes a kind of sense, given that this dribble of territory in northeastern France has a culture that in many respects is as German as it is French and given that Alsace's wines resemble those of Germany more than they do those of the other French regions. (Historically, Alsace was fought over by the two countries, and its ownership changed hands several times.) No matter how small a space the wine merchant accords them, however, they stand out—a neat little row of the slender, almost shoulderless green and brown bottles called *flûtes d'Alsace*, sometimes sporting pencil-yellow labels that make that make them even more distinctive, visually.

Despite their relatively small impact on typical American wine drinkers' consciousness, I've chosen to highlight Alsatian wines several times in this book. That's because Alsace's Pinot Gris wines (see pages 167–168), Rieslings (page 182), Gewürztraminers (page 190), and Pinot Blancs (pages 194–195) are all so outstanding. Having mentioned these four varietals— remember that alone among French wines, those of Alsace are given varietal names under the AC system—we've almost covered the field, albeit fleetingly. There are just two other kinds of still Alsatian white wine that you *might* find at your local wine emporium: Muscat (made either of Muscat Blanc à Petits Grains, here called Muscat d'Alsace, or another variety called Muscat Ottonel) and, even more rarely, Sylvaner. Alsace produces only one sort of red wine: Pinot Noir. And though some Alsace vineyards are classified, the system is simpler than classifications elsewhere in France; the fifty top vineyards are denominated as *grands crus*. (That's it. Wines from *grand cru* vineyards are labeled as such.)

Again admitting that it's dangerous to generalize, let's throw caution to the winds: Aside from the Alsatian Pinot Noirs (which with rare exceptions merely point toward what Burgundy's makers do with this grape), the wines of Alsace are all very *definite* wines—as distinctive as the bottles that contain them. Though their acidity can be razorlike, they're seldom if ever "austere." On the contrary, they can be amazingly aromatic and can pack a fruit wallop that is unusual, to say the least, for wines hailing from such a northerly latitude.

In short, Alsatian whites are about as far from innocuous as you can get—which means they may not immediately appeal to people habituated to milder white wines. But stay with them, and in no time you'll abandon mass-produced Italian Pinot Grigio forever. As I've said elsewhere, they are also extremely reliable, quality-wise. Only the region's better wines get exported, so feel free to experiment, within your price range, with whatever your neighborhood store carries. Among the makers you're likely to encounter are Domaine Weinbach, Hugel et Fils, and F. E. Trimbach. (Alsatian producers generally make a full range of varietals, including "reserve" wines—a term that has no legal meaning in Alsace but that denotes wines of special quality.)

(Just a Glimpse of) the Rhône. The Rhône isn't *one* wine region; it's two. Though the **northern Rhône** and the **southern Rhône** are linked by the river whose name they share, their topographies, their climates, and their wines are very different.

In the northern Rhône, which begins not too far south of the city of Lyon (which, in turn, lies just a little below Beaujolais), the river winds through steep-sided hills. Many of the vineyards are terraced; the topsoil is poor; and the climate is continental—the summers sometimes blistering, the winters often harsh. Many of the northern Rhône's appellations—including all of the most famous ones—are small; some are infinitesimal. That means, of course, that output is also small, and this limited production, combined with how very fashionable the wines of the northern Rhône have become, means that the prices of the most highly regarded northern Rhône wines lie well beyond *Drinkology WINE*'s budget. ("Millionaires' wines," critic Hugh Johnson calls some of them.) Just in case some distant relative should die and leave you a safe-deposit box filled with doubloons, however, it might be worth trying to remember a few of the names:

Prices are astronomic for some northern Rhône wines

- **Côte-Rôtie.** This, the northernmost Rhône appellation, produces Syrah-based red wines—perhaps with a little Viognier added—noted for being aromatic and silky-textured (though also often highly tannic). (Recent-vintage Côte-Rôties start at about $60 and go up—*way* up—from there.)

- **Condrieu** and **Château-Grillet.** These appellations produce the world's most highly praised Viognier-based white wines. You might find a Condrieu for as little as $40; much rarer, the wines of Château-Grillet—which, with only about nine acres, is the tiniest Rhône appellation of all—start at about $75 and then disappear from *Drinkology WINE*'s radar.

- **Hermitage.** The most famous northern Rhône appellation of all, Hermitage's renown extends back centuries. Thomas Jefferson, noted among other things for his propensity to exhaust his fortune on French wines, liked red Hermitage quite a bit. The vineyards that cling to the south face of the hill of Hermitage are planted with Syrah and with two white wine varieties—Roussanne and Marsanne—seldom grown outside the Rhône. Red Hermitage is routinely described as "masculine" or "manly"—so dark and muscular that it was once used to color and pump up pallid, limp-wristed Bourdeaux and Burgundies. Though you may find a white Hermitage for as little as $30, you can forget about red Hermitage (unless, that is, you get the key to that doubloon-laden safe-deposit box).

- **Cornas.** Cornas' Syrah-based reds vie with those of Hermitage for sheer robustness, but the prices won't punch you quite as hard (though they rarely drop below $40 a bottle).

Your checkbook's anorexia need not exclude you from all northern Rhône wines, however. You might try, for example, a red or white from **Crozes-Hermitage**; this **shadow appellation**—as appellations that incorporate the name and trade on the renown of their more famous neighbors are sometimes called—used to be the object of wine-snob contempt, but everyone agrees that its wines' quality has risen extraordinarily in recent decades. (You may find Crozes-Hermitage reds for as little as ten bucks, though they're more often priced in the $15 to $20 range.) And then there's the northern Rhône's largest appellation, **St.-Joseph**, whose lighter-styled Syrah-based reds and Roussanne/Marsanne-based whites are applauded for their compatibility with a wide range of foods. (You'll find lots of St.-Josephs in the $15 to $35 range.)

The inexpensive, often lively and fresh blended wines (mostly red) that simply carry the **Côtes du Rhône** appellation provide us with a sensible segue into the southern Rhône, since they may come from either the northern or southern part of the Rhône Valley. Very drinkable Côtes du Rhônes—Grenache often accounts for a largish percentage of the reds' blend—can be had for $10 and under. You're almost certain to run across Côtes du Rhônes made by E. Guigal, a very important and extremely trustworthy Rhône Valley *négociant.* A rung up the quality ladder are the wines labeled **Côtes du Rhône-Villages**; these, however, come only from the southern Rhône. Sixteen southern Rhône communes are permitted to attach their names to the Côtes du Rhône-Villages appellation, which can make for monikers that are absurdly long. (By the time you get done asking for a Côtes du Rhône-Villages St.-Maurice-sur-Eygues you really need a drink.) Experiment fearlessly: Côtes du Rhône-Villages, with or without a commune's name appended, can be very satisfying, and they're usually only a smidge more expensive than Côtes du Rhônes.

Cheap Côtes du Rhône can be quite drinkable

The southern Rhône's vineyards aren't so precipitously perched as many of the northern Rhône's; the climate is Mediterranean (we're now in Provence)—and the region's sunshine and warmth can make for wines that are exuberantly fruity and full bodied. Among the southern Rhône wines you might consider sampling are the Grenache-dependent rosés of the **Lirac** and **Tavel** appellations and the hearty reds from **Vacqueyras** and **Gigondas**, but these are sidelights to the region's truly great appellation: **Châteauneuf-du-Pape** (shah-toh-nerf-doo-PAP).

It's on Châteauneuf-du-Pape that you should focus, though "focus" seems like the wrong word, since there are scores upon scores of reputable-to-outstanding producers—and since AC regulations allow up to thirteen different varieties to be used in (always blended) Châteauneuf-du-Pape reds. (Grenache, Syrah, Mourvèdre, and Cinsault are major constituents; very little white Châteauneuf-du-Pape is made.) The variation in taste, however, isn't so wide as to render generalization meaningless: whatever else they are, good red Châteauneuf-du-Papes are dark, full-bodied, dense, rich, and spicy. In a word, these are *wonderful* red wines—and the kicker is that many, many, many are not exorbitantly expensive. You may find delicious Châteauneuf-du-Papes for as little as $25 a bottle; if you're willing to go up $15 in price, you'll do very well, indeed. The evening before writing this passage, I had a Châteauneuf-du-Pape made by Château de la Gardine (a very well-regarded producer) that was *heaven*—and forty bucks isn't, I don't think, too much to pay for a taste of the divine.

And speaking of the sacred: the name Châteauneuf-du-Pape translates as "New Castle of the Pope"; it hearkens back to the so-called Babylonian captivity of the papacy, a period in the late Middle Ages during which the popes ruled their spiritual/temporal kingdom from the nearby Provençal city of Avignon rather than from Rome. I bring this up only because it explains an unusual feature of many Châteauneuf-du-Pape bottles: they're embossed, above the label, with the papal coat-of-arms. That's a nod to history, not a Vatican imprimatur! (Many are distinctively shaped, as well: the body of the bottle isn't round but softly triangular.)

The papal seal is a nod to history

For a comprehensive treatment of the Rhône, north and south, turn to Robert Parker's *Wines of the Rhône Valley*. Whatever one thinks of Parker, he's certainly indefatigable, and his enthusiasm for Rhône wines bursts from every page.

ITALY

Don't worry—we'll get to the *fuhgeddaboudit* part in a moment—but let it be said that Italy presents a puzzle to the wine newbie that seems, at first glance, even less figure-out-able than that of France. For one thing, wine is made *all over* Italy—in all twenty of the country's political/geographical regions, stretching from Trentino–Alto Adige in the alpine north to the island of Sicily in the sweltering south. By some estimates more than eight hundred (others put the number at over a thousand) different wine-grape varieties are grown, and many of these, including some of the most famous, are rarely or never grown outside Italy—meaning that learning about Italian wine entails expanding your varietal vocabulary significantly. Add to this the crazy-making way (or, rather, *ways*) in which Italian wines are named: some are named for grapes, some are named for places, some are named for grapes *and* places, and some—many, in fact—have proprietary names. (The Italians call them "fantasy names.")

And then there are the intricacies of Italian wine law. The system now in place, which began to be introduced in the 1960s and is modeled on the French AC system, specifies four ranks. In ascending order, these are (1) *Vino da Tavola* ("table wine"; VdT, for short), (2) *Indicazione Geografica Tipica* ("typical geographic indication"; IGT), (3) *Denominazione di Origine Controllata* ("controlled denomination of origin"; DOC), and (4) *Denominazione di Origine Controllata e Garantita* ("controlled and guaranteed denomination of origin"; DOCG).

As your newfound familiarity with the French system surely leads you to assume, regulations grow stricter as you climb up this pyramid. VdT wines, which fall outside the classification system, are often very simple wines, including, for example, the red *(rosso)* or white *(bianco)*

STICKER SHOCK

A low price can cause its own kind of sticker shock. It seems to happen almost every time a group of friends gathers for a wine-tasting party, especially if the wines are tasted blind. After all the wines have been looked at, swirled, sniffed, and sipped and everyone's declared his or her favorite, the labels are uncovered and the wines' prices disclosed—and one or two people will have preferred the *cheapest* wine of the bunch. Occasionally, the results seem simply ridiculous, with *everyone* having chosen the $7.99 wine over its twenty-, thirty-, and forty-dollar competitors.

How can this be? Can it be true that a wine's price tag doesn't necessarily have anything to do how good the wine is?

Well, momentarily setting aside differences in taste—which always enter into judgments of quality—this question doesn't admit of an easy answer. Lots and lots of factors interact to determine a wine's price. We've encountered a few of them already, but here's a more complete list:

- *The rarity of the wine.* Does it come from a large Australian maker or hail from one of those tiny appellations in the northern Rhône? In many cases, the mere fact that not much of a given wine is produced drives up its price.

- *The vintage of the wine.* Wines from better vintages may cost more than those from less-good vintages. This is especially true of wines from certain Old World regions (e.g., Bordeaux, Burgundy) where vintage is extremely important in determining overall quality.

- *The age of the wine.* Obviously, wines get rarer as they get older. (They get bought; they get stashed away; they get drunk.) Prices can sometimes accelerate surprisingly quickly: a prestigious wine from a good vintage that was released just a few years ago might be significantly—maybe even astronomically—more expensive than a good-vintage wine from the same maker that's just now being released.

- *How fashionable the wine is.* The more sought-after a wine is, the higher its price may go. Certain wines graduate to the rank of status symbols: they may be great wines, but their prices reflect their *social* desirability as luxury goods as much as their inherent quality.

- *The reputation of the region.* Some regions just have more cachet than others. For example, no matter how good Pinot Noirs from New Zealand become, as a class they'll probably always cost less than the top red Burgundies (again, considered as a class) because of Burgundy's centuries-old renown.

- *The critics' opinions.* The critics who shepherd so many wine consumers' purchasing decisions can cause a wine's price to blast off or skid from the runway.

- *The cost of production.* Labor, the cost of equipment (e.g., oak barrels), and other production-related factors can have a big impact on a wine's price. Champagne and Amarone (to take just two examples) are expensive in part because they're comparatively difficult, time-consuming, and costly to produce.

- *The economy of the wine's home country—and of the world.* In the early 2000s, Argentine Malbecs were cheap in part because Argentina's economy was recovering from collapse. At the same time, European wines were growing ever more expensive in the United States because the dollar was falling against the euro.

And then there's a vague but all-embracing factor: *what the market will bear.* Wine—like virtually every commodity—commands higher prices during booms than during busts. And vintners set their wines' prices based in part on how much they think they can get. Sometimes they—and the importers and distributors who handle their products—make a killing; sometimes they get burned.

None of this, however, exactly answers the question about the relation of quality and price. Some wines are overpriced; others are undervalued. So where's the surprise in that? We all know that markets provide only imperfectly reliable guarantees of quality: A hackneyed, clumsy painting by a "blue chip" artist will fetch a higher price at auction than an inventive, beautiful work by an unknown. But it's hardly as if quality and price are totally unrelated. It would be no less than astonishing if, say, a $15 California Cabernet beat one costing $150 at a blind tasting conducted by experts. (It could happen, of course, but probably not.) Things become much more uncertain, though, when the wines being compared are more or less within the same ballpark, price-wise. As I found out in my own comparison of "moderately priced" California Cabs (see page 230), there's no telling whether a $40 wine will outperform all its $20 competitors.

Of course, my taste factored heavily into my judgment. So will yours. If you participate in a few blind tastings and find that you almost always favor the less-expensive wines, it may simply be that you prefer simpler wines—not *bad* wines, mind you, but wines that other tasters might find lacking in depth or complexity or ageworthiness or varietal fidelity or whatever. (And no harm in that.)

But whatever your taste, rest easy about one thing: In an era of excellent winemaking (and given the global wine glut), there's no reason to pay an arm and a leg for a good, drinkable bottle. Even if you stay within the $8 to $15 range, you'll find lots and lots of interesting wines from all over the world—reds, whites, rosés, and maybe even a few sparklers—that meet your budgetary requirements.

house wines *(vini di casa)*—often drawn directly from a barrel's tap—that you might order at a neighborhood *trattoria* in any Italian town. IGT wines are Italy's rough equivalent to French *vins de pays*—that is, they're "expressive" of the rather broadly demarcated areas they come from. (Regulations for IGT wines are limited to requiring that they come from where the label says they do.) The DOC and DOCG wines are the "appellation wines" of Italy, and it's at these levels that precise stipulations about distinct (often small) geographic **zones**, varietal content, yield, alcohol level, and vinification and maturation procedures come into force. Regulations for DOCG wines are more exacting than those for DOC wines. (The list of DOCG wines keeps growing; as of 2005, this extra "guarantee" applied to twenty-three kinds of wine.)

The thing is, these four classifications don't *necessarily* correspond to levels of quality. We saw something like this happening in France, but the situation in Italy is, if anything, even more unpredictable. One reason is that so many Italian makers disregard the system, for instance by creating wines from varieties disallowed by DOC regulations for their **Fuhgeddaboudit** zones. Remember the Super Tuscans we met back in chapter 5 (pages 156–157)? Many of them are non-DOC wines, as are countless others whose makers give them "fantasy" or varietal names (or both). Though relegated to IGT or sometimes even VdT status, these can be every bit as good—and occasionally better than—DOC/DOCG wines.

Sounds like an awful lot of information to sort out and digest, huh? Well, it is complicated, but, hey, *fuhgeddaboudit*, since you don't really need to know very much to begin your exploration (and enjoyment!) of Italian wine. Most of Italy's best-known wines come from the northern/north-central part of the country, and despite the ever-greater diversity of Italian wines you'll find on your local wine shop's shelves—an indication of their increasing popularity in America—it remains true that those you're likeliest to encounter hail from only a few places: the **Piedmont** (It., Piemonte) region in the northwest; the trio of regions called the **Tre Venezie** ("Three Venices") in the northeast, including **Friuli–Venezia Giulia**, the **Veneto**, and **Trentino–Alto Adige**; and **Tuscany** (It., Toscana).

We've met some of these wines already, including the Nebbiolo-based, Piedmontese reds **Barolo** and **Barbaresco** (pages 150–151); the Muscat-based **Asti** and **Moscato d'Asti**, also from the Piedmont (page 193); Pinot Grigios from the Venezie (pages 168–169); the sparkling wine, mostly from the Veneto, called **Prosecco** (page 219); and the Sangiovese-dominated Tuscan reds **Chianti**, **Chianti Classico**, and **Chianti Classico Riserva** (pages 152–153). Here's a little pronouncing dictionary of a few of the others—reds and whites—your wine shop probably stocks, with brief notes on each kind.

REDS

Amarone (ah-mah-ROH-neh)
From the Valpolicella zone of the Veneto (see below), this wine's original name was Recioto della Valpolicella Amarone—"bitter *recioto* of Valpolicella." *Recioto* wines are made from dried, sometimes botrytized, grapes whose sugars are therefore extremely concentrated. Most *reciotos* are sweet; Amarone's the exception. Made from a blend of local grapes (Corvina is the most important) and fermented to dryness, Amarone is Italy's most profoundly extracted dry red wine—and it is *exceptional*, with a multidimensional richness few other wines can approach. Amarones are

far from cheap—it's doubtful you'll find one for less than $45, and $70 is a more common price—but this is a wine worth breaking the piggy-bank for. Reputable makers include Allegrini, Bertani, Masi, and Zenato.

Barbera (bar-BEH-rah)

Barbera is the name of a grape; attach the name of a town (or, more accurately, zone) to it, and you've got the name of a DOC wine. **Barbera d'Alba** and **Barbera d'Asti**, both from the Piedmont region, are the two you'll run across most frequently. I remember that during my own wine-newbiehood I would always confuse Barberas with Barbarescos. Don't make this mistake!—they're both Piedmontese reds, but the similarity stops there. Nebbiolo-based Barbarescos are majestic wines priced for the deep-pocketed collector; Barberas, for the most part, are friendly, fruity-acidic, everyday reds. You can get a drinkable one for as little as eight bucks (try Michele Chiarlo's Barbera d'Asti), though you're more likely to spend $10 to $15. I *love* the Camp du Rouss Barbera d'Asti, though it's a notch up the price scale (about $22).

Brunello di Montalcino (broo-NELL-oh dee mawn-tahl-CHEE-noh)

Brunello means "little dark one" and refers to the strain of the Sangiovese grape grown in the zone surrounding the hilltop Tuscan town of Montalcino. Widely considered the greatest—best structured, most ageworthy—of Sangiovese-based wines, Brunellos (which are DOCG-category wines) are not for the down-at-heels. (Forty dollars is the *least* you'll pay.) Elegant *and* lush, tannic without being assaultive, Brunellos are wonderful wines, but the price tag's a barrier. Castello Banfi's Brunello (about $60) is widely available. I think it's just grand, but if I'm spending this kind of dough I'd rather have an Amarone.

Dolcetto (dole-CHET-oh)

Dolcetto ("little sweet one") is the name of a grape grown mostly in the Piedmont. (**Dolcetto d'Alba** is the most commonly available DOC-category Dolcetto.) Dolcettos resemble Barberas in being lively, fruity, and easy to enjoy; their darker color (often a deep purple-red) and lower acidity sets them apart. They're like Barberas, too, in how friendly they are to the pocketbook. The La Serra Dolcetto d'Alba made by Manzone is a delightful wine for $14. You'll find plenty of others to choose from in the $15 to $25 range.

Valpolicella (val-poh-lee-CHELL-lah)

The Valpolicella zone, near the city of Verona in the Veneto region, produces an array of red wines that, though they're all blends of the same set of local grapes (Corvina being the most important), differ markedly in character. The lightest is "standard" Valpolicella—often a quaffing wine best suited to washing down a slice of pizza. The most robust and complex is the incomparable Amarone, discussed above. But in between are the wines called **Valpolicella Classico**—often serious, highly scented, well-structured reds from a demarcated area of terraced, hillside vineyards within the larger Valpolicella zone—and **Valpolicella Ripasso**. It's the latter that I think you ought to keep an eye out for. The must for ripasso-style Valpolicellas—the word *ripasso* means to "pass [over] again"—is allowed to rest for a time on the lees (including the pressed grape skins) left behind from an Amarone fermentation, imparting a measure of Amarone's richness and tannic stamina to these wines. No, they're not Amarone, but they play a virtuosic second fiddle—*and* they're much less costly (generally $15 to $25 a bottle). I happened upon one I adore: the Classico Superiore Ripasso made by Remo

Farina (about $15). (Note: The often light-hued. light-bodied red wines from **Bardolino**, also in the Veneto, resemble simple Valpolicellas.)

Vino Nobile di Montepulciano (VEE-noh NOH-bee-lay dee mawn-teh-pool-CHAH-noh)
Quite a mouthful to say, the name means "the noble wine of [the Tuscan hilltown of] Montepulciano," and this wine is *not* to be confused with wines made from the Montepulciano *grape* (for example, Montepulciano d'Abruzzo; see page 300). Vino Nobile, like the reds from neighboring Chianti zones, is based on Sangiovese, either alone or as the dominant variety in a blend. Despite the aristocratic name and the fact that this wine was the first ever to be accorded DOCG status, Vino Nobile di Montepulciano has a reputation for being uneven—a rep borne out in my own (albeit limited) samplings. Vino Nobiles aren't hugely expensive—$25 to $40 is the usual range—but for that kind of money, I'd advise you to choose a similarly priced Chianti Classico Riserva (see page 153) instead.

WHITES

Gavi (GAH-vee)
This Piedmontese white, made from a grape called Cortese, comes from a DOCG zone centered on the town of Gavi; you'll sometimes see Gavis labeled **Gavi di Gavi** (best translated as "*the* Gavi of Gavi"), but this is more a marketing ploy than an indication of superior quality. Gavi's been enjoying a certain fashionability, showing up in more and more American wine shops. Unless you know the maker, though, it can be hard to predict the style of a Gavi—some are light, clean, and applely; others (given some time in wood) are fatter, sultrier, more deeply colored. Among the latter is the Gavi di Gavi made by Villa Sparina (about $21), one of the few wines

I've ever bought because of how much I liked the bottle—an unusual and striking ovoid shape. I was less enthusiastic about the wine, perhaps because its lush fruit and oak undertones reminded me—oh, no!—of a typical California-style Chardonnay, which is not what I usually look for in an Italian white. (In fairness, this wine does have its followers.)

Soave (SWAH-veh)
Twenty and thirty years ago, the dry white wine called Soave (from the Veneto region, and made from a blend of grapes in which Garganega figures most importantly) played a role in American wine-drinking culture similar to that filled, today, by mass-produced Italian Pinot Grigio. The very definition of *light* white wines, many Soaves (like many P.G.'s) are indescribable because there's not very much *to* describe. Luckily for those who prefer wine to water, there *are* some Soaves that do more than just quench your thirst. For the ones labeled **Soave Classico Superiore**, yields are somewhat more tightly controlled, and these wines, unlike garden-variety Soaves, are given some ageing before release. Better yet, try a Soave that doesn't call itself a Soave: San Vincenzo, made by the well-known producer Anselmi. In the late 1990s, Roberto Anselmi opted out of the Soave DOC, disgusted by the high yields permitted and the general nothingness of the resulting wines. His San Vincenzo white—though officially only an IGT wine—epitomizes, for me, what an Italian white wine should be: fresh and crisp while solidly fruity and having an incisive acid edge. It costs about $15.

Tocai Friulano (toh-KYE free-yool-LAH-noh)
Though its appearances on American wine-shop shelves remain infrequent, this unusual wine—produced in the Friuli sector of Friuli–Venezia Giulia, in Italy's northeastern corner—merits a place on this list for no bet-

ter reason than that I happen to like it. You may, too. Despite its name, the Tocai grape is no relation to the grape used in the famous Hungarian sweet wine, Tokaji. (That grape's name, by the way, is Furmint.) In Friuli, fruity-minerally Tocai is drunk with the region's smoked ham and bacon; you might have a glass with a brunchtime BLT. Because of its relative rarity here, I hesitate to recommend a specific maker; if you see a Tocai Friulano by anybody, give it a try. (You probably won't pay more than $20.)

Vernaccia di San Gimignano (vair-NAH-chah dee sahn jee-mee-NYAH-noh)

Vernaccia's the name of the grape; San Gimignano is the medieval Tuscan town, famous for its many stone towers, where this wine has been made at least as far back as the thirteenth century. Tuscany's only well-known white wine, it gets a decidedly mixed welcome from critics, who tend to dismiss many Vernaccias as insipid and to criticize others—newer-style wines into which some Chardonnay is blended, and which spend a little time in oak—as too big for their britches. But I like the leaner, crisper (more insipid?) ones, maybe because this was the first white Italian wine I ever drank and I'm sentimental about it. The S. Quirico Vernaccia di San Gimignano is a quaffing wine, most definitely, but it's not without personality; it'll set you back about ten or twelve bucks. (Note: The dry white wines called **Orvieto**, from the Umbria region immediately southeast of Tuscany, are made from different grapes—Trebbiano dominates the blend—but are similarly personable and refreshing.)

Having told you just a little bit about some of the most frequently encountered *northern* Italian wines, let me report that the breaking news, Italian wine–wise, is coming from the central and southern parts of the country. The time was—and not so long ago—that most of the wines made in regions like Le Marche (The Marches), Abruzzo, and Molise, midway down the "boot" on Italy's east coast; Puglia (the heel of the boot); and Sicily stayed pretty close to home. The embrace of modern winemaking techniques that began in northern Italy in the 1960s and

The breaking wine news is from central and southern Italy

'70s—and that raised the profile of Italian wines worldwide—only gradually filtered down through the rest of the country, but it led, eventually, to a new generation of "local" wines capable of exerting international appeal.

Some of these wines employ indigenous—sometimes ancient—grape varieties heretofore unfamiliar to the rest of us. The sidebar on pages 302–305 talks about some of what's been happening in Sicily, but let me quickly mention a few other wines, from a few of the other central and southern Italian regions, that you might consider trying.

The best-known, probably, is **Montepulciano d'Abruzzo**. (This is the wine that is *not* Vino Nobile di Montepulciano.) Reds based on the Montepulciano grape—especially those from Abruzzo—seem to have something for everyone: they're nicely structured without being overly tannic, often berrylike in flavor, sometimes briskly acidic, and food-friendly as can be. Try the scrumptious Valle Reale Montepulciano d'Abruzzo (about $18). (Note: This wine is imported into the U.S. by a company called Winebow, Inc., and carries a seal on its back label identifying it as a "Leonardo Locascio Selection." I point this out because months of tasting have convinced me that Winebow's Italian imports are extraordinarily trustworthy, and that Mr. Locascio has a taste that's spot-on—or at least accords with my own!)

Even more interesting are red wines made from two varieties grown in various places in Italy's south: **Aglianico** (ahl-YAHN-ee-koh) and

Primitivo (prih-mih-TEE-voh). Aglianico's an extremely ancient grape; it may have been introduced into Italy as early as 700 BC, by the Greeks. (*Aglianico* means "Hellenic," i.e., Greek.) This is a rough wine—which in this case I mean as a compliment. Tarry, leathery, and undomesticated, it can really stand up to powerfully flavored red-sauce pastas. The most acclaimed Aglianicos come from the Taurasi DOCG zone in the Campania region, near Naples, and Aglianico del Vulture DOC zone in Basilicata (where the sole of Italy's boot arches), but I'm more than content with the fairly commonly available Contado Aglianico made by Di Majo Norante, from the Molise region on the Adriatic coast (about $12, and another Winebow import).

You may recall the Primitivo grape from the discussion of Zinfandel (page 154); genetically, it's the same grape. But Italian Primitivo doesn't taste like California Zin. It's got the potency, but lacks the "dirtiness" that turns me off Zinfandel (but that others love). Knowing of the genetic connection, I tasted my first Primitivo with trepidation, . . . but, you know, I thought it was just great. The lushly fruity Sette Mare–brand Primitivo del Salento made by the Pugliese producer Rivini has become a *Drinkology WINE* household standard (a position that its $10 price tag helps it maintain).

These pages can, of course, provide only a sip of Italian wines' diverse wonders. For a comprehensive overview, get a copy of Joseph Bastianich and David Lynch's *Vino Italiano: The Regional Wines of Italy,* which has the distinction of being a genuinely *enjoyable* wine book (not an unknown phenomenon, but rare enough). Bastianich is also a restaurateur, winemaker, and wine seller: his handsome store, Italian Wine Merchants, is a must-visit destination in New York (108 East 16th Street, just east of Union Square).

CINDERELLA STORY

For the longest time, Sicily was a downtrodden stepsister to Italy's other wine regions. Not only were Sicilian wines mostly, and justifiably, disregarded as flaccid and uninteresting when compared to the reds and whites of continental (especially northern) Italy, but the island's extensive vineyards mostly played drudge to the Italian wine industry, producing untold tankerloads of highly alcoholic but otherwise featureless wine that was shipped north and blended with other wines to ratchet up their potency. Aside from the famous fortified wines of Marsala, Sicilian wine was all but unknown outside its homeland.

The Cinderella story began turning in the poor stepsister's favor about two decades ago, with the Fairy Godmother role acted by a number of vintners—some upstarts, but some the progeny of venerable Sicilian landowning/winemaking families—who were determined to create wines capable of competing on an international level. Beginning in the 1980s and gathering strength in the mid-'90s and beyond, this gradually expanding group of producers emulated the modernization efforts going on in the rest of Italy. Among other innovations, they introduced controlled fermentation and started aging some reds, and even some whites, in French oak. And, like some maverick growers in Tuscany and elsewhere, they began planting international varieties (Cabernet, Merlot, Syrah, Chardonnay) in their vineyards, and using these in blends with indigenous varieties—in part to make Sicily's wines more acceptable on a world market increasingly biased in favor of familiar varietal names.

The strategies worked, and today it's possible to find good quality and generally reasonably priced ($10–$20) Sicilian wines on many U.S. wine shop shelves. Among the trustworthy brands available here are Donnafugata, Duca di Salaparuta, Firriato, Planeta, and Tasca d'Almerita— the last also known as Regaleali, after an ancient estate in central Sicily long owned by the Tasca family. The Tasca family is the best known of the old, established winemaking families who embraced the newfangled ways. (Their flagship red, Rosso del Conte, is one of the great wines of Sicily.) Another is the Rallo family, long associated with the making of Marsala but since 1983 the producers of the Donnafugata line of table wines.

The best whites among the "new wave" Sicilian wines are densely fruity but dry, reasonably complex, and extremely versatile in pairing with food. They are, however, high in alcohol (14 percent isn't unusual) and low in acidity—functions of the island's hot climate and long growing season. The low acidity also condemns Sicilian whites to very brief lifespans; they should be drunk within eighteen months of bottling.

You may read elsewhere that only one of Sicily's several native white varieties—a grape known variously as Insolia, Inzolia (cen ZOH-lee-ah) or Ansonica (ahn-SOHN-nee-kah)—is suitable for the making of fine table wines, but this isn't true. The capable winemakers at the Firriato winery (in the town of Paceco, near Trapani) are, for example, creating very respectable wines from two other Sicilian whites, Grillo (GREE-loh) and Cataratto (kah-tah-RAH-toh), that are often dismissed as mere workhorse varieties. (Grillo is a major constituent of Marsala; much of the high-alcohol blending wine mentioned earlier is made from Cataratto, which still dominates Sicily's vineyards.) And Donnafugata combines an even less well known native grape, Damaskino (dah-muss-KEE-noh), with Cataratto to fashion the only Sicilian wine I've sampled that I'd describe as genuinely crisp. (Unfortunately, Damaskino is not among the Donnafugata wines exported to the U.S.)

Despite how good some Sicilian whites can be, however, star status definitely belongs to the island's red wines—most of which are based on the indigenous black grape called Nero d'Avola (NEH-roh DAH-voh-lah). At their best, Nero d'Avola varietals—garnet-colored and semitranslucent, like some Pinot Noirs—are unmistakably black cherry–flavored, with mild (though definitely present) tannins. For my taste, though, Nero d'Avola's true talent shines through when it's used as the foundation for blended wines, especially blends in which either Syrah or Cabernet Sauvignon figure. Of all the Sicilian reds I've drunk, my hands-down favorites are Firriato's Santagostino Baglio Soria, a Nero d'Avola–Syrah blend, and Donnafugata's Tancredi, a 70/30 blend of Nero and Cabernet, both of which *are* sold in the United States. The pepperiness of the Syrah and the structural girding imparted by the Cabernet make these blends terrific accompaniments to Sicilian red-sauce pastas. (At dinner in the Sicilian mountaintop town of Erice, I climbed even nearer the stars when I had the Firriato Santagostino with a red-sauce pasta dish incorporating rough-hewn chunks—shells and all—of Mediterranean lobster, or *aragosta*.)

A few other recommendations of Sicilian whites and reds you might try are given below, but it's impossible to close this sidebar without again mentioning the sweet wine known as **Passito di Pantelleria**. Not strictly Sicilian, in that it's made on the tiny island of Pantelleria, just off the Tunisian coast, *passito* is created through an unusual process in which sundried raisins of the Zibibbo grape (zih-BEE-boh; better known outside Sicily as Muscat of Alexandria) are combined with juice from late-harvested Zibibbo prior to fermentation. The result is an intense, viscous, amber-hued wine that, although exploding with honeyed-fruit flavor (apricots!) is not at all cloying. It's spectacular with simple desserts (think plain custard or flan) but also—because the raisiny quality is offset by the fresh-juice zip—very good sipped all by itself. Donnafugata makes a *passito* called Ben Ryé. The name means "son of the wind" in Arabic—appropriate because most of the inhabitants of sirocco-swept Pantelleria are of Arab descent. At about $35 a bottle, it's a little pricey for *Drinkology WINE*'s budget. But I promise it will blow you away.

Other Sicilian Wines Worth Trying

Donnafugata's Anthìlia (white): This half-and-half combo of Ansonica (Insolia) and Cataratto is fresh and fruity with surprisingly long finish.

Donnafugata's Vigna di Gabri (white): Though 100 percent Ansonica, this wine distinguishes itself from other, ordinary Sicilian whites in that 20 percent of the wine has been barrique-aged; just uncorked, it can be slightly harsh, but as it warms and opens, that woodiness is replaced by a delicate and pleasing caramel flavor. A very versatile wine—great with grilled meats, pasta, and seafood.

Duca di Salaparuta's Terre d'Agala (red): This blend of Nerello Mascalese (another native Sicilian variety) and Merlot is nicely structured, with light tannins. It's swell with spicy red-sauce pasta dishes—putanesca and arrabiata.

Firriato's Camelot (red): Proof that Sicilian winemakers can succeed with Super Tuscan–style reds, this Cabernet/Merlot blend is certainly a serious wine, but you can pleasurably drink it young.

Tasca d'Almerita's Leone d'Almerita (white): Lots of Sicilian producers are blending the native Insolia with Chardonnay; few are doing it this well. It seems custom-made for Sicilian seafood dishes, including smoked fish *(pesce affumicata),* grilled swordfish *(pesce spada),* and *fritto misto* (mixed fried seafood).

Spain

When it comes to international popularity, Spanish wines are beginning to give Italian wines a run for their (i.e., your) money. If your local wine shops are like those in my vicinity, they're carrying a much greater variety of Spanish wine than they did even two or three years ago; at one shop near me, the diversity of the Spanish wines on sale seems to increase from one month to the next. One reason for all the new attention is a dramatic improvement in quality, due to the relatively recent embrace of modern winemaking techniques—things like taking steps to prevent grapes from fermenting before reaching the winery, controlling white wines' fermentation, even simple winery hygiene—by many Spanish winemakers. Another is the ongoing revolution in Spanish cuisine; the relentless creativity of Spanish chefs has driven equally creative experimentation among the country's vintners.

This section focuses most of its attention on **Sherries**—fortified wines that are perhaps Spain's greatest contribution to the world of wine and that are given lengthy treatment here because they've been so unfairly neglected by most American wine drinkers (a situation that appears to be changing). But first a few notes on some other (unfortified) Spanish wines you're likely to encounter.

Reds. The most famous, and those that make the most frequent appearances on U.S. wine shop shelves, are the reds of **Rioja** (ree-OH-hah), a region of north-central Spain renowned for Tempranillo-dominated blended wines traditionally given long barrel-ageing—traditionally in American oak. Those traditions are changing, however, and today's Riojas are likely to have spent less time in barrel (now sometimes French oak) than would have been customary in the past. At their best, red

Riojas are powerful (often tannic) wines with a complex medley of fragrances and flavors. The Rioja Crianza made by Antigua Usanza is fantastically aromatic. At about $15, it's a great wine to use in sangria (a great recipe for which appears in this book's companion volume, *Drinkology*).

That term **crianza**, which you're likely to see on the labels of many of the Spanish wines carried by your local merchant, is, by the way, an indication of how much time the wine has spent in barrel. *Crianza* wines are "younger"—that is, have received less barrel ageing—than those labeled **reserva** or **gran reserva**. The specific requirements for these categories differ from one Spanish region to another (and some regions don't even use them); just remember that *crianzas* are likelier to be more **fruit forward**—because they're less mature—than *reservas* or *gran riservas*.

Spain has more than fifty winegrowing regions possessing appellation status—the Spanish terms are ***Denominación de Origen*** (DO) and the more elevated ***Denominación de Origen Calificada*** ("qualified denomination of origin"; DOCa). Besides those from Rioja (the first region to be accorded the DOCa designation), other Spanish reds you'll want to look out for include those from the Catalonian regions of the **Penedès** and **Priorato**, and—a personal favorite—those from the **Jumilla** (inland from the cities of Valencia and Alicante, in eastern Spain).

The Penedès (pay-NAY-dess) is best known for the sparkling white wine called *cava* (see page 219), but its still red wines—typically blends, and often (not always) dominated by Tempranillo (here traditionally called Ull de Llebre)—are showing up increasingly often in American wine shops and on restaurant wine lists. Although it's unusual in that it contains no Tempranillo, the branded wine called Sangre de Toro

("Blood of the Bull"), made by the big Barcelona-based maker Torres, offers a robust introduction to Penedès reds at a price that won't make you stamp your hooves and snort: about $10. (Sangre de Toro's blend is about two-thirds Garnacha, and one-third Cariñena—a variety called Carignan in France.)

Priorato (pree-oh-RAH-toh; called Priorat in the regional Catalan dialect) is a tiny region southwest of Barcelona that fifteen years ago was hardly on Spain's wine map. But a group of enterprising small producers reinvigorated the wine industry here, creating lush blended reds—often dependent on Garnacha and/or Cariñena but also incorporating French varieties like Cabernet Sauvignon and Syrah—that knocked the wine world's silk socks off. (Priorato came so far so quickly that in 2000 it was named Spain's second DOCa region.) Priorats tend to be expensive ($40 and up), but you can find some within *Drinkology WINE*'s preferred range. The Cartoixa Reserva made by Scala Dei (a Cabernet-Garnacha-Syrah blend; about $25) is an awesomely extracted wine that seems custom-built to accompany a leg of lamb or a beef roast.

I choose to round out our little list with Jumilla (hoo-MEE-yah) only because I've had such wonderful experiences with its red wines, mostly blends dependent on a variety the Spanish call Monastrell—the same grape called Mourvèdre in France. Actually, one Jumilla that wowed me was a Monastrell *varietal*; the Altos de la Hoya Monastrell made by Bodegas Olivares. It retails for about $12—too little to pay for a wine with such a complex nose (floral, earthy, banana-like) and one so gorgeously round in the mouth (a quince or apple-peel flavor predominated). Other Jumillas—blends, but in the same price range—that I've enjoyed include those carrying the Altos de Luzón and Casa de la Ermita labels.

But don't let my hurried and narrow summary circumscribe your exploration of Spanish reds. Among others you'll want to sample are those of **Ribero del Duero**, in north-central Spain—mostly blends whose major constituent is a local strain of Tempranillo called Tinto Fino—and of **Navarra**, which lies just to the northeast of Rioja and whose blended wines rely more or less equally on Tempranillo and Garnacha.

Whites. There's space enough to mention just two Spanish whites—but don't think this is just a mention "in passing," since these white wines are among the most characterful and delicious you'll ever encounter. Though both may be DO wines, their labels are more likely to identify them by varietal rather than place-of-origin names: **Verdejo** (vair-DAY-hoh), which mostly comes from the Rueda region, northwest of Madrid (though the grape is grown in several other Spanish regions), and **Albariño** (ahl-bah-REEN-yoh), from the Rías Baixas region of Galicia, in Spain's northwestern corner just above Portugal's northern border. Recommendations: the Albariño made by Peitán (about $14) and the Naia-brand Verdejo (about $12). I can't shout the Naia Verdejo's praises loudly enough: densely fruity but with a definite acid tickle, it rates only slightly below my beloved Mosel Rieslings. Naia's bold, abstract orange-and-white label is instantly recognizable. So buy a bottle.

Sherry. I remember when I first heard of Sherry—or, rather, read of it. I was eleven or twelve years old and reading Edgar Allan Poe's stories for the first time. They were, I discovered to my great excitement, even scarier than the Vincent Price movies based on them that I'd seen, and one of the scariest was "The Cask of Amontillado." I didn't know what

Amontillado was—the dictionary's definition, "a medium dry sherry," didn't help much—and I was left wondering what about this stuff was so enticing that it could lure Fortunato, the hapless victim of the tale, to his murder deep in the "catacombs of the Montresors." The story, thrilling as it was, provided nary a clue as to the attraction.

Neither, frankly, did my early adult experience of Sherry. As a young man, I hung out with an Episcopalian priest—he was a chaplain at my college—and, though he himself was a bourbon drinker, he introduced me to a larger high-church Anglican circle in which Sherry was the aperitif of choice. In the tasteful, understated parlors of this set, Sherry was always served from crystal decanters, whose elegance belied the fact that the Sherry inside them was usually the cheapest available rotgut. I didn't know that then, of course; I just figured that this was what Sherry was—rancid, nasty-tasting hooch that, try as I might, I'd never develop a taste for. Poor old Fortunato began to seem even more foolish.

And that's pretty much where I left it until it came time to work on this book. Oh, sure, I'd long before taken to keeping a bottle of (inexpensive) Sherry in the kitchen cupboard, since so many recipes call for it. Liking the nutty, aromatic character it lends to food, I even began using it in some of my own creations—and on a friend's advice began adding a teaspoonful to hearty soups, just before serving. But *drink* the stuff? You've got to be kidding.

Unfortunately, my image of Sherry—as the drink of prim, churchy gentlewomen of a certain caste and a certain age, and as a wine whose chief value is in the kitchen—is one that many Americans share. Our ignorance of Sherry is reflected in our wine shops, whose selection of Sherries is often slight. What a shame.

In truth, Sherry is one of the great fortified wines of the world. Our word "Sherry" is a corruption of the name Jerez (hare-ETH), a town in southwestern Andalusia that has given its name to the Sherry-producing region that surrounds it. (The town's full name is Jerez de la Frontera; it and two nearby Andalusian towns, Puerto de Santa María and Sanlúcar de Barrameda, are the only places Sherry is made.)

Actually, to speak of "Sherry" as if all Sherries were similar is a mistake. All Sherries are white wines that have undergone deliberate, long-term oxidation, but there are two basic styles—**fino** ("fine") and **oloroso** ("fragrant")—and these are divided into several subtypes, for a total of seven styles in all.

First, though, the basic distinction. Fino Sherries are dry; rather light in color, body, and flavor; and, though fortified, lower in alcohol (about 15 percent) than olorosos. Darker, fuller-bodied, and fuller-flavored (nut and caramel flavors predominate), olorosos may be dry or sweet, and they generally weigh in at about 18 percent alcohol. The differences result from the different ways finos and olorosos are made.

Fino Sherries are made from better-quality grapes. (The major variety is Palomino, though two other grapes, Pedro Ximénez and Moscatel—a Spanish name for our old friend Muscat of Alexandria—play minor roles.) Only the free-run juice from the crushing of the grapes is used for finos. Olorosos are made from grapes (also mostly Palomino) from lesser vineyards, and free-run juice is mixed with juice from pressing before fermentation. Olorosos' darker color is partly—though only partly—accounted for by the fact that the pressed juice remains in somewhat longer contact with the skins.

Virtually all Sherries—dry or sweet—are fermented to dryness before the additional alcohol (in the form of distilled grape spirits) is added; most sweet Sherries become so through the addition of sweet wine later on. More alcohol is added to Sherries destined to become olorosos than to those that will be finos, and this disparity has a big effect on what happens to the wines as they mature.

All Sherries are barrel matured, but the method of maturation is unique to the Jerez region. It's called the **solera** method, and it involves transferring wine from barrel to barrel as it ages. It's easiest to understand the process by beginning at the end and working our way backward. After the

The *solera* method is unique to Jerez

Sherry has sat for a time in the last barrel in the series, a portion is withdrawn and bottled. The same amount is then extracted from the next-to-last barrel and used to replenish what was taken from the final one. An equal quantity of wine is removed from the barrel that's third from last and added to the next to last. And so on—until we get to the first barrel in the *solera*, which is replenished with "new" wine (actually, wine that's been barrel aged for a year following fermentation before entering the *solera* system). Depending on the complexity of a bodega's *solera*, the wine may travel through as few as five or as many as fourteen barrels before bottling. The ranks of barrels—the proper term for these large casks is **butts**—that make up a *solera* have a Spanish name that wine babies will love: they're called *criaderas* ("nurseries").

Notice something important about this process: the butts are never completely emptied, so some older wine always remains behind to mix with the younger wine that's added to it. This **fractional blending**, combined with the fact that the butts are old—used in many cases for a hundred years or longer—is partly responsible for Sherries' distinctive flavor.

But there are other factors, and here we come back to the difference between finos and olorosos. None of the butts in a *solera* is ever filled to the top—an airspace occupying one-sixth to one-fourth of the butt's volume is allowed to remain. As they develop, higher-alcohol oloroso Sherries interact directly with the oxygen in this airspace, which is another reason they're comparatively dark in color. But a weird thing happens to the fino Sherries: they're low enough in alcohol to permit the growth, on the surface of the wine, of a kind of yeast unique to the Jerez region: it's called *flor*, because it appears to "flower" across the surface of the wine. Feeding off the oxygen in the airspace and nutrients in the wine (which are replenished whenever younger wine is added to the barrel), the *flor* can form a thick crust atop the wine; though this layer of yeast is porous, it greatly restricts the amount of oxygen reaching the wine, which is why fino Sherries are so much lighter in color—and brighter and livelier in taste—than olorosos.

That's about as much as you need to know about Sherry-making technique, but let's take a brief look at the subtypes of finos and olorosos. The lightest finos are called **manzanilla** Sherries; they're made only in the seaside town of Sanlúcar, where the humidity remains high enough to permit the *flor* to remain alive year round. (Elsewhere in the Jerez region, the *flor* dies off during the dry summer, meaning that standard finos interact more directly with the oxygen in their casks for a couple of months each year.) Manzanillas are fragile wines; they should be drunk within a few months of bottling, their freshness intact. (Since Sherries are never dated, you should buy a manzanilla only from a wine shop that gets new shipments regularly and frequently.) Manzanillas should be served chilled—and should be kept (in the fridge!) for no more than two or three days after opening.

As should other finos. One of the big mistakes that people make with Sherry is to treat all Sherries as if they last forever. Manzanillas and finos don't—once a bottle of either has been opened, it's no more long-lived than any other white wine.

Amontillados are fino Sherries that are dosed with extra alcohol and given additional barrel ageing after they leave the *solera* system. The extra alcohol prevents the regrowth of the *flor*, and amontillados therefore take on some of the darker color and nutty flavor of olorosos. Manzanillas and finos are always dry, but many amontillados are sweetened through the addition of a little bit of a sweet Sherry called Pedro Ximénez (see below). **Palo cortado** Sherries, in turn, are amontillados allowed to age even longer in barrel, bringing them even closer in character to olorosos. Amontillados are best served chilled; palo cortados, like olorosos, at room temperature.

Drinkology WINE recommends that you introduce yourself to Sherry by sampling an oloroso: at their best, olorosos are incomparably rich and nutty—there's just no other wine like them. (And they take a little less getting used to than finos, which can have a sharp "chemical" flavor that's definitely an acquired taste.) Unlike finos, olorosos—which are on quite friendly terms with oxygen—can survive for a long time after being opened, so there's no rush to drink the whole bottle. (And, yes, you can transfer an oloroso to a decanter and serve it in elegant little glasses when the pastor comes to visit.) Today, most olorosos are slightly sweetened with a dash of Pedro Ximénez.

Cream Sherries are *very* sweet Sherries that were originally developed for the British market. (The most famous is Harvey's Bristol Cream.) Cream Sherries are generally cloying and uninteresting but can be great cocktail ingredients.

Pedro Ximénez Sherries, made from the grape of the same name, are also very sweet—but of an altogether different order from the creams. This viscous, dark brown Sherry is made from the juice of very ripe grapes, or even raisins—juice so sugary that it cannot be fermented to dryness. Pedro Ximénez isn't just used to sweeten amontillados, olorosos, and creams; in Andalusia, it's drunk by itself as a dessert wine. With its characteristic flavor of raisins, coffee, and chocolate, it's fantastic drizzled over vanilla ice cream.

Crisp, well-chilled manzanillas and finos are just *made* to be drunk with seafood. Olorosos, assuming their dark-and-handsome suavity suits your disposition, can be marvelous aperitifs, but it's a good idea—because of the potency of their flavor and alcohol content—to serve them with hors d'oeuvres. (In Spain, dry and off-dry Sherries of all types are served with the small-portioned dishes called *tapas*.)

Sherry's limited international market means that Sherries are surprisingly inexpensive—even shockingly underpriced, when you consider the amount of time and labor that goes into their making. Many respectable Sherries—including finos, olorosos, amontillados, and palo cortados—can be had for between $15 and $25 a bottle. (Try those by Emilio Lustau.) The Sherry-maker called Osborne produces a range of drinkable Sherries for even less. (It's a bottle of Osborne's oloroso that I keep in my kitchen for use in recipes calling for Sherry.)

PORTUGAL

Portugal gives three gifts to the wine world. The first two are the magnificent fortified wines **Port** and **Madeira** (the latter made on the Portuguese-owned island of Madeira, off the West African coast). The third isn't a wine at all—it's *cork*, of which this little country nestled into the Iberian Peninsula is the world's largest producer.

Though this section is mostly devoted to Port—by far the most important wine that Portugal produces—it's worth noting that non-fortified Portuguese wines have, by all accounts, improved enormously over the past twenty or so years. I'm old enough to have been introduced to the country's wine through the mass-market Portuguese brands Lancers and Mateus—whose semisweet, semi-sparkling rosés enjoyed astonishing popularity in the United States from the postwar years up through the 1980s. I don't mean to disparage them too harshly: they accompanied many an interesting—if déclassé!—evening during my young manhood. They're still made, of course, but today your local wine shop is also likely to carry a sampling of dry Portuguese reds (including some, probably, from the **Douro** region, where the grapes for Port are also grown; see below), as well as a small selection of the Portuguese white wines known as **Vinho Verde**

The name Vinho Verde means "green wine"

(VEEN-yoh VAIR-deh). Vinho Verde— the name means "green wine," an indication of its youthfulness, not its color—is produced in the northernmost part of Portugal, in a region called the **Minho**, just below the border from Galicia, in Spain. You might think of Vinho Verde as Portugal's version of the Spanish Albariño—it's often made from the same grape (here called Alvarinho). But unlike the often distinctly fruity and aromatic Albariño, Vinho Verde is usually a very simple, light, refreshing wine (and often the eensiest bit spritzy). Some wines are too much for me; Vinho Verde is too little—a white wine that, though dry, often *really is* like soda pop. (In fairness, many people like it as a summertime refresher.)

A Note on Madeira. Made on the Atlantic island of the same name (a Portuguese possession since the fifteenth century), Madeira was once the most popular fortified wine in America—in fact, it was the most popular *wine*, period. The signers of the Declaration toasted their independence with Madeira; it was served at George Washington's inauguration.

Madeira's fortunes have mostly fallen since the mid-nineteenth century, however. Today, much Madeira is mass-produced stuff suitable for cooking and not much else. But there are still good Madeiras being made— through an intricate process that involves heating the wine (sometimes by storing it in casks in attic lofts that broil under the island's subtropical sun) and then subjecting it to long (sometimes *very* long) barrel ageing. The best Madeiras are made from one of four white grapes—Sercial, Verdelho, Bual, and Malmsey (elsewhere called Malvasia)—and the grape that's used correlates with the wine's level of sweetness, with Sercial Madeiras being the driest and Malmseys the sweetest. Vintage Madeiras are the province of connoisseurs and can fetch hundreds of dollars a bottle. But there's a California firm, the Rare Wine Co., that oversees the production of a series of blended Madeiras intended to approximate the styles of Madeira that were popular in America during the colonial and Revolutionary era. The company's New York Malmsey, Boston Bual, and Charleston Sercial brands provide an excellent entrée into the world of Madeira for about $40 a bottle.

Port. War! What is it good for? Well, perhaps not *absolutely* nothing— for without war, we would never have had the exceptional fortified wine called Port.

The origin of Port, you see, is inextricably tied to the endless wars between Britain and France that roiled Europe from the sixteenth through the early nineteenth century. Whenever these nations squabbled, Britain would impose heavy duties on imported French wine; whenever actual fighting broke out, shipments of French wines to Britain would cease, and British tipplers would find themselves bereft of their beloved claret. Port was born during one of these contretemps, in the early 1700s, when British merchants, looking for another source of wine to keep their countrymen lubricated, decided to give Portugal a try. They set up shop in the Portuguese city of Oporto, at the mouth of the Douro River, and began shipping home wine from the vineyards that lay many miles upstream. (In case it isn't obvious, Port—or, more properly, *Porto*—takes its name from its hometown.)

To begin with there wasn't very much of this wine, and it wasn't very good, so the British shippers—eventually there came to be quite a number of them—took it upon themselves to build the industry from what amounted to scratch, overseeing the construction of terraced vineyards in the harsh terrain of the Upper Douro region and refining the methods by which Port was made. It wouldn't be too far off the mark to say that the British were virtual "colonizers" of northern Portugal during this period. Although the Portuguese did eventually gain some measure of control over the Port trade, Port remains closely identified with the numerous British-named firms—companies like Dow's and Graham's and Warre's and Taylor Fladgate & Yeatman—that continue to produce and market much of the Port made today.

Port is one of those kinds of wine—Bordeaux, Burgundies, and Champagne are others—that merit and reward a lifetime of study (and drinking). The complexities of Port production—and appreciation—go well beyond this little book's scope, so consider what follows as only the barest, most fleeting of introductions.

At its most basic, Port is a red wine whose fermentation has been deliberately interrupted through the addition of brandy—high-alcohol distilled grape spirits—to the fermenting must. (You'll remember from chapter 2 that yeast die off when the alcohol in the must reaches a certain level.) Adding the brandy not only **fortifies** the wine, raising its alcohol content to about 20 percent, but it also ensures that the wine remains sweet, since the yeast aren't given the chance to finish their job of converting all the sugar in the grape juice to alcohol. So now you know that Port is a sweet, fortified red wine—which means, unfortunately, that you know next to nothing.

That's because Port is made in *ten* distinct styles, which vary according to how long the wine is aged in barrel before being bottled, whether or not it's filtered before being bottled, how long it should be allowed to continue ageing in the bottle before being drunk, whether the wine is a blend of wines from different years or consists entirely of wine from a single vintage, where in the Douro region the grapes used to make the wine are grown, and yet other factors. Talk about too much wine information! The thing is, most of the Ports you'll find on **Port is made in ten distinct styles** American wine shop shelves belong to one of only five—or six, depending on how you count—categories, so let's focus our attention on those.

Ruby Ports are relatively simple young wines—blends of different vintages—that have been aged in barrels (or sometimes in metal tanks) for two or three years before being bottled, after which they're immediately released and are ready to drink. (The reason, by the way, for blending together wines from different vintages is twofold. First, it allows the **shipper**—Port makers are called *shippers*—to compensate for poorer-quality vintages by mixing those wines with ones from better years. Second, blending makes it possible for each maker to establish a consistent, recognizable house style by adjusting the blend, as necessary, from year to year.) Rubies can be densely fruity, very enjoyable wines, but they're a far cry from the serious Ports admired by connoisseurs.

Things become more complicated when we get to **tawny Ports**, which come in two—*very* different—basic varieties: ***young* tawny Ports** and *aged* tawny **Ports**. As their names imply, both of these are light in color, but the similarity stops there. Young tawnies are insignificant wines made from not-great grapes. (The French drink young tawny Port on the rocks, as an aperitif; there's no reason for your francophilia to extend this far.)

Aged tawnies, by contrast, can be extremely impressive. The label will tell you how long an aged tawny Port has spent in the barrel: ten years, twenty years, thirty years, or forty years. Actually, since these, too, are blends from different vintages, the stated age is an average. (Young tawny Ports carry no age indication.) Barrel ageing giveth and it taketh away: long contact with wood gives aged tawnies a superbly nutty, sometimes caramelized flavor; the years spent in the cask also gradually divest these wines of their original deep-red color. Aged tawny Ports are ready to drink as soon as they've been bottled and released, and unlike vintage Ports (see below) they don't require decanting before serving. Though aged tawny Ports can be drunk as aperitifs, they're perhaps better reserved for the end of a meal—or, even better, drunk as nightcaps.

Vintage Ports are what Port aficionados usually mean when they say "Port." Since most Ports are blends of several years' wines, they don't carry a vintage. Vintage Ports, by contrast, are made entirely of grapes from a single harvest—and it has to be a great harvest, yielding superlative grapes, for a shipper to "declare a vintage." (Actually, the decision doesn't belong just to the shipper; an official body called the Port Wine Institute has to test the wine and approve the shipper's intention.) Although Port shippers declare vintages individually, there's usually some degree of consensus as to what constitutes a great harvest. The years in which a large number of shippers declare a vintage aren't exceedingly rare: they happen, on average, about three times per decade.

Unlike aged tawnies, vintage Ports don't spend a great deal of time maturing in barrel: only two years. But they're capable of evolving in the bottle for decades after their release. In fact, opening a vintage Port before it's undergone lengthy bottle maturation is considered, in some circles, a crime against nurture. (I hereby confess that during the writing of this book I opened—and, yes, drank—a vintage 1997 Port by a less-well-known shipper called Delaforce. I

Vintage years are declared about three times per decade

know I should've waited, but let me report that it was one of the most delectable, satisfying wine-drinking experiences of my life. I'm committed, however, to holding onto the vintage 2000 Delaforce I bought to replace it, at least until . . . .)

Vintage Ports are not filtered or fined before being bottled, and they throw a shocking amount of sediment as they age, which means they must be carefully decanted before serving. (For a little lesson on decanting wines, see page 350.) Younger vintage Ports are costly, but compared with some other kinds of wine not breathtakingly so—meaning that you can find many in the $40 to $70 range. For *Drinkology WINE*'s penny-laden change-purse, that's a lot of money, but we're less miserly when it comes to Port than virtually any other wine.

There *are* cheaper alternatives to vintage Ports that provide more or less close-ish facsimiles to the epiphany that vintage Port bestows. The names of these other styles are somewhat deceiving, so be careful. The first is what's called a **late bottled vintage Port**. These "LBV" Ports carry a vintage year, but they're not *true* vintage Ports, because (1) they're made every year, and (2) they're given longer barrel ageing and are filtered before bottling. They're ready to drink when released, and they usually don't have to be decanted. (But be careful—I've had LBV Ports that threw a little bit of sediment.) The other of these styles is called **vintage character Port**—an even more annoying name, since these Ports are blends from different years (their labels aren't dated) and because they don't, in fact, have the character of vintage Ports. Irritatingly imprecise nomenclature aside, LBV and vintage character Ports *can* be very nice wines. One vintage character Port—the Six Grapes brand, made by Graham's (about $20)—has been a frequent visitor to the *Drinkology WINE* household.

Except for young tawnies, Ports of all these stripes are powerfully flavored wines whose sweetness and magnitude makes them most suitable for serving *after* dinner. That doesn't mean that they're good "dessert" wines, however, since they'll simply overpower virtually any cake, pastry, pudding, or other dessert. The best accompaniment is

Stilton is Port's ideal partner

a cheese course, preferably one that includes a robust blue cheese. (The English blue called Stilton is an ideal partner.) Or Port can be served all by itself, as a "digestive" to punctuate dinner's conclusion or—my favorite—as a late-evening libation.

Speaking of conclusions, I can't take my leave of this brief introduction to Port without a few concluding notes. Number one: Some Ports sport the credential **single *quinta* vintage Port**. *Quinta* (KEEN-tah) is the Portuguese word for "farm"; single *quinta* vintage Ports are therefore Ports made from grapes produced in a single year by a single vineyard. Number two: Lots of winemakers outside Portugal make fortified wines that they call "port." These wines may be good or bad, but they are *not* Port; the term should be applied only to the fortified wines of Portugal. Number three: Though British firms continue to dominate the Port trade, a number of Portuguese makers have, over the years, elbowed their way into the business. One of these companies, Quinta do Infantado, produces spectacular Ports in the range of styles described above. Infantado's ruby Port—at less than $20 the bottle—has become my "default" Port. It is plain delicious.

GERMANY AND AUSTRIA

I went into a neighborhood wine shop recently—not one that I ordinarily patronize—and asked the manager to direct me to the German wines. (I'd poked around a bit myself and couldn't locate them.) "We don't sell any," he responded. "We used to carry a few, but nobody bought them."

Granted, this particular shop's an extreme case—but not all *that* extreme. Even at the very best American wine shops (I'm thinking of places like Sherry-Lehmann, on Madison Avenue in New York City), the German-wine inventory is mostly limited to Rieslings, and these Rieslings mostly come from only four of Germany's thirteen winegrowing regions: **Mosel-Saar-Ruwer**, the **Rheingau** (RINE-gow), the **Pfalz** (FAHLTZ), and the **Rheinhessen** (RINE-hess-en). (These and several other German wine regions are strung along the Rhine River and several of its tributaries in the southwestern part of the country.)

Walk into a shop whose holdings are less extensive than the redoubtable Sherry-Lehmann, and you're likely to find a few Mosel Rieslings—and that's it. Now, it's true that Riesling is by far the most important of German fine-wine grapes, and that Mosel Rieslings—see pages 178–181 for detailed treatment—are among the world's most wondrous wines. But so long as you remain stateside, your experience of the wines of Germany is going to remain circumscribed. And that goes double for Austria—Germany's southeasterly neighbor, and the other great winemaking country of middle Europe—since your wine shop's selection of Austrian wines will probably consist of a dry Riesling or two and perhaps a couple of Grüner Veltliners, if you're lucky. (For more on Grüner Veltliner, Austria's most important white grape, see page 191.)

Given these realities, there are just a few things that you need to know about German and Austrian wines. As you learned in chapter 6, the best German wines are those categorized as *Qualitätswein mit Prädikat* ("quality wines with special attributes"). Fortunately, you don't have to know how to pronounce this term—just remember the acronym QmP, and you'll do fine. (The six classes of QmP wines are explained on pages 179-181.)

Since few poor-quality German wines are exported, by far the greater majority of German wines you'll find in U.S. shops are QmPs, though it's possible you might encounter wines from one of two lesser categories: ***Qualitätswein bestimmter Anbaugebiet*** ("quality wine from a specified region"; **QbA**) or, much more rarely, ***Qualitätswein garantierten Ursprungs*** ("quality wine of guaranteed origin"; **QgU**). Though the analogy is far from exact, you might think of these two categories as very roughly equivalent to French regional- and village-appellation wines, respectively. German wine laws take greater account of the ripeness of the grapes used in a wine than do other nations' appellation systems, but they're similarly hierarchical, with regulations regarding such things as alcohol content and winemaking techniques growing stricter as you move up the scale from QbA to QgU to QmP. (Note: QbA wines are typically chaptalized, which means that sugar is added to the must before or during fermentation, the purpose being to raise the alcohol level of the finished wine. **Chaptalization** is unlawful in some winegrowing regions and frowned upon in others, since it's often employed to disguise the fact that the grapes were underripe when harvested or to compensate for lack of concentration where yields are too high. But in some northern winegrowing regions—Germany, Alsace, and others—it's legal and accepted for *some kinds* of wines.)

The labels of QmP wines tend to look more difficult to figure out than they actually are. For instance, sitting on my desk is a bottle labeled "Bert Simon/Serrig Würtzberg/Riesling Spätlese/2003/Mosel-Saar-Ruwer." "Bert Simon" is the most prominent line on the label—indicating that this is the name of the producer. The second line, "Serrig Würtzberg," consists of the name of the village from which this wine comes (Serrig, in the Saar Valley) and the name of the vineyard in which the grapes were grown (Würztberg). (Note: Often, the suffix "-er" is added to the village's name; thus a wine labeled "Serriger" would also come from the village of Serrig.) "Riesling," obviously, is the name of the grape, and "Spätlese" the QmP classification (see page 179). The vintage is 2003; the region Mosel-Saar-Ruwer. (This is a pretty good wine, by the way, with a creamy-citrusy flavor reminiscent of key lime pie; it costs about $20.)

What's complicated isn't the deciphering of a German label so much as the understanding of what all these names and terms signify about a wine's probable quality—and this requires familiarity and a level of expertise similar to that needed to make an educated guess about the quality of a Burgundy. If your

Knowing the importer can give you a leg up

choice is to be more than just haphazard, you've got to know something about the maker, something about the village and—more important—the vineyard, and something about the vintage. As I've mentioned before, recognizing a good importer's name can give you something of a leg up; the Terry Thiese Selection wines imported by Michael Skurnik are terrifically trustworthy. (Also, the weather gave you a break during the decade 1993–2003; with the exception of 2000, German vintages during this period were good to outstanding.)

There are two other words that appear on some German wine labels that you ought to know: ***trocken*** and ***halbtrocken***, meaning "dry" and "half-dry" (or "semi-dry"), respectively. *Trocken* wines contain negligible amounts of residual sugar; *halbtrocken* wines only a little (less than 2 percent), so they, too, are likely to taste dry. And don't be confused—as I once was—if you see the word *Weingut* preceding a producer's name. This word, which you might mistranslate as "good wine," doesn't signal anything about quality; it's simply the German word for "winery" (literally, "wine estate").

Austria's wine classification system differs subtly from that of Germany, but there's no need to go into the details here. Just remember that the dry Austrian white wines you're likely to encounter—Rieslings and Grüner Veltliners—will, on the whole, be more fruit-forward and higher in alcohol than German whites (both functions of Austria's more southerly latitude). Austria's wine regions are concentrated in the eastern part of the country, near the Slovakian and Hungarian borders; the most important is **Lower Austria** (the "lower" refers to the area's downstream location along the Danube River).

You won't see "Lower Austria" on a wine's label, however; you'll see the name of one of the districts into which Lower Austria is divided: Carnuntum, Donauland, Kamptal, Kremstal, Thermenregion, Traisental, Wachau, and Weinviertel. **Wachau** (vahk-AOW) is generally regarded as the most important of these, not for the quantity of wine produced but for its quality. But—wouldn't you know?—the Wachau district has a classification system all its own, categorizing wines as **Steinfeder** (SHTINE-fay-der; the lightest-bodied), **Federspiel** (FAY-der-shpeel; more or less equivalent to a German Kabinett), or **Smaragd** (smah-RAHGT; roughly equivalent to a Spätlese). Among the Austrian wines that do manage to make their way to the United States, those made by the Wachau estate called Nikolaihof are very reliable (and they're produced following biodynamic principles; see page 282). Try the Nikolaihof von Stein Riesling Federspiel; wonderfully balancing

Wachau has a system that's all its own

mineral and fruit flavors, it's a great accompaniment to Wiener schnitzel or chicken paprika (cost: under $15).

The vast majority of German and Austrian wines imported into the United States are whites, but I can't close this section without mentioning an Austrian red that's been making occasional appearances at wine shops near me—and that you, too, may be lucky enough to find. It's made from a grape called **Blaufränkisch** (BLAOW-frehn-kish), and it has the fresh-fruit scrumptiousness of a Beaujolais. A maker called Glatzer, located in the Lower Austria district of Carnuntum, makes a very pleasant Blaufränkisch that sells for about $15. (Glatzer also makes a respectable Grüner Veltliner Kabinett that's about the same price.)

The paucity of German and Austrian wines in our shops sometimes makes me wonder whether American wine drinkers are really aware that World War II ended more than sixty years ago. Until the de facto embargo is lifted, your only way of gaining an acquaintance with the full range of these countries' wines is to travel there. If such a trip's in your stars, you might want to consider signing up for one of the tours offered by the German Wine Academy, which aim at quickly equipping participants with the basic knowledge and skill necessary to understand and differentiate among the wines produced by all of Germany's thirteen wine regions. The tours are, in fact, more like wine classes that trundle from place to place:

It wasn't too long ago that American Jews who keep kosher met with a very limited selection at the wine shop. Aside from the thick, sweet, grape-juicy wines made by two big producers, Manischewitz and Mogen David, there wasn't much, if anything, to choose from. The situation today couldn't be more different. Some wine shops in cities with a large Jewish population carry a wide variety of fine kosher wines—of types ranging from California varietals, to Bordeaux, to Champagne, to . . . why, there's even a kosher Moscato d'Asti.

And kosher wines continue to improve, with the best being indistinguishable, on the level of overall quality, from their non-kosher counterparts. That's especially heartening when you consider that it's rather difficult, from a practical point of view, to create fine kosher wines that can compete taste-wise with non-kosher wines. Among the many religious requirements are that, from the moment the grapes enter the winery, all the winemaking must be performed by Sabbath-observing Jewish men and that no work whatsoever can be performed between sundown on Friday and sundown on Saturday—a prohibition that can cause problems if, for example, something goes wrong with a fermentation during the Sabbath.

But it's a particular requirement for kosher wines labeled *mevushal*—wines that remain kosher even if opened and poured by a non-Jew—that can cause the most trouble, at least potentially. *Mevushal* wines must be heated (the Hebrew term literally means "cooked," or "boiled"), and heat is notorious for injuring wine's aromas and flavors. Today, makers of fine kosher wine overcome this difficulty by passing the must through a flash pasteurization unit that quickly raises its temperature to 185 degrees Fahrenheit, then immediately cools it down, eliminating or minimizing any flavor loss. Or such is the claim. Some wine critics do maintain that white wines endure the process somewhat better than do reds, which are more susceptible to heat damage.

The practical hurdles haven't stopped winemakers from entering the kosher market, now estimated at $27 million a year, domestically. One wine shop in the Bronx, in New York City, stocks no fewer than 450 different kosher wines, including wines from Australia, Chile, France, Hungary, South Africa, Spain, and, of course, Israel—whose wines, especially those from the Golan Heights, have been improving at lightning speed. (Note that not all Israeli wine is kosher.)

Among American kosher-wine makers, two California firms, Baron Herzog and Hagafen, earn consistently high marks for their red and white varietals. Baron Herzog's beat Hagafen's on the affordability scale, with the former's Cabernet Sauvignon retailing for about $13 (the Hagafen Cab goes for a little less than $40). For a good kosher sparkler, turn to the Champagne house of Nicholas Feuillatte; its kosher nonvintage brut costs about $40. Don't think of these wines as wines meant only for observant Jewish wine-drinkers; they're top-notch wines that just happen to be kosher.

the course ends with a blind taste-test, and participants are presented with certificates of achievement. (How *echt Deutsch* can you get?) You can find out more about the academy's tours by visiting its website: the English-language version is at www.deutscheweine.de/Frame.asp?Sprache=E. (The website does not explain, however, what happens to you if you *fail* the blind tasting.)

EVERYPLACE ELSE

A friend gave me a bottle of Chardonnay from, of all places, India. (It was O.K.) *The New York Times* tells me that Baja California is fast becoming the "Napa Valley of Mexico." In the summer of 2004, long-neglected Greek wines suddenly got hot (in the good sense) because the Olympic games were being held in Athens. Israeli wines are up and coming, as are those of former Soviet-bloc countries gradually recovering from the deleterious effects of communism. The magazines tell me that I've just *got* to try the red wines from Virginia that are made from the indigenously American Norton grape. The wine industry's exploding in Texas, New Mexico, and Arizona. English white wines, or so I read, are "increasingly respectable." And in Brazil, Amazonian forests are being felled so that upstart growers can plant rows of Cabernet Sauvignon vines . . .

You get the picture. Wherever it's possible to do so, wine grapes are being grown and wine's being made. A lot of it is good; a lot of it is plonk. (But, after all, the same could be said of French wine.) Of course, most of these wines will never make even the briefest cameo at your local wine shop. But who knows? Maybe in a decade or three we'll all be regularly quaffing wines from Uruguay, Moldova, and Arkansas. In the history of wine, stranger things have happened.

In the meantime, be adventurous. Drink the local wines when you're traveling abroad. (In many places, that won't cause you much trouble, since *only* the local wines will be available.) And if a bottle of Turkish wine, or Slovenian wine, or—omigod!—*New Jersey* wine should show up on the sale rack, why not give it a go? You might lose ten bucks. But you might lose your prejudices.

CHAPTER NINE

Of Wine Sellers and Wine Cellars

WINE FAQS

WELL, WE'RE NEARING THE END—THE END *OF THE BEGINNING*, that is, of your wine education. By this point, you're far from being the wine baby you were when you picked up this book. But you've probably still got all sorts of questions that *Drinkology WINE* has yet to touch on, and it's my guess that many of these have to do with your own interaction with wine—how to buy it, order it in a restaurant, store it, and serve it. You may also be wondering about the business of wine and, more important, about what else you should do to further your wine knowledge. I can't anticipate all your questions, but here are some that may have occurred to you—along with my answers, of course. (Beware: Some of the answers are what you might call *opinionated*.) I'll set out the questions as if they were FAQs—with you doing the asking.

BUYING WINE

Just curious: How does wine get from the producer to the wine shop?
As with many other questions you might ask about wine, this one doesn't
have a simple answer that applies to every case (no pun intended), but
for imported wines the process generally works like so:

Producers sell their finished, bottled wine to **importers**, who arrange
for shipment to the United States. Importers make their decisions as to
which wines to buy based, of course, on taste and price—and, even more
essential, on whether they believe a given maker's wine or line of wines
will succeed in the American market. Once the wine arrives in the U.S.,
it is sold to **distributors** (sometimes called **wholesalers**), which are
licensed on a state-by-state basis and which, in turn, handle the sale to
retail outlets (and, in most states, restaurants, as well).

Some importers have their own distribution operations, but this is
comparatively rare, so for foreign wines there are usually three layers of
middlemen—importer, distributor, and retailer (or restaurateur)—
between the winemaker and you, the consumer. (Sometimes, however,
there's an additional layer. In some wine-producing regions—Bordeaux,
for instance—it's traditional practice for winemakers to sell their product to local *brokers,* which sell to importers, which sell to distributors,
which sell to stores/restaurants, which sell to you.)

Obviously, there's no role for an importer when it comes to domes-
tically produced wines, but otherwise the process is the same, with wine
moving from the maker to the distributor to the retailer to you. Needless
to say, the house-that-Jack-built process that eventually delivers wine
from the maker to your (home or restaurant) table adds considerably to
a wine's price. Typically, importing and distribution together double the

cost: a bottle that the importer buys for $5 is sold to the shop or restaurant for $10. And then, of course, the shop or restaurant adds its own markup. Retailers generally mark up the price they pay by 50 percent, selling the bottle they've paid $10 for to you for $15.

But then why does the price of a given wine sometimes differ from shop to shop?

Why can you so often find a bottle of wine that costs $14.99 at one store selling for just $12.99 at another shop nearby? (Let's assume that the second shop isn't trying to rid itself of excess inventory by running a special sale on the wine.) Setting aside the possibility that the shops may have different overhead costs and that their precise markups may therefore differ (or that one proprietor may simply be greedier than the other), there's an industry-related reason for such differences. Distributors offer discounts to retailers depending on how much of a particular wine they buy: if the shop buys just one case (i.e., twelve bottles), it will pay a certain unit amount; if it buys two or three at once, it will pay less; and if it buys five cases or more, it'll be rewarded with an even greater discount—and can pass those savings on to the consumer. So it may well be that shop number one, above, just doesn't have the storage space or just doesn't move the merch fast enough to buy in larger, discounted quantities.

Shouldn't *I* get a discount for buying wine by the case?

Yes, you should. What's good for the goose *should be* good for the gander, and you—the wine shop customer—should likewise be rewarded for buying in bulk. Many, many retailers offer their customers a discount (sometimes 10 percent, more often 15) for buying a **full case** of a given wine. (Sometimes they'll post a sign advertising this practice; sometimes you have to ask. So ask.) And some wine shops (the *nice* shops, the ones we *like*) give you a 10-percent discount even if you order a **mixed case** of wine.

I've been invited to dinner, and I want to bring along a bottle of wine— but I don't know what kind of food's being served. What should I buy?

Well, you could call the host back, or email him or her and *ask* what's for dinner, but let's assume all the land lines are down and your cell phone and cable are on the blink. In that case, my opinion is that you should take a light-bodied red—something that's not going to be too tannic or deeply extracted (something, in other words, that's probably going to work whether or not there's red meat on the menu). My personal inclination would be to buy one of the Beaujolais Cru wines discussed on page 277: a Côte de Brouilly, perhaps, or a Fleurie, Juliénas, or Morgon. Not only is this kind of wine extremely versatile, but it's a sure-ish bet that everyone will like it—and probable that some guests will never have drunk it before and will be pleased that you've expanded their known wine universe. Another advantage is that Beaujolais Crus work well with both winter and summer meals. (They're best served ever so slightly chilled.) Plus, you'll probably spend only $15 or so.

On the other hand, if your purpose in bringing a bottle of wine is not so much to provide a beverage to be drunk with dinner but rather to give a thank-you gift to the host, I'd recommend spending more, and taking along a bottle of Champagne or perhaps an interesting fortified or dessert wine— an aged tawny Port, perhaps, or a Pedro Ximénez Sherry, or a Hungarian Tokaji, or a good Madeira (see pages 320, 314, 173, and 316, respectively). Just about everybody loves being given Champagne, and people who drink a lot of wine and are reasonably knowledgeable about it like being given unusual wines that they might not ordinarily buy for themselves.

At a party recently, I had a wine I really liked, but my local wine shop doesn't carry it. Can I ask them to get a couple of bottles for me?

Well, you can ask—and you *should* ask—but whether the shop will be able to help you is another matter. First, the shop's manager will have to check to see whether the wine you want is carried by any of the distributors serving your area. Even if it is, there's another possible hurdle: Distributors set minimums below which they won't deliver. If the wine you want is an expensive wine, that may not present a problem, since the cost of even a few bottles may exceed the distributor's minimum. If, however, the wine is relatively cheap, the shop may have to piggyback your order onto the next large order it places with that distributor—so you'll have to wait. Note, too, that the retailer will probably tack an extra markup—maybe as little as a dollar, maybe more—on each specially ordered bottle.

ORDERING WINE IN RESTAURANTS

Restaurant wine lists confuse and humiliate me. I hardly ever recognize *anything* on the list, and I get nervous whenever a dinner companion asks me to choose the wine. Help!

I sympathize. Restaurants are particularly forbidding environments for the wine newbie—much scarier, I think, than wine shops. First off, in a wine shop, you can actually *see* the bottles, which means you may be able to recognize a wine you've had—and liked—in the past even if you can't quite remember the name. You can examine the bottles, turning them over to see whether there's any helpful information on the back label—a familiar importer's name, some tasting notes, some food-pairing suggestions. Also, in a wine shop, you're seldom required to *say* the name of the wine you want: you can pluck it off the shelf or rack, take it to the register, and be mutely done with the transaction without having to reveal your ignorance of how the wine's name is pronounced.

Quite a difference from just looking at a list of unfamiliar names, with prices attached—and being called on to choose and say one of those names in the presence of attentive others.

But do try to relax. If you feel rudderless when staring at a restaurant wine list, you're hardly alone. Even among people who are reasonably knowledgeable about wine, it's the rare person who—perusing an unfamiliar wine list—will know more than a few of the wines being offered. Oh, he or she may recognize most or even all of the *types* of wine on the list, but when it comes to the particular makers and the vintages, this "knowledgeable" person is likely to be as at-sea as you, the neophyte. You're in good company, in other words, so do yourself a favor and try to think of your choice of a wine as an interesting gustatory experiment rather than an occasion for potential embarrassment.

Of course, I can't tell you *what* to order, but I can provide you with some general tips:

- Be adventurous. If you do happen to recognize any of the wines on the list, don't automatically choose one of those simply because you're familiar with it. Make a resolution to boldly go where you haven't gone before. Tell your dining companions, "You know, I've never had this wine before, and I'd really like to try it." Chances are, they'll be pleased to accompany you on your journey into the unknown (and forgiving if what you choose turns out to be a dud).

- Bone up, electronically. Many restaurants today post their wine lists, along with their menus, on their websites. This gives you an opportunity to plan ahead.

- Ask for help from the waiter. Of course, there's some risk in this. The waiter may possess as little knowledge about wine—even about the wines on that restaurant's list—as you, and may cover by suggesting a wine that he or she knows is popular with the restaurant's clientele. (Be wary of remarks like, "Well, we sell a lot of such-and-such.") If the waiter seems to know little or nothing about the wine list, and assuming the restaurant has no sommelier (see below) on staff, you might ask whether you could talk to whoever buys the wine for the restaurant (probably the general manager or, in smaller places, the proprietor).

- Before asking for a wait-staff recommendation, decide how much you want to spend. If you can't spend a lot, do *not* be embarrassed—be fearless, explicitly asking for a recommendation in the thirty- to thirty-five–dollar price range (or whatever). In all probability, the waiter will greatly appreciate your forthrightness, since it makes his or her job so much easier.

- If you and your dining companions are ordering a wide diversity of dishes, think about choosing a relatively light-bodied red wine: one of the Beaujolais Crus mentioned above, or perhaps an Oregon or New Zealand Pinot Noir, or maybe a Chianti or Chianti Classico. These wines share the virtue of great versatility. Of course, if there are four or more people in your party and it's likely that everyone will drink a couple of glasses, there's no harm in ordering two different bottles—a full-bodied red and a dry, light white, perhaps—and having them brought to the table simultaneously, so that people can pour themselves what they like over the course of the meal. And don't forget that, among white wines, dry Rieslings are companionable with a fairly wide range of foods (red meats and heavy tomato-sauce pastas are exceptions to this rule).

- Point. If you're afraid of tripping over your tongue when ordering a wine whose name you're not sure how to pronounce, use your finger to indicate your choice, saying, "I think we'll have a bottle of this." If the waiter's a kind-hearted sort, he or she will say the wine's name aloud (and slowly and distinctly)—and compliment you on your choice. Then again, *why* worry so much about this? If you fear that your dining companions will laugh at you if you mispronounce a wine's name, maybe you need a new circle of friends. (If you just can't conquer your xylophataquieopiaphobia—that's the easy-to-say term for the fear of mispronouncing words—you might get in the habit of always carrying with you a book called *How to Pronounce French, German, and Italian Wine Names,* by Diana Bellucci. Understand, though, that whipping this out every time you place a wine order will seem much more pathetic than simply stumbling over a name.)

- If you're dining with a single companion and the wine list offers half-bottles, considering ordering two different half-bottles—one for the first course, one for the second—rather than a whole bottle. This strategy serves two purposes: (1) it offers some protection against your getting stuck with a wine you don't care for for the entire meal, and (2) it doubles your ability to experiment.

Half-bottles, by the way, are useful in another regard. If it seems to you that you and your dinner companion(s) are likely to drink more than one bottle of wine but probably not so much as two, half-bottles are a great backup. These days, more and more restaurants are offering a sizable selection of half-bottles—an admirable trend.

If you select a wine previously unknown to you and do end up enjoying it, do remember to take note of what it was. Newly gained wine "knowledge" can be get lost in your neural pathways very quickly—especially if you've had a bit too much to drink! So take a moment to write down all the important information on the label—the type of wine, the maker, the vintage—or tote the bottle home with you. (Some restaurants will try to remove the label for you, if you ask.)

I'm taking a date to a classy restaurant—one with a sommelier on the wait staff. What should I expect?
Well, that's a little hard to say. At some such places, the **sommelier** (saw-mull-YAY), or **wine steward**, is extremely interactive with diners—presenting them with the wine list, inquiring about the kinds of food they're intending to have, and suggesting wines to accompany each course. At others, the sommelier remains more or less in the background—keeping track of the restaurant's wine inventory, working with the chef to develop special wine-and-food tasting menus, and so on, but appearing at diners' tables only to open the wine (if then). The best sommeliers (in the best-run restaurants) don't just have an intimate and extensive knowledge of their establishments' cellars; they make it their job to help patrons plan their meals—with the aim, of course, of heightening the dining experience's pleasure. If you receive this kind of attentive service, the tip you leave should reflect your satisfaction, since the sommelier gets a cut of the "floor"—a percentage, that is, of all the tips received by the waiters. There's absolutely no excuse for a sommelier's acting in a haughty or smug manner. (If he or she behaves condescendingly, you might find the opportunity to point out to him or her that the word *sommelier* derives from the medieval French for "pack animal driver.")

These days, only a very few sommeliers wear what used to be the badge of their trade—a silver necklace from which depends a small, shallow silver cup called a **tastevin** (taht-VAAⁿ—that's right, you don't pronounce the "s"). Traditionally, these flattish little vessels—sometimes called "wine tasters"—were used for tasting and examining wine siphoned from barrels in a wine cellar. (The faceted pattern inside the tastevin was designed to capture whatever light was available in the dimly lit cellars of yore.) If collecting wine paraphernalia interests you, you can buy yourself a newly minted tastevin from virtually any wine-accessories catalog or online emporium. Antique tastevins regularly appear on eBay—and, of course, in shops that specialize in wine-related antiques.

TASTEVIN

What's the etiquette of restaurant wine service?

The onus is on the waiter to follow the proper procedure, not on you. First of all, the waiter should present the bottle to the person *who ordered the wine*. It's astonishing, really, how unconsciously sexist and ageist (in a reverse way) some waiters can be, automatically bringing the wine to the oldest male at the table. Don't put up with this. The waiter should remember who ordered the wine, or, if the wine's brought to the table by a waiter different from the one who took the order, he or she should *ask* who did the ordering.

The waiter should show you the label of the *unopened* bottle so you can make sure that it is, in fact, the wine you requested. Take a moment to look at it, checking (especially) to see whether the wine is the same vintage as that given on the wine list. If you're not knowledgeable about vintages, a difference might not be terribly meaningful to you—but it could be an indication that the restaurant is careless about updating its wine list. It could also be a mistake on the part of whoever retrieved the wine. In any case, point out the discrepancy.

It used to be common practice for waiters, after opening a bottle, to present the cork to the person who'd ordered the wine, but at many restaurants today this step has been dropped from the ceremony. Does it matter? Maybe. If the waiter hands you the cork (or, more likely, sets it on the table beside you), you do get the chance to check the cork's condition and, if you wish, to smell it. How much you can learn from this examination is debatable, however. A dried-out-looking cork may indicate that the wine was improperly stored (and that it may have oxidized). A cork that smells "off" *may or may not* be a sign that something's wrong with the wine. To really tell whether the wine's O.K., you have to smell and taste it—

Which is the reason the waiter will pour just a little bit of wine—half an inch or so—into your glass. The point of this essential part of the ritual is *not* to determine whether you *like* the wine; it's to let you make sure that the wine is free of any fault—especially that it isn't afflicted with cork taint. (For more on cork taint and some other faults, review the sidebar on pages 115–120.) Take this step seriously: look at the wine; swirl it; give it a good, long sniff; and taste it. If there is something objectively wrong with the wine, this is the best time to identify the problem.

It's my experience that once the wine's been accepted and glasses have been poured all around, some waiters become a bit *too* attentive, rushing to the table to refill any glass that's growing empty. This annoys me. Sometimes it seems that such waiters are hurrying you along, hoping that you'll finish the bottle quickly and order another. But even if the waiter's intention is concernful rather than mercenary, it's still irritating, since I like to determine for myself the speed at which I drink. If a waiter jumps to refill the glasses without asking the diners whether they'd like more, don't be shy about telling him or her that you'd prefer to pour the wine yourselves.

Dare I send a bottle back?

By all means. But do so *only* if the wine has an identifiable technical fault. It's very bad behavior to send a bottle back just because you don't happen to like it or find that the wine doesn't go very well with your meal. Of course, in a good restaurant, the waiter won't argue with you, no matter how suspicious your reason for rejecting the wine. But do keep in mind that, by sending back a perfectly good bottle, you're doing the restaurant financial harm. (You'll pay for it in the afterlife. There's a rung of hell reserved for those who make a habit of sending back the wine for no good reason—where such sinners are forced to drink "light chablis" for all eternity.)

Why is wine so expensive in restaurants?

Restaurants have traditionally tripled or even *quadrupled* their wines' whole-sale price, selling for $30 or $40 a bottle they buy for $10. The restaurant trade has, with some justification, defended such sizable markups by point-ing to the costs involved. Restaurants must cellar the wine; they lose a cer-tain amount of inventory through breakage and employee theft; and, of course, they suffer additional losses when customers send the wine back for illegitimate reasons. (More to the point, however, is the fact that the profit margin on the meals they serve is very small, and many restaurants make most of their money on the wine and liquor they sell.)

The custom of tripling/quadrupling the wholesale price of each wine sold by the bottle has begun, in some quarters, to give way to pricing practices that are more customer-friendly. Restaurateurs, or many of them, appear to have noticed that they sell more wine if they charge less for it. So some have adopted a graduated scheme in which the markups they add grow smaller as the wine becomes more expensive: that is, they may charge diners $30 for a bottle that cost the restaurant $10 but only $50 for a bottle that they paid $20 for (and so on up the scale). Other eateries are using a simpler method for pricing their wines: they simply add a given dollar amount—$15, say—to every bottle of wine they sell. If they pay $10, they sell the bottle for $25; if they pay $100, they charge $115. And yet other restaurants are simply doubling the wholesale price. As a waiter at one such restaurant put it to me, "We just want people to drink a lot of wine and have a good time." Bravo.

STORING AND SERVING WINE AT HOME

How should I store the wine I buy?

Good question—but there are several prior questions. How much wine do you ordinarily keep on hand? Do you usually drink the wine you buy within a few days or weeks, or are you beginning to collect wines—buying the occasional "ageworthy" bottle that you hope to keep for several years or longer before opening? And—perhaps most important of all—how much space have you got? (And, if you're intending to start a collection, do you have the right *kind* of space for long-term wine storage?)

If you don't keep much wine around and tend to quickly drink whatever you buy, there's no need to be overly fastidious about storage. Get a wine rack that accommodates your needs, and place the rack in a spot that doesn't get too cold or too warm—and where the variation in temperature isn't very great. (Note: The top of the refrigerator is a *terrible* place to situate a wine rack. Hot air rises, remember. Not only does the temperature atop your fridge shoot up every time you cook, but it's usually warm up there anyway, because heat from the refrigerator's compressor vents up the back.)

If you're not really interested in collecting wines but want always to have a couple of cases on hand, approach your storage strategy a little more carefully. Besides making sure that all the bottles are stored on their sides (which keeps the wine in contact with the cork, preventing it from drying out and possibly allowing oxygen to penetrate the bottle), you should choose a storage location within your home that (1) is usually dark, (2) is reasonably cool (but that never gets colder than 45°F or so), (3) is neither too dry nor too damp, and (4) isn't near a source of vibration. Don't drive yourself crazy, but do your best: A closet that's not near a heat source might work well—but *not* if you live in a high-rise apartment building and the closet is adjacent to the elevator shaft. (Vibration, like light and heat, accelerates physical/chemical changes occurring in the wine.) If you have a basement, that might be an O.K. place—but not if the basement room also contains a furnace or boiler, or if it's dank or occasionally floods during heavy rainstorms. (You don't want the corks to dry out, but neither do you want the labels to detach or disintegrate because of the excess moisture.)

If, however, you're intending to lay down wines for consumption in the fairly distant future, you've got to get more serious about storage. If you're lucky enough to own a manse with a network of catacombs below, no problem—store the wine in the caverns along with your ancestors' bones. But let's assume your housing situation is a little more average. You still need a space that closely approximates the environmental conditions of a real underground cellar: a constant, cool year-round temperature (about 55°F is ideal), moderate relative humidity (about 60–70%), and an absence of sunlight and vibration. And, of course, your "cellar" (below ground or not) has to be large enough to accommodate the collection you amass. (A good rule of thumb is to *double* the amount of space you think you could possibly need.)

Can you create such a space at home? Well, if you've got an actual basement, you might be able to—so long as your wine-cellar room is properly insulated from any heat given off by the boiler or furnace. If that option isn't available to you, you might consider investing in one of the many **refrigerated cellars** on the market. These thermostatically controlled, stand-alone units come in an incredible array of styles and sizes. Some are made of stainless steel and look like high-tech appliances; others are enclosed in cabinetry designed to evoke traditional pieces of furniture (breakfronts and credenzas). The smallest models hold only eight bottles; the largest accommodate hundreds upon hundreds. As you might imagine, these specialized appliances don't come cheap. You can get an eight-bottle mini-cellar for as little as $150, but the big cabinet-style models run into the thousands. (To get an idea of what's available, visit International Wine Accessories' website, at www.iwawine.com.) Besides their hefty price tags, the big refrigerated cellars have a couple of other disadvantages worth mentioning: (1) they're *heavy*—especially when filled with wine!—so you *must* make sure that your floor is structurally capable of supporting such a unit before buying one; and (2) the compressors of some of these units produce low-level vibrations that might, over the long haul, injure the wines inside.

But there's yet another alternative for the would-be wine collector who's pinched for space and who'd rather spend the big bucks on the wine, not a storage unit. That's to store your wine "off site," at a professional wine storage facility (a.k.a. **warehouse cellar**). Most sizable cities have such services—look in the Yellow Pages, under "Wine Storage," or ask at your local wine shop. (Wine shops often have partnership arrangements with storage companies.) Warehouse cellars' fees are typically calculated on a per-case/per-month basis, and this storage option can be surprisingly *in*expensive—at least as compared with laying out the cash for a big at-home unit. So long as your wine stays in the warehouse, you'll probably pay less than $2 per case per month. (Additional fees for pickup and delivery are, of course, tacked onto the basic warehousing cost.)

It may go without saying, but if you're cellaring a large number of wines at home, you're going to have to come up with some system of organizing them and also of keeping track of them to make sure that you drink them during the interval—sometimes years-long—when they're mostly likely to be at their peak. (It makes little sense to collect wines unless you consult vintage charts and other sources to determine how long they should be held.) And, please, do store your wines label side up—it makes locating the bottle you want so much easier.

You've talked about storage temperature, but at what temperature should wine be *served*?

Oh, my. Wine experts can get terrifically persnickety over this issue, specifying (for example) that American Chenin Blanc varietals should be served at between 43 and 48°F, whereas dry Rieslings should be served at between 48 and 53°F. I don't know about your life, but mine's growing much too short to fret about such hair-splitting distinctions. It's therefore my opinion that you'll do well enough if you understand a few basic principles.

Cooler temperatures accentuate a wine's acidity and (if it's a red wine) its tannins; warmer temperatures accentuate aroma and flavor, since the volatile organic molecules responsible for smell and taste bounce around a lot more as a wine warms up. Knowing this, it's possible to establish a few simple rules. Light-bodied dry white wines are probably best served reasonably cold—anywhere from 42–43°F up to 48°F or so. (Rosés do well within this same cool temperature range.) Fuller-bodied, aromatic whites (whether dry oaked Chardonnays or dessert whites like Sauternes) show better at a slightly higher temperature: about 50 to 55°F. Light-bodied reds—wines like Beaujolais and Valpolicella—are best served in the low to mid-50s; full-bodied, tannic reds in the 58 to 67°F range. No wine is at its best over about 70°F.

But, hey, are you actually going to take your wine's temperature before serving? If you want to, there are a number of wine thermometers (like the one pictured) on the market. Since most of these are of European make, however, they're usually graduated in degrees Celsius. Personally, metric conversions are the last thing I want to deal with when serving wine, so here's *Drinkology WINE*'s lazy-guy approach:

WINE THERMOMETER

- Thoroughly chill all white wines (this takes about four hours in the refrigerator), but remove all but the lightest-bodied (and sparkling wines) from the fridge twenty minutes to half an hour before serving. (The temperature inside your refrigerator, by the way, is probably about 40°F.) At table, keep sparkling wines and light-bodied still whites in a Champagne bucket that's half-filled with equal parts ice and water. If you're worried about a fuller-bodied white warming up too much over the course of a meal, place the bottle in a **wine cooler** to maintain temperature. (Tabletop wine coolers come in an array of models. Some are Thermos-like; the insulation alone keeps the wine cool. Others have slots between their exterior and interior walls into which you slip fitted ice packs that you keep in the freezer between uses.)

- Unless you keep your wines under ideal cellar conditions, briefly chill (for about an hour) light-bodied reds before serving. (Again, you can maintain the temperature, more or less, by keeping the bottle in an insulated cooler at table.)

- Serve full-bodied reds at room temperature. If the room temperature exceeds 70°F, so what? If it exceeds 80°F, why in the world are you serving red wine, anyhow?

The most important thing to remember is that once a bottle's been opened, the wine's nose and palate will keep changing over the course of a meal or an evening, no matter what temperature-control measures you take. The wine's interaction not just with the ambient temperature but also with the oxygen in the air, with the warmth of your hand holding the glass, with whatever food you're eating, and with your increasingly besotted palate causes your experience of the wine to change from moment to moment. This is *interesting*, so try to squelch your control-freak impulses, and go, as it were, with the flow.

Besides wineglasses and a corkscrew, what kind of equipment do I need to serve wine at home?

I've just mentioned the usefulness of wine coolers and Champagne buckets for maintaining a wine's temperature at table. Besides these items (and a foil cutter; see page 78), you'll probably want a decanter of some sort and, if it's likely that you'll occasionally serve wines that have thrown sediment, a wine funnel, as well. If you seldom finish a whole bottle of wine in an evening, you may—emphasis on the *may*—also want some sort of device for preserving leftovers. The next two Q&As deal with decanting and preservation.

When should I decant wine? (And how do I do it?)

Oh, what a contested issue! Everyone agrees that red wines that are likely to have thrown substantial sediment while in bottle should be carefully decanted before serving. (We'll talk about how to do that in a sec.) But there's no such agreement—in fact, there's an extreme variance of opinion—about whether to decant other reds.

The pro-decanting faction insists that virtually all still red wines benefit from being decanted before serving. (In this case, decanting simply means pouring the wine from the bottle into a decanter or pitcher.) It's

DECANTER

their contention that decanting, by aerating the wine, helps it "open"—not just softening the tannins through exposure to oxygen but revealing the wine's fuller character. (There are even some extremists who think that fuller-bodied, more aromatic white wines should be decanted, as well.) The anti-decanting faction thinks that, for most wines, decanting makes little if any difference—and that sufficient aeration will occur anyway, as the wine is

swirled in the glass and as what remains behind in the opened bottle remains in contact with the air. (This faction, too, has its extremists, who maintain that decanting can actually damage delicately scented/flavored reds, robbing them of the fragile smells and tastes they'd maintain slightly longer if left in the bottle.)

Which side is right? Who knows? One thing's for certain: wine can look *awfully* attractive in a glass or crystal decanter—which I unashamedly admit is why I often decant the red wines I serve. (The squashed body of the decanter pictured is designed to maximize contact with the air, but I like it because it's an interesting shape.) I do exercise a little caution, though, not decanting until a short while before serving.

At any rate, this is one wine-related issue that you are utterly free to decide for yourself . . . *except* when it comes to decanting wines with sediment.

As you've learned, vintage Ports are not filtered before bottling and tend to deposit lots of additional sediment as they age in bottle. Bottles of mature red Bordeaux—in fact, of any mature red that began its life as a deeply colored, highly tannic wine—are also likely to contain a fair amount of sediment consisting of tannin and pigment particles that have precipitated out of the wine over time. Because the sediment can be unpleasantly gritty and bitter-tasting, the sediment must be separated out of the wine before it reaches the drinker's glass. This calls for a more meticulous method of decanting.

If you're going to serve a vintage Port, a mature Bordeaux, or another wine that may contain significant sediment, you've got to make this decision at least a day ahead of time, so that you can set the bottle upright for a long enough time to allow sediment deposited along the side of the bottle to settle to the bottom. Be careful not to move it around during this period, and try your best not to agitate the wine when opening the bottle. Once it's opened, begin pouring it into a decanter *very* slowly and carefully. If it's a non-fortified wine you're decanting, you might position a light source—a candle or, better, one of those flashlights with a head that tilts—behind the bottle, so that you can see the sediment as it gathers in the bottle's shoulder and approaches the neck. When you see the sediment reach the neck, it's time to stop pouring.

A light source won't do you much good, though, if you're decanting a Port, since the bottle's glass will be much too dark for you to see what's going on inside. That's one good reason for employing a **wine funnel**, or **wine horn**, when you decant wines with sediment. This specialized funnel, which contains a fine wire-mesh screen, will catch the sediment particles if you overshoot the mark. Actually, I think it's a good idea to use a wine funnel whenever you're performing this kind of decanting. It provides a measure of safety against too-slow reflexes.

The lazier among us—a group to which I sometimes pledge my allegiance—dispense with the background light source altogether, pouring carefully but counting on the funnel's screen to catch any sediment that escapes the bottle. The drawing shows a funnel in use; note that the funnel depicted, like some other wine funnels, has a curved spout; the hole—which is on the side, not at the bottom, of the spout—directs the wine against the decanter's interior wall. Whether this "soft launch" actually "promotes maximum aeration and clarity" (I steal these words from a catalog blurb) is anybody's guess. But the wine cascading down the decanter's wall makes for a pretty effect.

USING A WINE FUNNEL

If you haven't got a wine funnel, there's a quick 'n' dirty method that works nearly as well. Pour the wine through a (white, unscented) paper towel folded inside an ordinary kitchen funnel. (Don't use a coffee filter for this—its fine pores will filter too much out of the wine.)

Since it can be hard to tell just how much, if any, sediment has gathered in the bottle until it's opened and poured, I think it's a good rule of thumb to carefully decant any full-bodied red that's more than seven or eight years old. But—as always, it seems—there's a caution in order. Very, very old wines shouldn't be decanted at all, since their fragile bouquets and flavors will fall apart very quickly once the wine has left the bottle.

What should I do with leftover wine?
Here's an idea: Re-stopper the bottle, and put it in the refrigerator. (Try to drink what's left within a day or two.)

Well, sure, I do that with *white* wine—but how about red?
Re-stopper the bottle, and put it in the fridge. Take it out a couple of hours before you intend to drink it. (And again, try to drink what's left within a day or two.)

Sounds radical, huh? But why? If I remember correctly, the purpose of a refrigerator is to preserve—at least for a time—the foods and beverages you put in it. I'm well aware, of course, that wine is perishable, and that the oxygen that remains inside the bottle will continue, even in the fridge, to interact with the wine, changing it and eventually doing it harm. If you want to drive yourself nuts, there are lots of wine-preservation "systems" on the market—vacuum pumps that remove all the air from the bottle; aerosols that squirt a layer of inert nitrogen gas into the bottle, displacing the oxygen. If you want to spend money on this stuff, be my guest. (But it's my guess that these devices are purchased more often than they're actually used—and some wine experts question whether such preservation strategies do any good whatsoever.)

And here's an even more radical idea: If you can't finish a bottle of a full-bodied, reasonably tannic red wine the same evening you open it, re-stopper it and *don't* put it in the fridge. (Set it in a cool spot, though.) It just might survive beautifully until the following evening. And there's even a small chance—if it's a very good, robust wine—that it might be *better* the second day.

I'm giving a dinner party. How much wine should I buy?
Ah, the host's eternal question. Back in the day when people drank more than they tend to nowadays, the rule was lay in one bottle per guest (not one bottle of each *kind* of wine to be served, but the same total number of bottles as guests). Call me old-school, but I think this rule's as sensible as ever. If there are bottles left over (so long as they haven't been opened), so what? You'll enjoy the wine yourself during the days and weeks ahead—or you'll throw another party. Besides, it's always better to have too much wine on hand than too little.

I gave a dinner party and one of the guests—a real slob—spilled red wine all over the tablecloth. I'll never invite *him* back, of course, but how do I get the stains out?
Remind me not to be your friend. But assuming you were using a washable cotton tablecloth, spray the stains with Spray 'n Wash (or another spray-on laundry stain remover) and launder it as you usually would. Our table linens suffered many a red wine stain during *Drinkology WINE*'s tasting parties—and this couldn't-be-simpler method always worked. (But do try to spray the stains as soon after the party as possible.)

On the off-chance that Spray 'n Wash alone *doesn't* work, you might want to try a well-regarded product called Wine Away, manufactured by a Washington State outfit called Evergreen Labs. A number of retailers carry it, but you can also order direct from www.evergreenlabs.com.

And while we're on the subject of housekeeping, how should I clean wineglasses?

What you should *not* do is to wash them in the dishwasher. Dishwasher detergent—even the purportedly "fragrance-free" kind—leaves a residue behind that will strongly, and negatively, affect wine's aroma and flavor.

The best method, I think, is to wash the glasses by hand in *hot water only*, rinsing and re-rinsing them thoroughly and allowing them to air-dry. If you must use detergent—if the glasses are greasy or lipstick-stained, say—use only a minimal amount, and continue rinsing until you're certain the detergent has all been washed away. Dish-soap residue, by the way, can impede the formation of bubbles in sparkling wine—so be extra-fastidious in rinsing Champagne flutes or tulip glasses.

LEARNING (MORE) ABOUT WINE

What's the next step in my wine education?

These days, acquiring hands-on knowledge about wine couldn't be easier. If you live in or near a decent-size city, your opportunities are nearly endless. Tastings abound. (Though be aware that most wine-shop tastings are promotional rather than educational in nature.) Wine classes—on both introductory and more advanced levels—are thick on the ground, being offered by adult/continuing education programs, university extension programs, local culinary schools, and even wine shops. Many wine classes are just a single evening long (and not too costly—often less than $100, including the "materials fee" for the wines you'll sample), though multi-session classes are also common.

If the wine bug's really bitten you—and you've got the time and money—you might consider enrolling in a wine class at a top culinary school. The Culinary Institute of America, for example, offers a wide variety of two- to five-day intensive wine classes—some geared toward beginners, others aimed at professionals—at its Greystone campus in Napa Valley, California. The cost of these intensives varies, but they average around $900 to $1,000. (That's just tuition, of course.) To find out more, visit the CIA's website, at www.ciachef.edu. If an east coast locale is more convenient, you might consider investigating the multi-day "Fundamentals of Wine" courses (also about $900) offered by the French Culinary Institute in New York City; more information can be found at www.frenchculinary.com.

And what about reading? There are so many wine books out there, and I just don't know which are "must-haves" for my library.
Yeah, the Wine & Spirits section of your local Barnes & Noble—groaning with hundreds of titles—can be almost as intimidating to the wine newbie as a wine shop itself. Over the course of this book, I've recommended several works that deal with specific kinds of wine or specific wine-producing countries and regions, but I can winnow your must-have list of general or comprehensive wine books down to just four:

The Oxford Companion to Wine, 2d ed., edited by Jancis Robinson. This single-volume encyclopedia is a phenomenal reference book. Liberally and intelligently illustrated (with many very good maps), it contains entries on virtually every wine-related topic imaginable, all written by experts in their respective fields. But it's not only comprehensive; it's opinionated and occasionally witty—a rarity in reference books of whatever type. (One favorite example: the entry "wine writing," which begins, "a parasitical activity . . . .") One caution: The *Oxford Companion* is meant to be used by professionals as well as laypeople, so some entries—particularly those on vinification processes and techniques—are highly technical and almost opaque to the nonscientist reader. But the book will answer virtually any wine-related question you might have. (Whether you'll *understand* every answer is another matter.)

The New Wine Lover's Companion, 2d ed., by Ron Herbst and Sharon Tyler Herbst. This "companion" is a dictionary rather than an encyclopedia—its brief entries are designed for at-a-glance reference. One of the book's great values is that it gives a pronunciation key for every entry term that's a foreign word or phrase. The extensive appendixes—covering grape varieties, common wine-tasting terms, the Bordeaux classifications, and so on and on—are tremendously useful.

The World Atlas of Wine, 5th ed., by Hugh Johnson and Jancis Robinson. A stupendous book, the *World Atlas* contains scores of highly detailed maps that "put you where the wine is" with an exactitude equaled by no other wine book. Plus, there are lots of color photos that underscore the diversity of the world's winegrowing terrains, as well as hundreds of reproductions of wine labels representative of the regions covered by the atlas. The text, though immensely informative, does tend to focus on the minutiae of climate and geology—as well it should, though this can make it tough going for the wine newbie.

The Wine Bible, by Karen MacNeil. This, in my opinion, is *the* comprehensive wine guide for the non-expert. Written in a clear, lively, and utterly *friendly* manner, this "Bible" is a salvation for readers (like me) who find much wine writing off-putting and oppressive. MacNeil is unable, it seems, to write a boring sentence. The organization of the book is predominantly geographical, and each section contains numerous interesting sidebars on topics related—directly or, sometimes, tangentially—to the wines of the region under discussion. Even better, the book contains extensive information on the foods of each winemaking country and region, as well as travel tips. Despite its heft (nine hundred–plus pages), this is a book I'd carry along if I were doing a wine tour abroad. Complaints? Only that the maps are less informative than they might be, and that MacNeil recommends wines seemingly without regard to price or (more important) their availability in the United States. But, given the book's many merits, these are quibbles.

Finally, if you think you might enjoy reading some wine journalism, I have just a few recommendations. The *Wall Street Journal*'s wine column, by the wife-and-husband duo Dorothy J. Gaiter and John Brecher, epitomizes wine writing at its *least* snobby. Called "Tastings," it appears in the *Journal*'s Weekend section every Friday. Read just one of Gaiter and Brecher's pieces, and you'll find your fear of wine subsiding significantly. Much more erudite—and intellectually stimulating—are the writings of longtime *Gourmet* wine editor Gerald Asher. Asher doesn't just know everything about wine; he seems to know everything about *everything*. There are several collections of his essays in print, including *Vineyard Tales: Reflections on Wine* and *The Pleasures of Wine: Selected Essays*. No matter how reader-friendly or stimulating, however, most wine writing shares an unfortunate deficit: it's virtually humor-free. An exception to this dour rule is Lawrence Osborne's *The Accidental Connoisseur: An Irreverent Journey through the Wine World*; Osborne's encounters with winedom's denizens—the powerful and the obscure—are a hoot and a holler.

Indexes

GENERAL INDEX

Abruzzo region (Italy), 300
AC. *See* Appellation d'Origine
    Contrôlée system
acidity, 42, 50, 108–9, 160–61;
    temperature's effect on, 347
Aconcagua Valley (Chile), 250
aged tawny Port, 320, 321,
    335
ageing of wine, 14, 55–56, 66;
    barrel, 57, 58, 59, 60, 106,
    136, 306, 320, 321; bottle,
    66, 107, 258, 321
ageworthiness (definition), 87
Aglianico, 300–301
Aglianico del Vulture zone
    (Italy), 301
Alaska, 67
Albariño, 309, 316
alcohol content, 13–14, 99,
    109, 146, 154–55; of de-
    alcoholized wines, 234; and
    formation of legs, 97; and
    yeast, 41–42
Alexander II, 213
Aligoté, 273
Aloxe-Corton, 274
Alsace, 27, 32, 33, 47,
    167–68, 177, 178, 182, 190,
    193, 194, 195, 224, 257,
    283–84, 325
Alto Adige region (Italy), 169,
    190. *See also* Trentino–Alto
    Adige

Alvarinho, 316
Amarone, 175, 291, 294–95,
    296
American hybrids, 239, 243
American vine species,
    122–23. *See also* Norton
American Viticultural Areas,
    229, 230, 233, 235
amontillado Sherry, 310, 314,
    315
Andalusia, 71, 311, 315
Anderson Valley (California),
    143
Anjou region (Loire Valley),
    279
Anjou-Villages, 279
Anselmi, Roberto, 298
Ansonica, 303, 305
antioxidants, 134–35
AOC. *See* Appellation
    d'Origine Contrôlée system
Appellation d'Origine
    Contrôlée system, 25–27,
    129, 254–56
appellations, 25–26. *See also*
    communal appellations,
    regional appellations
Argentina, 33, 72, 150,
    244–46, 291
Arizona, 330
Arkansas, 330
aromatized wines, 14, 30
Asher, Gerald, 358

Asti, 193, 294
attack (definition), 110
Auslese, 173, 179, 180,
    182–83
Australia, 17, 28, 33, 35, 137,
    138, 139, 145, 146, 149,
    162, 177, 184, 193, 196,
    224, 239–42, 243, 329;
    Phylloxera in, 122
Austria, 120, 177, 178, 181,
    191, 195, 222, 323–24,
    326–27; *Phylloxera* in,
    122
autolysis, 209
Auvergne region (Loire
    Valley), 278
AVA. *See* American
    Viticultural Areas

Baja California, 330
balance, 108
Balthazar (bottle size), 216
Barbaresco, 150–51, 294, 295
Barbera, 295, 296, 297
Barbera d'Alba, 295
Barbera d'Asti, 295
Bardolino, 297
Barolo, 150–51, 294
Barossa Valley (Australia), 242
barrel ageing, 57, 58, 59, 60,
    106, 136; of Port, 320–21;
    of Rioja, 306. *See also solera*
    system

barrel fermentation, 55, 59, 60
barrels, 54–61
barriques, 61
Barsac, 173, 176, 196, 260, 263, 266; classification of, 262
Basilicata region (Italy), 301
Bas-Médoc, 259
Basque winemakers, 248, 249
Bastianich, Joseph, 301
Beaujolais, 33, 142, 147–48, 236, 269, 273, 276–77, 285, 327, 348
Beaujolais Crus, 277, 335, 338
Beaujolais Nouveau, 148, 276
Beaujolais-Villages, 148, 276–77
Beaune, 274
Beerenauslese, 173, 180, 181
Belluci, Diana, 339
berry (definition), 9
"Big Six," 32
biodynamic viticulture, 280, 282, 327
blanc de blancs Champagne, 165, 207–8
Blaufränkisch, 236, 327
blending, 242; of Champagne, 208; of clonal wines, 19; of rosés, 198. *See also* fractional blending
body, 97, 105–6
Bordeaux, 20, 24, 26, 27, 29, 31, 32, 33, 34, 47, 61, 72, 74, 82, 90, 94, 100, 104, 128, 129, 130, 135, 137–38, 140, 147, 149, 156, 170, 196, 245, 251, 253–54, 256, 257–66, 277, 286, 318, 328, 333, 351; map, 260
Bordeaux-type bottles, 224, 225

Botrytis (Botrytis cinerea), 172–73, 180. *See also* noble rot
botrytized wines, 172–73, 260. *See also* Auslese, Barsac, Beerenauslese, Eiswein, Sauternes, *sélection des grains nobles,* Tokaji, Trockenbeerenauslese
bottle ageing, 66, 107, 160, 258; of vintage Port, 321
bottles, 61, 170, 207; shapes of, 224–25, 283; sizes of 214–16. *See also* half-bottles
bottling, 65
bouquet (definition), 103
Bourgueil, 279, 280
Bourgogne. *See* Burgundy
Brazil, 330
Brecher, John, 358
Britain: and Port trade, 317–18, 322
Brix, 50
brokers, 333
Brouilly, 277
Brunello de Montalcino, 152, 295
brut (definition), 211
Bual, 317
Bulgaria, 140
Burgundy, 20, 25, 27, 33, 35, 82, 95, 128, 129, 130, 142–43, 156, 164–65, 167, 195, 200, 237, 244, 251, 253, 254, 256, 257, 266–77, 286, 290, 291, 318, 325; map, 268
Burgundy labels, 272
Burgundy-type bottles, 224, 225

Cabernet Franc, 47, 137, 138, 147, 258, 279

Cabernet Sauvignon, 17, 20, 31, 32, 33, 36, 47, 74, 90, 95, 108, 129, 130, 135, 136, 137–39, 140, 146, 147, 156, 157, 184, 199, 224, 226, 227, 230–32, 234, 235, 236, 240, 250, 258, 259, 263, 264, 292, 302, 304, 305, 308, 329, 330
California, 16, 19, 27, 28, 31, 33, 35, 36, 60, 72, 74, 91, 121, 125, 129, 130–31, 135, 137, 138, 139, 141, 143, 144, 147, 149, 151, 154–55, 161, 162, 165, 166, 169, 184, 185, 186, 187, 188, 189, 190, 197, 199, 218, 224, 226–34, 244, 274, 292, 298, 317, 328, 329; *Phylloxera* in, 124–25; and Prohibition, 126–27
Campania region (Italy), 301
Canada, 174
canopy management, 48
cap (definition), 53–54
Carabantes, Francisco de, 247
carbonation, 222
carbonic maceration, 276
Carignan, 308
Cariñena, 308
Carmenère, 249, 250
Carneros AVA (California), 143, 233
Carnuntum district (Austria), 326
Casablanca Valley (Chile), 249, 250
Catalonia, 71, 219, 307
Cataretto, 303
cava, 71, 219, 307
cellar conditions, 56–57, 345–46

cellars, 54, 56–57; refrigerated, 346; warehouse, 346–47

Chablis, 27, 28, 33, 99, 113, 165, 269

Chalonnaise. *See* Côte Chalonnaise

Chambolle-Musigny, 274

Champagne, 31, 33, 36–37, 118, 144, 165, 203, 206–18, 256, 291, 318, 335; classified vineyards in, 256–57; definition of, 12; kosher, 328, 329; rosé, 198; sweetness of, 176

Champagne bottles, 214–16, 225

Champagne houses, 209

Champigny-Saumur, 279

chaptalization, 324–25

Chardonnay, 17, 28, 32, 33, 42, 47, 55–56, 59, 60, 129, 130, 137, 159, 160, 161–65, 166, 183, 192, 194, 195, 207, 208, 219, 224, 226, 227, 229–30, 232, 234, 236, 237, 240, 249, 252, 269, 273, 274, 275, 298, 299, 302, 305, 330, 348

Charmat, Eugène, 219

Charmat method, 219

Chassagne-Montrachet, 164, 274, 275

château (definition), 253

Château-Grillet, 197, 285

Châteauneuf-du-Pape, 29, 145, 148–49, 287–88

Chénas, 277

Chenin Blanc, 17, 33, 187–89, 197, 227, 236, 251, 252, 279, 280, 347

Chianti, 25, 27, 152, 153, 157, 294, 297, 338

Chianti Classico, 152, 153, 294, 338

Chianti Classico Riserva, 153, 294, 297

Chile, 20, 35, 72, 137, 138, 139, 162, 177, 184, 244, 245, 247–50, 259, 328

Chinon, 147, 279, 280

Chiroubles, 277

Cinsault, 200, 252, 288

claret, 259, 317

classifications, 27; in Alsace, 284; in Bordeaux, 261–62; in Burgundy 270–71; in Champagne, 256–57

classified growths (definition), 261

Clicquot-Ponsardin, Nicole Barbe, 210

clones, 18–19, 20, 48

Clos de Vougeot, 271, 273

cloudiness (wine fault), 120

cold filtration, 234

cold soaking, 53, 133

collecting wines, 108, 344, 345–47

Columbia Valley (Washington), 235

communal appellations, 26; in Burgundy, 270, 274

Condrieu, 197, 285

Constantia, 251

Coonawarra region (Australia), 139, 242

cork, 315

cork pullers, 80

cork taint, 100–101, 115–17, 342

corks, 170, 207; Champagne, 214; condition of, 80, 342; natural, 115–17; stopper, 225; synthetic, 77, 117

corkscrews, 75–80

Cornas, 286

Corsica, 251

Corton, 164

Corvina, 294, 296

Côteaux du Layon, 279

Côte de Beaune, 269, 274, 275

Côte de Brouilly, 277, 335

Côte Chalonnaise, 269, 275

Côte de Nuits, 269, 271, 274

Côte d'Or, 164, 269, 274

Côte du Rhône, 287

Côte du Rhône–Villages, 287

Côte du Rhône–Villages St.-Maurice-sur-Eygues, 287

Côte-Rôtie, 197, 285

coupe, 220–21

cream Sherry, 314

criaderas (definition), 312

crianza (definition), 307

Crozes-Hermitage, 286

cru (definition), 256

cru bourgeois, 262

Culinary Institute of America, 356

cult wines, 265

Curicó Valley (Chile), 248, 249

cuvée (definition), 212

Damaskino, 303

dealcoholized wines, 234

decanters, 349, 350

decanting, 90, 350–53; of Port, 321

demi-sec (definition), 211

Denominación de Origen (DO), 307

Denominación de Origen Calificada (DOCa) 307

Denominazione di Origine Controllata (DOC)156–57, 289

Denominazione di Origine Controllata e Garantita (DOCG), 289

dessert wines, 15, 30, 31, 106. *See also* Barsac, Beerenauslese, Eiswein, ice wine, icewine, Moscato d'Asti, Passito di Pantelleria, Sauternes, *sélection des grains nobles,* Tokaji, Trockenbeerenauslese

disgorgement, 211, 212

distributors, 333–34, 336

DOC wines, 162, 293, 295, 296, 298, 301. *See also Denominazione di Origine Controllata*

DOCa wines, 308. *See also Denominación de Origen Calificada*

DOCG wines, 293, 295, 297, 301. *See also Denominazione di Origine Controllata e Garantita*

Dolcetto, 296

Dolcetto d'Alba, 296

domaine (definition), 253, 267

Donauland district (Austria), 326

dosage, 211

Douro region (Portugal), 316, 318, 319

doux (definition), 212

DO wines, 309. *See also Denominación de Origen*

dryness, 41, 109; bone, 111

dry wines (definition), 14

"dumb" wines, 99

Edna Valley (California), 165, 229

egg-white fining, 65, 108

1855 Classification, 261–62

18th Amendment, 125

Eiswein, 174, 180–81

élevage (definition), 39

England, 43, 330

enologist (definition), 43. *See also* flying winemakers, winemaker

Entre-Deux-Mers, 261

estate bottled wines, 45

extra brut (definition), 211

extra sec (definition), 211

extreme value wines, 227

Faith, Nicholas, 273

fantasy names, 289, 293

faults. *See* wine faults

Federspiel wines, 326–27

fermentation, 11, 12, 39, 40–42, 52–56, 61, 133, 171, 175–76, 206; barrel, 55, 59, 60, 160. *See also* carbonic maceration, malolactic fermentation, refermentation, second fermentation

festivals, 68–69

fighting varietals, 227

filtration, 64

Finger Lakes region (New York), 178, 238–39

fining, 64–65, 108

finish (definition), 55, 110

fino Sherry, 311, 312–13, 314, 315

"five S's," 74, 92–93

Fleurie, 277, 335

flight (definition), 74

flor, 313, 314

flutes, 84; cleaning of, 355

flûtes d'Alsace, 283

flying winemakers, 242

foil cutters, 78, 349

fortified wines, 14, 30. *See also* Madeira, Marsala, Port, Sherry

foxy wines, 124

fractional blending, 312

France, 16, 20, 21, 24, 25, 26–27, 29, 31, 32, 33, 61, 91, 124, 137, 145, 150, 166–67, 184,193, 196, 197, 199, 201, 222, 227, 253–88, 289, 317, 328; *Phylloxera* in, 122

Frank, Konstantin, 238–39

free-run juice, 11, 160

French Culinary Institute, 356

French hybrids, 174, 239

French paradox, 134

Friedrich, Jacqueline, 283

Friuli–Venezia Giulia region (Italy), 168, 169, 294, 298

frizzante wines, 13, 30, 118, 136

fruit wines, 67

Fumé Blanc, 185. *See also* Sauvignon Blanc

Furmint, 299

Gaiter, Dorothy J., 358

Galicia, 316

Gamay, 136, 147–48, 236, 273, 276

garage wines, 265

Garganega, 24, 298

Garnacha, 149, 199, 308, 309. *See also* Grenache

Gavi, 297–98

generic wines, 16, 27–28, 29, 30, 227

German-type bottles, 224, 225

German Wine academy, 327, 330

Germany, 16, 47, 119, 168,
173, 174, 177, 178, 190,
193, 195, 222, 227, 283,
323–26, 327, 328
Gevrey-Chambertin, 274
Gewürztraminer, 47, 48,
50–51, 52, 62, 95, 162,
189–91, 236, 274, 283
Gigondas, 149, 287
glasses. *See* wineglasses
glycerol, 106
grafting, 123–24
gran reserva (definition), 307
grape (definition), 9–10
Grauburgunder, 168
Graves, 184, 196, 259–60, 263
gray rot, 172
Greece, 16, 199, 330
green harvest, 47
Grenache, 148–49, 199, 200,
287, 288. *See also* Garnacha
Grillo, 303
grower Champagnes, 209
Grüner Veltliner, 191, 324, 326
gyropalette, 210

halbtrocken wines, 326
half-bottles, 216, 339
hangovers, 135
Haut-Médoc, 26, 259, 261
haziness (wine fault), 64, 120
health: and red wine, 133,
134–35
Herbst, Ron, 357
Herbst, Sharon Tyler, 357
Hermitage, 145, 286
Hohnen, David, 243
horizontal tasting, 74, 236–37
Hungary, 140, 328
Hunter Valley (Australia), 196

ice wine, 62–63, 174

icewine (Canadian), 174, 176,
239
IGT wines, 293, 298. *See also
Indicazione Geografica
Tipica*
importers, 325, 333–34
India, 330
Indicazione Geografica Tipica,
289
Insolia, 303, 305
irrigation, 49–50, 248
Israel, 328, 330
Italy, 16, 21, 24, 33, 47, 61,
137, 138, 140, 150, 152,
162, 166, 168, 169, 193,
219, 289–305; *Phylloxera* in,
122

Jefferson, Thomas, 286
Jerez region (Spain), 311
Jeroboam (bottle size), 216
Johannisberg Riesling, 182,
238
Johnson, Hugh, 273, 285, 357
jug wines, 27, 149, 227
Juliénas, 277, 335
Jumilla region (Spain), 307,
308

Kabinett, 179, 181, 182
Kamptal district (Austria), 326
Koestenbaum, Wayne, 278
kosher wines, 328–29
Kramer, Matt, 273
Kremstal district (Austria), 326

labels, 19; Burgundy, 272;
German, 325
Lalande de Pomerol, 266
Lambrusco, 13, 136
late bottled vintage Port, 321,
322

late harvest wines, 167, 227.
See also Auslese, Barsac,
Beerenauslese, Eiswein, ice
wine, icewine, Sauternes,
sélection des grains nobles,
Spätlese, Tokaji, Trockenbeerenauslese, *vendange
tardive*
LBV Port. *See* late bottled vin-
tage Port
Lebanon, 137
lees, 56, 201. *See also sur lie*
left bank (Bordeaux), 259
leftover wine: preservation of,
221, 353–54
legs, 97
Lemberger, 236
lever corkscrews, 78–79
Liebfraumilch, 191
Liger-Belair, Gérard, 202
Lirac, 149, 287
Locascio, Leonardo, 300
Loire Valley, 20, 32–33, 91,
100, 147, 184, 187, 188,
199, 201, 257, 277–81, 283
Long Island (New York),
43–51, 147, 190, 239, 242
Los Carneros. *See* Carneros
Lower Austria region
(Austria), 326, 327
Luján de Cuyo region
(Argentina), 245
Lynch, David, 301

Macabeo, 219
maceration, 11, 53, 133. *See
also* carbonic maceration
MacNeil, Karen, 357–58
Mâcon-Lugny, 276
Mâconnais, 164, 269, 275–76
Mâcon-Villages, 276
Mâcon-Viré, 276

Madeira, 14, 315, 316–17, 335
magnum (bottle size), 216
Maipo Valley (Chile), 139, 249
Maipú region (Argentina), 245
Malbec, 33, 138, 149–50, 245–46, 258, 291
Malmsey, 317
malolactic fermentation, 42, 60
Malvasia, 317
manzanilla Sherry, 313, 315
Le Marche (The Marches) region (Italy), 300
Margaux, 26, 259, 263
Marlborough region (New Zealand), 243, 244
Marsala, 14, 302, 303
Marsanne, 286
maturation. *See* ageing
mead, 67
Médoc, 259, 261, 262
Melon de Bourgogne, 201
Mendocino County (California), 143, 228
Mendoza region (Argentina), 150, 245–46
Mercurey, 275
Meritage wines, 29, 138
Merlot, 19, 20, 32, 33, 47, 48, 50, 51, 63, 136, 137, 138, 139–41, 146, 147, 156, 157, 166, 226, 232, 234, 235, 236–37, 249, 250, 258, 261, 263, 302, 305
méthode ancestrale, 222
méthode champenoise, 203, 208–11, 218
Methuselah (bottle size), 216
Meursault, 164, 274, 278
mevushal wines, 328–29

Mexico, 228
microchâteaux, 265
micro-oxidation, 117
mid-palate (definition), 110
Minho region (Portugal), 316
Missouri, 121, 124, 125, 127
Moldova, 140, 330
Molise region (Italy), 300, 301
Monastrell, 308. *See also* Mourvèdre
Mondavi, Robert, 185
Monroe, Marilyn, 213
Montepulciano. *See* Montepulciano d'Abruzzo, Vino Nobile di Montepulciano
Montepulciano d'Abruzzo, 300
Monterey County (California), 230, 232
Montlouis, 279, 280
Le Montrachet, 164
Morey-St.-Denis, 274
Morgon, 277, 335
Moscatel, 311
Moscato d'Asti, 193, 294; kosher, 328
Mosel (Mosel-Saar-Ruwer) region (Germany), 74, 178, 181, 182, 224, 309, 323, 325
mother vines, 18
Moulin-à-Vent, 277
Mourvèdre, 288, 308
mousse, 212
mouthfeel, 53, 105, 106–9
Müller-Thurgau, 191–92
Muscadet, 200–201, 278–79
Muscadet Côtes de Grandlieu, 201
Muscadet de Sèvre-et-Maine, 201
Muscat, 236

Muscat of Alexandria, 193–94, 304, 311
Muscat d'Alsace, 283
Muscat Blanc à Petits Grains, 193, 251, 283
Muscat grape family, 111, 175, 192–94
Muscat Ottonel, 283
must (definition), 52

Nantais region (Loire Valley), 278
Napa Valley (California), 34, 36, 130, 143, 228, 229, 230–31, 233; *Phylloxera* in, 124
Napoleon, 251
Napoleon III, 261
Navarra region (Spain), 199, 309
Nebbiolo, 136, 150–51, 295
Nebuchadnezzar (bottle size), 215, 216
négociants: in Beaujolais, 277; in Burgundy, 267, 275; definition, 264; in the Rhône, 287
Nerello Mascalese, 305
Nero d'Avola, 303–4
New Jersey, 67, 141, 331
New Mexico, 330
New South Wales, 196
New World (definition), 16–17
New York State, 177, 178, 182, 190, 238–39. *See also* Long Island
New Zealand, 17, 20, 33, 72, 143, 184, 186, 242–44, 274, 291, 338
Le Nez du Vin 102
noble rot, 167–68, 172–73, 196. *See also Botrytis*, botry-tized wines

nonalcoholic wines. *See* dealcoholized wines
nonvintage Champagne, 208–9, 217
nonvintage wines, 34, 37
North America, 17; *Phylloxera* in, 122. *See also* Canada, Mexico, United States
Norton, 127, 330
nose (definition), 98
Nuits-St.-Georges, 270, 272, 274

oak, 54–55, 57–61, 95, 136, 162, 164
oenophile (definition), 43
off-dry (definition), 14–15
old vine Zinfandel, 155, 232–33
Old World (definition), 16–17
oloroso Sherry, 311, 312–13, 314, 315
Ontario, 174
ordering wine in restaurants, 336–44
Oregon, 20, 33, 74, 143, 144, 169, 190, 192, 234, 237–38, 244, 274, 338
organic viticulture, 282. *See also* biodynamic viticulture
Orvieto, 299
Osborne, Lawrence, 358
oxidation, 54, 57, 64, 91, 107, 117–18, 159–60, 170; of Sherry, 313

Paarl region (South Africa), 252
palate (definition), 98
palo cortado Sherry, 314, 315
Palomino, 311

Pantelleria, 175, 176, 194, 304–5
Parallado, 219
Paris Tasting, 128–31, 237
Parker, Robert M., Jr., 86–89, 246, 254, 263, 288
Passito di Pantelleria, 175, 176, 194, 304–5
Pauillac, 259, 263
Pedro Ximénez (grape), 311
Pedro Ximénez Sherry, 314–15, 335
Pellegrini, Bob, 43–59, 62–63, 190
Pellegrini, Joyce, 44, 62
Penedès region (Spain), 153, 307–8
Pennsylvania, 67
Pérignon, Dom, 207
Pessac-Léognan, 184, 196, 260, 261, 263, 264
Peterson, James, 171
pétillant wines, 13, 30
Petite Sirah, 145, 151–52, 227
Petit Verdot, 138, 258
Pfalz region (Germany), 323
pH, 50
phenolics, 134–35, 160
Phylloxera (Phylloxera vastatrix), 122–24, 125, 127, 235, 243, 247–48, 249
Piedmont (Piemonte) region (Italy), 150, 193, 294, 295, 296
Pinotage, 252
Pinot Blanc, 194–95, 283
Pinot Grigio, 32, 33, 104, 159, 166, 168, 169, 183, 187, 284, 294,
Pinot Gris, 32, 33, 166–69, 195, 237–38, 283
Pinot Meunier, 207

Pinot Noir, 17, 20, 28, 32, 33, 74, 95, 113, 136, 140, 141–44, 147, 150, 160, 164, 167, 195, 199, 207, 224, 226, 232, 233, 237–38, 244, 249, 250, 252, 273, 274, 276, 281, 284, 291, 304, 338
plonk (definition), 115
Poe, Edgar Allan, 309
Pomerol, 140, 261, 262, 263, 264, 266
Pommard, 274
Port, 14, 36–37, 84, 136, 175, 315, 317–23, 351
Port bottles, 225
port-style wines, 227
Portugal, 309, 315–23; *Phylloxera* in, 122
Port Wine Institute, 320
Pouilly-Fuissé, 164, 200
Pouilly-Fumé, 20, 184, 185, 281
preservation: of leftover wine, 221, 353–54; of wine, 64–65
prestige cuvées, 212–13
Price, Vincent, 309
pricing of wine, 290–92; 334–35, 343–44
Primitivo, 155, 301
Priorato (Priorat) region (Spain), 149, 307, 308
Prohibition, 121, 125–27, 155, 228; in New Zealand, 243
proprietary names, 16, 28–29, 30, 289. *See also* fantasy names
Prosecco, 219, 294; bottles, 225
Provence (France), 287
pruning, 48
P.S. I Love You, 151

Puglia region (Italy), 300, 301
Puligny-Montrachet, 164, 274
pump corkscrews, 79
punt, 214
pupitre, 210

*Qualitätswein bestimmter
Anbaugebeit* (QbA), 324
*Qualitätswein garantierten
Ursprungs* (QgU), 324
Qualitätswein mit Prädikat
(QmP), 178, 181, 324, 325
quinta, 322

Rabbit corkscrew, 78, 79
racking (definition), 56
Rallo family, 303
Rapel Valley (Chile), 249, 250
Recioto di Soave, 175
Recioto della Valpolicella, 175
Recioto della Valpolicella
Amarone. *See* Amarone
recioto wines, 294
Red Mountain AVA
(Washington), 235
red wine: characteristics of,
132–33, 136; colors of, 91,
94–95, 136; and health,
133, 134–35; making, 11,
41, 53–54, 57, 59; serving,
90, 348–49
red wine headache syndrome,
135
red wine stains, 354
refermentation: of
Champagne, 208; as wine
fault, 118–19
refrigerated cellars, 346
regional appellations: in
Burgundy, 270. *See also
Indicazione Geografica
Tipica, vins de pays*

Regnié, 277
Rehoboam (bottle size), 216
release (definition), 65
remuage, 210
reserva (definition), 66, 307
reserve (definition), 66
residual sugar, 109, 171
restaurants: ordering wine in,
116, 117–18, 336–44
resveratrol, 134
retailers. *See* wine shops
Rheingau region (Germany),
182, 323
Rheinhessen region
(Germany), 323
Rhône Rangers, 149
Rhône Valley, 29, 33, 145,
148, 197, 199, 200, 240,
257, 284–88, 290;
Phylloxera in, 122
Rías Baixas region (Spain),
309
Ribero del Duero region
(Spain), 153, 309
riddling, 210, 212
Riedel, Claus Josef, 82
Riedel Crystal, 82, 83
Riesling, 32, 33, 74, 82, 95,
99, 119, 159, 160, 162, 169,
173, 177–83, 190, 191, 224,
236, 238, 283, 309, 323,
324, 325, 326, 338, 347
right bank (Bordeaux), 261
Rioja region (Spain), 24, 149,
153, 306–7, 309
ripasso-style Valpolicella, 296
riserva (definition), 66
Robinson, Jancis, 273, 356,
357
Rolland, Michel, 242
Romania, 194
rootstocks, 124–25

rosé, 10, 31, 149, 161,
198–200, 281, 287, 316;
Champagne, 144, 217;
making, 12, 198; serving,
199, 348
Rothschild family, 248
Roussanne, 286
ruby Port, 319, 323
Rueda region (Spain), 309
Ruländer, 168
Russia, 137
Russian River Valley
(California), 143
Ruwer Valley, 178. *See also*
Mosel

Saar Valley, 178, 325. *See also*
Mosel
St.-Amour, 277
St.-Émilion, 140, 261, 263,
264; classification of, 262
St.-Estèphe, 259, 263
St.-Joseph, 286
St.-Julien, 259, 263
Saintsbury, George, 128
St.-Véran, 164, 200
Salmanazar (bottle size), 216
Sancerre, 20, 184, 278, 281;
rosé, 199, 281
Sancerrois region (Loire
Valley), 281
San Francisco Zinfandel
Festival, 69
Sangiovese, 152–53, 156, 157,
294, 295, 297
Santa Barbara County
(California), 228, 233
Santa Ynez Valley
(California), 232, 233
Santenay, 274
Saumur region (Loire Valley),
279

Sauternes, 24, 31, 82, 106, 170, 173, 176, 184, 194, 196, 260, 263, 264, 266, 348; classification of, 262

Sauvignon Blanc, 17, 20, 24, 32, 33, 47, 62, 91, 100, 137, 159, 162, 163, 170, 183–87, 196, 226, 232, 236, 243–44, 248, 249, 251, 252, 258, 263, 280,

Savennières, 279

Savoie region (France), 222

scoring wine, 85, 86–89

Screwpull Table Corkscrew, 77

Screwpull Table Model, 76

screw tops, 75, 117

sec (definition), 211

second fermentation, 12, 42; of Champagne, 208. *See also* tank method

sediment, 64, 94, 107, 350, 351–52

Sekt, 222

sélection des grains nobles (SGN), 167

Sémillon, 24, 170, 196, 258, 263

Sercial, 317

serving: of rosés, 199; of sweet wines, 176; of white wines, 161; temperatures, 347–49

shadow appellation (definition), 286

shelf talkers, 88

Shenandoah Valley (California), 155

Sherry, 14, 84, 160, 176, 305, 309–15

sherry-style wines, 227

Shiraz, 32, 33, 95, 136, 144–46, 151, 225, 235, 240–41, 243, 251. *See also* Syrah

Sicily, 157, 242, 289, 300, 302–5

Sideways, 141, 233

single *quinta* vintage Port, 322

single-vineyard wines, 233

Slovenia, 331

Smaragd wines, 327

Soave, 298

Soave Classico, 24

Soave Classico Superiore, 298

solera method, 312–13

sommeliers, 338, 340–41

Sonoma Valley (California), 74, 143, 190, 228, 229, 231, 233; *Phylloxera* in, 124

South Africa, 17, 33, 72, 145, 146, 177, 184, 186, 187, 188, 189, 193, 251–52, 328

South America, 17, 244–50

Spain, 16, 21, 24, 71, 149, 153, 193, 199, 219, 248, 306–15, 316, 328; *Phylloxera* in, 122

sparkling wines, 12–13, 30, 31, 42, 71, 95, 118, 202–22; bottles, 225; California, 227

Spätlese, 179, 181, 182, 325

split (bottle size), 216

Spurrier, Steven, 128–29

stabilization, 64–65

stain removal, 354

Steen, 187, 251. *See also* Chenin Blanc

Steiner, Rudolph, 282

Steinfeder wines, 326

Stellenbosch region (South Africa), 252

still wines (definition), 12

storing wines, 220, 344–47

structure, 107, 111; of Bordeaux reds, 138

stuck fermentation, 42

sulfites, 64, 65

sulfur content, 100

Super Tuscans, 156–57, 293, 305

sur lie (definition), 201

sweet wines, 15, 30, 109, 161, 170–76, 211–12, 260, 280, 304, 311–12, 317, 319

Switzerland: *Phylloxera* in, 122

Sylvaner, 283

Syrah, 32, 33, 136, 144–47, 150, 151, 197, 200, 227, 235, 236, 240, 285, 286, 288, 302, 304, 308. *See also* Shiraz

table wine (definition), 13–14. *See also vino da tavola, vins de table*

Tămîioasă, 194

tank method, 219

tannins, 53, 90, 99, 106–8, 109, 133, 138, 140, 160; removal of, 65; temperature's affect on, 347; wood, 59, 60

tartrate precipitation (wine fault), 119–20

Tasca family, 303

tastevin, 341

Taurasi zone (Italy), 301

Tavel, 200, 287

tawny Port, 319–20

TCA (2,4,6-trichloroanisole), 115

tears, 97

Tempranillo, 24, 149, 153–54, 199, 306, 307, 309

terroir, 21, 22–23, 44, 142, 163, 241; in Burgundy, 267

Texas, 67, 234, 330

thermal amplitude, 246

Thermenregion district (Austria), 326

Thienpont family, 265
Thiese, Terry, 181, 325
Tinto Fino, 153, 309
tirage, 208
Tocai Friulano, 298–99
Tokaji, 173, 176, 299, 335
Tokay, 251. *See also* Tokaji
tongue map, 82
Torres, Miguel, 248
Touraine AC wines, 280–81
Touraine region (Loire), 278, 279
tours. *See* wine tours
Traisental district (Austria), 326
Traminer, 190
transparency, 178
trellises, 49
Trentino–Alto Adige region (Italy), 168, 169, 289, 294. *See also* Alto Adige
Tre Venezie regions (Italy), 294
Trockenbeerenauslese, 173, 180, 181
trocken wines, 326
tulip glasses, 84; cleaning, 355
Turkey, 331; *Phylloxera* in, 122
Tuscany region (Italy), 25, 138, 152, 156–57, 294, 295, 297, 299, 302
21st Amendment, 125
two-buck Chuck, 227

ullage (definition), 57
Ull de Llebre, 153, 307
Umbria region (Italy), 299
unfiltered wines, 120
United States, 67, 226–39; Prohibition in, 125–27. *See also* American Viticultural Areas, wine laws, *and individual state names*

Uruguay, 330
Uzbekistan, 193

Vacqueyras, 149, 287
Valpolicella, 294, 296–97, 348
Valpolicella Classico, 296
Valpolicella Ripasso, 296
varietal character, 139
varietal names, 17, 20–21, 22–23, 27, 30, 31; in Alsace, 27, 183; and clones, 19
VDQS wines, 255
VdT wines, 289, 293
vegetative propagation, 18, 123
vendange tardive (VT), 167
Veneto region (Italy), 24, 157, 169, 219, 294, 296, 298
Verdejo, 309
Verdelho, 317
vermouth, 14
Vernaccia di San Gimignano, 299
vertical tasting, 74, 78, 236
la Veuve Clicquot (the Widow Clicquot), 210, 222
Vidal Blanc, 174, 239
village appellations, 26; in Burgundy, 270, 274
Vin de Constance, 251
Vin Doux Naturel, 175
vinegar, 57, 100
Vin de Liqueur, 175
Vin Santo, 175
vines: grafting, 123–24; propagation of, 18; training, 48–49; and yield, 47. *See also* American hybrids, American vine species, clones, French hybrids, *Vitis vinifera*
Vinho Verde, 316
vinifera. See Vitis vinifera

vinification (definition), 39
Vino Nobile di Montepulciano, 152, 297, 300
vino da tavola (definition), 289. *See also* VdT wines
vins de pays, 255, 293
vins de table, 255
vintage, 31, 34–37; and price, 290
vintage Champagne, 212
vintage character Port, 322
vintage charts, 34–35
vintage Port, 320–21, 351
vintage years: declaring, 37, 320
Viognier, 17, 189, 197, 227, 285
Virginia, 234, 330
viticulture (definition), 39
Vitis vinifera (vinifera), 10, 32, 46, 123, 228, 235, 239, 243
Volnay, 274
Volstead Act, 126
Vosne-Romanée, 274
Vouvray, 33, 187, 188, 189, 279–80
Vreeland, Diana, 221

Wachau district (Austria), 182, 326–27
waiter's friend corkscrew, 75–76
Walla Walla AVA (Washington), 235
warehouse cellars, 346–47
Washington, George, 316
Washington State, 33, 140, 141, 177, 232, 234–37
Weingut (definition), 326
Weinviertel district (Austria), 326

Weissburgunder, 195
Weisser Burgunder, 195
Western Cape Province
    (South Africa), 186, 252
white wine: characteristics of,
    159–61; colors of, 91,
    94–95, 117, 159–60; mak-
    ing, 11–12, 41, 54–56, 57,
    160; serving, 90, 161,
    348–49
White Zinfandel, 155
wholesalers, 333
Willamette Valley (Oregon),
    143, 192, 237–38
wine: age of, 91, 94; blending
    of, 242; business of, 63,
    333–35; collecting, 108;
    color of, 10–12, 30, 91, 94;
    cost of, 59; definition of, 9;
    descriptions of, 112–13; eti-
    quette, 341–43; fashions in,
    133, 291; and food, 81, 85,
    89, 107; fruit, 67; history
    of, 61, 121–31; labels, 19,
    272, 375; ordering in
    restaurants, 116, 117–18,
    336–44; preservation of,
    64–65; pricing of, 290–92,
    334–35, 343–44; religious
    use of, 126; scoring of, 85,
    86–89; serving, 161, 176,
    199, 347–49; stabilization
    of, 64–65; storage of, 220,
    344–47; transport of, 170
Wine Advocate, 86–89, 235
wine books, 356–58
wine bottles. See bottles
wine classes, 355–56
wine coolers, 348–49
wine critics, 291. See also
    Parker, Robert M., Jr.;
    Johnson, Hugh; scoring;

Wine Advocate; Wine
    Spectator
wine faults, 90–91, 115–20;
    342. See also sulfur content,
    vinegar
wine festivals, 68–69
wine funnels, 349, 352
wineglasses, 81, 82–84; clean-
    ing of, 355. See also coupe
wine laws: German, 324;
    Italian, 289, 293; New
    Zealand, 243; U.S., 9, 17,
    34, 65, 151. See also
    American Viticultural
    Areas, Appellation
    d'Origine Contrôlée sys-
    tem, Denominación de
    Origen, Denominación de
    Origen Caficada,
    Prohibition
wine lists, 336–39
winemaker (definition), 43. See
    also flying winemakers
winemaker's dinners, 69
wineries: visiting, 67–68
wine shops, 35, 36, 88, 223,
    226, 238, 301, 323, 327,
    333–35, 336
Wine Spectator, 35, 86–89, 235,
    264
wine stewards. See sommeliers
wine tours, 70–72
wing corkscrew, 76
wood. See barrel ageing, bar-
    rels, oak
wood tannins, 59, 60, 106

Xarel-lo, 219
Xynomavro, 199

Yakima Valley AVA
    (Washington), 235

yeast. See fermentation
yield, 47
young tawny Port, 319–20

Zack, Joel, 71
Zibbibo, 304
Zinfandel Advocates and
    Producers (ZAP), 69
Zinfandel, 69. 82, 90, 95,
    154–55, 226, 232–33, 234,
    301

Index of Makers, Négociants, Importers, and Retailers

Alamos (Argentina), 150, 246
Allegrini (Italy), 295
Alliance (Australia), 240
Almaden (California), 28, 31
Altos de Luzón (Spain), 308
Amador Foothill (California), 155
Anselmi (Italy), 298
Antigua Usanza (Spain), 307
Archery Summit (Oregon), 144
Ariel (California), 234
Au Bon Climat (California), 233

Castello Banfi (Italy), 295
Baron Herzog (California), 329
Barton & Guestier (France), 264, 266
BearBoat (California), 144, 233
Beaulieu Vineyard (California), 228
Graham Beck (South Africa), 218
Berger (Austria), 191
Bertani (Italy), 295
Billecart-Salmon (Champagne), 217
Bogle (California), 151
Bonny Doon Vineyard (California), 28–29, 31, 149, 227
Casa del Bosque (Chile), 250
Bouchard Père & Fils (France), 275
Henri Bourgeois (Loire), 184
Bründlmayer (Austria), 222

Camp du Rouss (Italy), 295
Cateña (Argentina), 150, 246
Charles Heidsieck (Champagne), 209
Charles Krug (California), 228
Charles Shaw (California), 227
Chateau Montelena (California), 130, 131
Chateau Ste Michelle (Washington), 235
Château Cheval Blanc (Bordeaux), 147
Michele Chiarlo (Italy), 295
Château du Cléray (Loire), 201
Cloudy Bay (New Zealand), 243–44
Columbia Crest (Washington), 235, 237
Concha y Toro (Chile), 249, 250
Francis Ford Coppola (California), 146
Cordoníu (Spain), 219
Cousiño-Macul (Chile), 139
Covey Run (Washington), 235, 236, 237

Delaforce (Port), 321
Donnafugata (Italy), 302, 303, 304–5
Dow's (Port), 318
Joseph Drouhin (Burgundy), 275
Dry Creek (California), 188
Georges Duboeuf (Burgundy), 277
Dubonnet (France), 14

Duca di Salaparuta (Italy), 302, 305

Viña Echeverría (Chile), 249
Casa de la Ermita (Spain), 308
Viña Errazuriz (Chile), 250
Étude Wines (California), 233
Eyrie Vineyards (Oregon), 238

Fairview (South Africa), 252
Faiveley (Burgundy), 275
Remo Farina (Italy), 296–97
Livio Felluga (Italy), 168
Nicholas Feuillatte (Champagne), 217, 329
Firestone Vineyard (California), 232
Firriato (Italy), 157, 302, 303, 304, 305
Foppiano (California), 151
Dr. Konstantin Frank Vinifera Wine Cellars (New York), 238
Freixenet (Spain), 219
Fürst Löwenstein (Germany), 182

E&J Gallo (California), 28
Château de la Gardine (Rhône), 288
Gatinois (Champagne), 144
Glatzer (Austria), 327
Goats Do Roam (South Africa), 252
Golden Valley (Romania), 194
Gosset (Champagne), 217
Graham's (Port), 318, 322

Grgich Hills (California), 184, 185

Domaine Jean Grivot (Burgundy), 270

Château Jean de Gué (Bordeaux), 266

E. Guigal (Rhône), 287

Haag (Alsace), 190

Hagafen (California), 329

Château Haut-Brion (Bordeaux), 260, 261, 262

Hitching Post (California), 233

Hogue Cellars (Washington), 235, 236, 237

Hopewell Valley (New Jersey), 141

Domaine Huet (Loire), 280

Hugel et Fils (Alsace), 284

Hugo (Australia), 241

Quinta do Infantado (Port), 323

Inglenook (California), 228

Inniskillin (Canada), 174

Iron Horse (California), 218

Italian Wine Merchants (retailer), 301

Jacob's Creek (Australia), 240

Louis Jadot (Burgundy), 275

King Estate (Oregon), 238

Kir-Yanni (Greece), 199

Klein Constantia (South Africa), 251

Kris (Italy), 168

Krug (Champagne), 209

Labouré-Roi (Burgundy), 275

Château Lafite-Rothschild (Bordeaux), 248, 262

Lancers (Portugal), 316

Casa Lapostolle (Chile), 250

Château Latour (Bordeaux), 138, 262

Louis Latour (Burgundy), 275

Lenz (New York), 190, 239

Lillet (Bordeaux), 14

J. Lohr (California), 234

Emilio Lustau (Sherry), 315

Maculan (Italy), 157

di Majo Norante (Italy), 301

Manischewitz (U.S.), 328

Manzone (Italy), 296

Viña Mar (Chile), 250

Château Margaux (Bordeaux), 262

Louis M. Martini (California), 231, 232

Masi (Italy), 296

Mateus (Portugal), 316

Domaine Louis Max (Burgundy), 275

Mayo Family Winery (California), 229

Milz (Germany), 181

Mirassou (California), 186

Moët & Chandon (Champagne), 212, 217

Mogen David (U.S.), 328

Château de Montfort (Loire), 188

Morgan Winery (California), 230

Château Mouton-Rothschild (Bordeaux), 29, 138, 262

Mulderbosch (South Africa), 188–89

G. H. Mumm (Champagne), 209

Naia (Spain), 309

Nikolaihof (Austria), 327

Bodegas Olivares (Spain), 308

Ornellaia (Italy), 156

Osborne (Sherry), 315

Parducci (California), 151

Peitán (Spain), 309

Pellegrini Vineyards (New York), 44–59, 63, 66, 67, 141

Penfolds (Australia), 240

Château Petrus (Bordeaux), 140

Château Le Pin (Bordeaux), 265

Pine Ridge (California), 189, 231, 232

Piper-Heidsieck (Champagne), 218

Piper-Sonoma (California), 218

Pisano (Italy), 219

Planeta (Italy), 302

Les Plantiers du Haut-Brion (Bordeaux), 264

Joh. Jos. Prum (Germany), 181

Rare Wine Co. (importer), 317

Ravenswood (California), 231–32

Rivini (Italy), 301

Louis Roederer (Champagne), 209, 212–13, 217

Roederer Estate (California), 218

Baron Philippe de Rothschild (France), 29

Ruffino (Italy), 165

Rust en Vrede (South Africa), 146

Felipe **Rutini** (Argentina), 246

S. **Quirico** (Italy), 299

Viña **Santa Ema** (Chile), 249

Viña **Santa Rita** (Chile), 184, 186, 249

Sassicaia, 156, 157

Scala Dei (Spain), 308

Schloss Gobelsberg (Austria), 191

Clos de **Sénaigerie** (Loire), 201

Sherry-Lehmann (retailer), 323

Bert **Simon** (Germany), 325

Michael **Skurnik** Wines (importer), 181, 325

Stag's Leap Wine Cellars (California), 130, 229

Sterling Vineyards (California), 231, 232

Taittinger (Champagne), 212

Tasca d'Almerita (Italy), 302–3, 303, 305

Taylor Fladgate & Yeatman (Port), 318

Thabani (South Africa), 184, 186

Tiefenbrunner (Italy), 168

Tignanello (Italy), 29, 156, 157

Torres (Spain), 307–8

F. E. **Trimbach** (Alsace), 168, 284

Les **Trois Chênes** (Loire), 280

Trumpeter (Argentina), 150, 246

Valle Reale (Italy), 300

Vega Sindoa (Spain), 199

Veramonte (Chile), 250

Veuve Clicquot-Ponsardin (Champagne), 210, 215, 217, 244

Villa Puccini (Italy), 157

Villa Sparina (Italy), 297–98

Vintage New York (retailer), 238

Warre's (Port), 318

Domaine **Weinbach** (Alsace), 284

Hermann J. **Wiemer** (New York), 182, 238

Willm (Alsace), 190

Winebow, Inc. (importer) 300

Château d'**Yquem** (Bordeaux), 170, 196, 262

Zenato (Italy), 297

ABOUT THE AUTHORS

JAMES WALLER lives in Brooklyn, New York. His previous books include *The Moviegoer's Journal, The Well-Bred Cat* and *The Well-Bred Dog* (both with Lisa Zador), and, most recently, *Drinkology: The Art and Science of the Cocktail.* He has been known to mix the grain with the grape.

ELIZABETH ALDRICH lives outside Washington, D.C., and is the executive director of the Dance Heritage Coalition. Several times a year she sips wines while admiring the ocean from the terrace of her house in Tunquén, Chile.